Guide to the BBC ROMS

GUIDE TO THE BBC ROMS

Don Thomasson

IN THE UNITED KINGDOM —
Melbourne House (Publishers) Ltd
Castle Yard House
Castle Yard
Richmond, TW10 6TF

IN THE UNITED STATES OF AMERICA —
Melbourne House Software Inc.
347 Reedwood Drive
Nashville TN 37217

IN AUSTRALIA —
Melbourne House (Australia) Pty Ltd
Level 2, 70 Park Street
South Melbourne, Victoria 3205

Cataloguing in Publication

Thomasson, Don.
Guide to the BBC ROMs.

ISBN 0 86161 184 5

1. BBC Microcomputer. 2. Operating Systems (Computers) I. Title

001.64'25

Edition: 7 6 5 4 3 2 1
Printing: F E D C B A 9 8 7 6 5 4 3 2 1
Year: 90 89 88 87 86 85 84

Contents

1 Introduction 1
2 Initialisation 7
3 Interrupts 19
4 The OSBYTE and OSWORD Calls 33
5 Input and Output 51
6 Buffers 57
7 Keyboard 65
8 Command Line Interpreter 81
9 VDU Control 93
10 Save and Load 151
11 The Sound System 155
12 Files 167
13 The BASIC Interpreter 199
Appendices:
Disassembler and Sort Programs 219
Index 225

Chapter 1
INTRODUCTION

When a soldier or airman arrives at a new base, his first and most urgent need is for a 'map of the camp', by which he means something that will tell him where to find the cookhouse, the orderly room and other essential places. This book is intended to perform a similar service for those who wish to investigate the BBC computer ROM-borne programs.

The normal approach to this is via the provision of a commented disassembly, but that would be difficult in the case of the BBC system, because there are a number of different versions of the operating system and the BASIC interpreter. Even in the case of O.S. 1.2Ø two variants have been found, one in a fairly basic machine for cassette working, the other in a machine equipped with disc drives.

The solution adopted is based on the fact that each reader can easily generate a disassembly of the ROMs in his own machine. The result may not be easy to understand, in the absence of comments, so this book provides comments which are based on one particular version, but which should be generally applicable to other versions.

Rather than attempting to creat artificial link-names, the link addresses of the cassette-based OS 1.2Ø version are used. This means that users of other versions may need to create cross-reference tables, because their link addresses are different, an unfortunate but unavoidable necessity.

In short, the book may not provide an exact map of the camp you want to explore, but it should give you sufficient guidance to make exploration profitable.

The Overall Concept

Most small computers combine their operating systems and BASIC interpreters in a single program, with the two main elements inextricably entangled with each other. The BBC system keeps the elements separate, with the operating system occupying C∅∅∅ to FFFF and the interpreter occupying 8∅∅∅ to BFFF. The latter area of store, however, is not reserved solely for BASIC. Other ROMs can be switched in to replace the interpreter, allowing other languages and specialities to be implemented.

The operating system is essentially an interface, in that it deals with control of the display, keyboard and other peripheral systems and interlinks the relevant data streams. This greatly simplifies the task of the language systems. For example, the implementation of the SOUND command in BASIC involves no more than the creation of a table of variables. The operating system uses this data to set up three bytes in the appropriate sound buffer, and later the main sound routine, working under interrupt control, decodes the bytes and generates the required sound chip control data. Once the intricacies of the system are understood, it is possible to reduce the process of setting up a sound to the insertion of three bytes in a buffer.

One consequence of this is that the operating system is a far more important part of the whole than might be expected. Apart from the floating point and other mathematical routines, the interpreter is comparatively humdrum and obvious, the main problem in following it arising from the need to keep track of the many variables.

Quite apart from that, one of the main reasons for understanding the ROM routines is to discover how they can be accessed from machine code, and a large proportion of that access must be to the operating system.

In these circumstances, no apology is offered for the fact that the operating system is examined in greater detail than the BASIC interpreter.

Finding Routines

The first problem in creating a disassembly is discovery of the entry points to particular routines, and details will be given of the way to find such entries. Some are defined quite explicitly, some are dependent on indirect links, and others are contained in look-up tables. In a few cases, the entries can only be determined by reference to other routines, and that has determined the order in which the various sections of the program are treated.

Once the entry address to a block of code is known, the disassembly program given in the Appendix can be used to translate the block into mnemonic instructions, but this process must end at an absolute jump, a return instruction, or a BRK instruction, which signals the start of text. It should also stop at some jump instructions which appear to be conditional, but which are always executed because of previous action. For example, a BEQ instruction following LDA #Ø will always be executed.

Each block is likely to yield further entry points, some of which may be within the block itself, others being to closely associated blocks, and others to different routines. A program is described in the Appendix which will help you to create ordered lists of the more important links.

Variables

Like the entry and link points, the addresses of variables will be those for the system on which the study was based, and some may differ in other versons. However, it appears that most of the vector (indirect) link addresses have been preserved.

It should be noted that the 'low byte first' convention is adopted in cases where numbers occupy more than one byte. This has been extended, in concept, to cases where a number is held in more than one register. X/A, for example, indicates a two-byte number held in X (low byte) and A (high byte).

Conventions

Two-digit hexadecimal numbers are prefaced by &, but four-digit hexadecimal numbers are not. Brackets round a four-digit number indicate the contents of that number, and on occasion a group of consecutive bytes will be indicated (ØØFA/B), which means the joint contents of locations ØØFA and ØØFB. Grammar may be sacrificed in places for the sake of brevity, but the main objective is always to seek reasonable clarity.

Presentation

The layout of the operating system routines is not always as logical as one might wish, some aspects involving widely scattered blocks of code. A table at the end of this section shows where a particular block is handled, and this should enable the reader to find what he wants, but as far as possible the modules within a section are presented in address order, except for the OSBYTE and OSWORD routines, which are taken in their own numeric sequence.

Some routines which can follow a number of alternative paths have not been traced through all those paths. A particular example is the block of code dealing with PLOT, which offers many different routes. These can best be followed on a paper-and-pencil basis, the action of each block being described separately to aid this process.

Since the comments are based almost entirely on the disassembled code, it is possible that misconceptions have crept in, but every effort has been made to avoid this.

Other Literature

This book is not intended to replace or duplicate the information given in the User Guide or Advanced User Guide, which provide specific information regarding the intended modes of operation. The object here has been to look at the way the system works, so that alternative modes of use, not necessarily intended, can be explored.

Index of Routine Addresses

The following list indicates the chapter in which a given section of code is examined.

	Chapter No.	
C4CØ - D93F	9	VDU Control
D94Ø - DC1B	2	Initialisation
DC1C - DE8B	3	Interrupts
DE8C - DEA8	4	OSBYTE
DEA9 - DEBA	2	Initialisation
DEBB - DFØB	7	Keyboard

DFØC	- DFØF	2	Initialisation
DF1Ø	- EØ33	8	Command Line Interpreter
EØ34	- EØ38	4	OSBYTE
EØ39	- EØA3	8	Command Line Interpreter
EØA4	- E1AC	5	Input/Output
E1AD	- E2ØD	6	Buffers
E2ØE	- E274	10	Save/Load
E275	- E29F	12	Files
E2AØ	- E3ØF	10	Save/Load
E31Ø	- E434	8	Command Line Interpreter
E435	- E4E2	6	Buffers
E4E3	- E4FØ	7	Keyboard
E4F1	- E514	6	Buffers
E515	- E5B2	7	Keyboard
E5B3	- E67E	4	OSBYTE
E67F	- E688	12	Files
E689	- E712	4	OSBYTE
E713	- E731	7	Keyboard
E732	- E743E	6	Buffers
E74F	- E7DB	4	OSBYTE
E7DC	- E7EA	12	Files
E7EB	- E82C	4	OSWORD
E82D	- E8DØ	11	Sound
E8D1	- E9C7	4	OSWORD
E9C8	- E9D8	8	Command Line Interpreter
E9D9	- E9FE	7	Keyboard
E9FF	- EA1C	4	OSBYTE
EA1D	- EA9B	8	Command Line Interpreter
EA9C	- EAE2	7	Keyboard
EAE3	- EBØ2	4	OSBYTE
EBØ3	- EE12	11	Sound
EE13	- EED9	12	Files
EEDA	- FØ94	7	Keyboard
FØ95	- FØB8	6	Buffers
FØB9	- FØCB	8	Command Line Interpreter
FØCC	- F134	7	Keyboard
F135	- F1A2	12	Files
F1A3	- F1C3	8	Command Line Interpreter
F1C4	- FBFF	12	Files

FCØØ - FEFF cover input/output addresses.
FFØØ - FFFF is mainly occupied by links and data.

Chapter 2
INITIALISATION

Some of the more complex components of a computer need to be set up to a given state when power is first applied. This is usually achieved by means of a Reset line which remains in its 'off' state for a few tens of milliseconds after the various power rails have stabilised. The BBC computer has two reset lines.

RSTA is controlled by a simple charging circuit, and is only effective when the computer is first switched on. RST is generated by a timer chip, and is effective both at switch-on and when the BREAK key is pressed. RSTA resets the internal VIA chip, and RST resets everything else. The distinction will be seen to be important.

When reset is removed from the 65Ø2 CPU, it reads an address stored at FFFC/D and jumps to the location specified. Check the address, remembering that the upper byte is in the higher location, and you know where to find the initialisation routine. It may not be at the address used here, but don't worry about that.

D9CD The first action is to set (ØDØØ) = &4Ø, which is an RTI instruction. This comes into play in the event of a non-maskable interrupt, which is 'vectored' to ØDØØ by the contents of locations FFFA/B. The interrupt is normally associated with the Econet system, and the RTI instruction is a precaution only if Econet is not fitted.

Set I then bars maskable interrupts, Clear D sets Binary mode in case the processor chose to come up in Decimal mode, and the stack pointer is set to &FF, this being its home position in page 1.

A = (FE4E) then reads the Interrupt Enable Register of the internal VIA. ASL moves the most significant bit into carry, and if that leaves A = Ø a jump to D9E7 is taken. Remember, the internal VIA is not reset by RST, so it is not cleared down by pressing BREAK. If this is a BREAK and not initial switch-on, one or more of the enable bits will be set.

A is pushed before the jump, to retain an indication of whether this was a switch-on or BREAK start.

If the jump is not taken, A = (Ø258), which determines the action taken in response to depression of the BREAK and ESCAPE keys. Bit 1 is examined, and it if is Ø the routine jumps to DAØ3, skipping the store clearance routine.

Bit 1 was brought into the bit Ø position by an LSRA before the check, and if the jump is not taken another LSRA zeroes A. (Unless someone has put a value greater than 3 in (Ø258), which would mess things up somewhat.)

D9E7 Whether reached by a jump or directly, this point finds A = Ø. (ØØØØ/1) = Ø4ØØ, the base address for store clearance, X=4 and Y=Ø.

D9EE ((ØØØØ) + Y) =A = Ø. If (ØØØ1) then equals Ø, the routine jumps to D9FD, because the RAM clearance is complete and the clearance routine has wrapped round to clear locations ØØØØ and ØØØ1. The RAM address system is arranged so that this happens as soon as all available RAM has been cleared, whether it extends to 16K or 32K.

Otherwise Y is incremented, and if Y is then non-zero the routine loops to D9EE. If Y = Ø, Y and X are incremented, (ØØØ1) is incremented to select a new page, and if (ØØØ1) is positive the routine loops to D9EE.

Look at that closely, and you will see that clearance of a fresh page begins with Y = 1. Location Ø is not cleared. Why? Well, it would be more difficult to arrange to skip location ØDØØ, which holds that RTI instruction, so all location Øs are left alone.

D9FD This point is reached when clearance is complete, and X holds the number of the last page to be cleared, plus 1, &8Ø for 32K RAM, & 4Ø for 16K RAM. This value is copied into (Ø284), the soft key consistency flag, and (Ø28E), which signals the size of available RAM.

DAØ3 Attention is now turned to the peripheral devices. (FE42) = &ØF sets Port B of VIA **1** to output on bits Ø - 3, input on bits 4 - 7. Then a loop outputs values &ØE to &Ø9 on Port B.
The port drives a set of addressable latches on bits Ø - 3, and the latches control eight functions, as follows:

Sound Chip	Enabled by &ØØ	Disabled by &Ø8
Speech Generator (RS)	Made low by &Ø1	Made high by &Ø9
Speech Generator (WS)	Made low by &Ø1	Made high by &ØA
Keyboard Auto-Scan	Disabled by &Ø3	Enabled by &ØB
CØ address modifier	Made low by &Ø4	Made high by &ØC
C1 address modifier	Made low by &Ø5	Made high by &ØD
Caps Lock LED	On by &Ø6	Off by &ØE
Shift Lock LED	On by &Ø7	Off by &ØF

Where devices are not fitted, selecting them can have no effect. The function of the Keyboard Auto-Scan will be discussed in the section dealing with the keyboard, which will also deal with LED control. The CØ and C1 flags are concerned with screen address modification in hardware scroll. The sound chip will be dealt with in the section on Sound.

While we are dealing with Port B, it is convenient to mention that its inputs are used as follows;

Bit 4: Fire button Ø

Bit 5: Fire button 1

Bit 6: Speech generator VSRDY

Bit 7: Speech generator VSPINT

It will be noted that the outputs to Port B leave out &Ø8 and &ØF. The sound chip is only enabled when it is being set up. and it will then go on sounding even if it is disabled. Fortunately, it is self-clearing to disable. The shift lock LED is left to its own devices for the moment.

DA11 A further loop is now entered in which X takes values 9 to 1. The keyboard interrogate subroutine FØ2A is

called for each value. This subroutine locks the keyboard by disabling auto-scan, and sets bit 7 of X high if the key defined by X on entry to the subroutine is pressed. In this case, wire links rather than keys are involved, except for the CONTROL key.
The meaning of the X values output by the interrogate subroutine are as follows:

X=1: CONTROL key pressed
X=2,3: Links 7,8: Not used
X=4,5: Links 5,6: Disc Drive Data
X=6: Link 4: SHIFT/BREAK action.
X=7-9: Links 1-3: Initial screen mode.

As each X value is output by the interrogation routine, bit 7 is shifted into the msb of (ØØFC). The last shift puts the lsb of (ØØFC) into carry, and the msb of (ØØFC) is 1 if CONTROL was pressed.

An option to use SHIFT with BREAK is mentioned in the manuals, but as the state of SHIFT would be checked by X = Ø, a value not used here, the option is not immediately relevant.

DA2Ø (ØØFC) is rotated left to put the carry into the lsb and put the msb into carry. The LED-setting routine at EEEB is then called. This transfers the CPU status byte on entry to A on exit, so a rotate right is needed to restore the carry bit to its rightful place.

It is now time to deal with the initialisation of page 2, which holds the indirect links and many system variables. There are three situations to be considered;

(a) A is pulled, restoring the value pushed early in the initialisation routine. If A = Ø, an initial start is being performed. X = &9Ø, Y = &9C, (Ø28D) = 1, and (Ø28F) = (ØØFC) inverted.

(b) If carry is set, CONTROL was pressed, calling for a cold restart. X = &9Ø, Y = &87, (Ø28D) = 2, and (Ø28F) = (ØØFC) inverted.

(c) if carry is clear, CONTROL was not pressed with BREAK, and a warm restart is required. Y = &7E, X = &9C, (Ø82D) = Ø, and (Ø28F) is unaffected, being set already.

The values in X and Y determine which parts of page 2 are cleared and which are initialised.

(Ø28D) is used to indicate which type of initialisation was last performed, and (Ø28F) provides an indication of the keyboard links which are set.

DA44 Page 2 can now be set up, partly by reference to a source table holding standard values. First, (Ø2ØØ + X) to (Ø2CD) are zeroed, then (Ø2CF – Ø2FF) = &FF. Rather out of context, (FE63) = &FF, setting Port A of the external VIA (printer interface) to output on all bits. Then, again rather out of context, (ØØE2 – ØØFF) = Ø. Finally, the lower part of page 2, up to (Ø1FF + Y), is set from the source table.

The full implications of these alternative changes to page 2 can only be appreciated by working them out at length. The bulk of the values set can be found by reference to the source table.

DA64 (ØØED) = A = &62, and subroutine FBØA is called to set up the ACIA (Asynchronous Communications Interface Adapter, or serial I/Ø chip.) Note the subroutine address. We will return to it in due course.

DA6E A positive orgy of peripheral initialisations comes next. (FE4D), (FE4E), (FE6D) and (FE6E) are all set to &7F, clearing the interrupt flag and enable registers of both VIAs. Interrupts are allowed briefly, to clear the air. With all significant interrupts disabled, nothing is affected.

If bit 6 of (ØØFC) = 1, subroutine FØ55 is called. This is a dead end if the disc system is not implemented.

(FE4E) = &F2:	Enable interrupts 1,4,5,6, of the internal VIA
(FE4C) = 4:	Set internal VIA PCR
(FE4B) = &6Ø:	Set internal VIA ACR
(FE46) = &ØE:	Set internal Via T1 counter (L)
(FE6C) = &ØE:	Set external VIA PCR
(FECØ) = &ØE:	Set up A/D converter

If (FE6C) ≠ &ØE increment (Ø277). (External VIA bit mask)

(FE47) = &27:	Set internal VIA T1 counter latch (H)
(FE45) = &27:	Set internal VIA T1 counter (H)

The internal VIA interrupts are used thus:

Ø	Keyboard. Enabled as needed.
1	Frame sync pulse
4	End of A/D conversion
5	T2 counter (for speech)
6	T1 counter (1Ø mS intervals)

Setting the internal VIA PCR to 4 gives:

CA1:	Interrupt on negative edge. (Frame Sync)
CA2:	Handshake output. (Keyboard)
CB1:	Interrupt on negative edge. (End of conversion)
CB2:	Negative edge. (Light pen strobe)

Setting the internal VIA ACR to &60 gives:

Latching disabled
Shift register disabled
T1 counter continous interrupts
T2 counter timed interrupt.

(For further information, consult details of the VIA chip.)

The T1 counter being set to 27ØE (9998 decimal), it generates an interrupt every 9998 clock pulses, i.e. every 10 mS.

Setting the external VIA PCR to &ØE gives:

CA1:	Interrupt on negative edge. (Printer Acknowledge)
CA2:	High output. (Printer strobe)
CB1:	Interrupt on negative edge. (User port)
CB2:	Negative edge. (User port)

If reading the external VIA PCR does not give the value just set in it, the chip is missing or defective. (Ø277) is incremented from &FF to Ø to bar all external VIA interrupts.

Setting (FECØ) = &ØE gives input channel 1 selected, and the ten-bit mode of the converter chip.

DAAA Subroutine EC6Ø is called to clear the sound channels. This is another address worth noting.

The actions which follow depend on the kind of initialisation being carried out, reference being made to page 2 locations unaltered in a warm start but reset during initial or cold start.

Subroutine E6A7 is called with A = (Ø282) AND &7F to set up the Serial ULA. Then, if (Ø284) ≠ Ø subroutine E9C8 is called to rest the function keys, this call being executed only for a cold or initial start.

DABD Attention now turns to the paged ROMs. First, subroutine DC16 sets (ØØF4) = (FE3Ø) = X = Ø. This sets the ROM select chip and its RAM copy. X = 3, Y = (8ØØ7). Y now holds the displacement of the start of the ROM heading text relative to 8ØØØ.

DAC5 A loop checks that the heading text begins with '(C)', the copyright symbol. If the check fails, a jump to DAFB is taken. Otherwise, X = Y = (ØØF4).

DAD5 Y is incremented, and if the result exceeds &ØF a jump to DAAF is taken. Otherwise, (ØØFA) = Y inverted, and (ØØFB) = &7F. (ØØFA/B) form an address equal to (7FFF – Y).

DAE3 (FE3Ø) = Y, selecting ROM Y, then A = ((ØØFA) + Y) = (7FFF). Then (FE3Ø) = X, and if ((ØØFA) + Y) ≠ A the routine loops back to DAD5. It might appear that there is an error here, but since (7FFF) is either the top RAM location or empty the first check will aways show equality.

If equality is found, (ØØFA/B) is incremented, and if (ØØFB) has not reached &84 the routine loops to DAE3 for a further comparison. As two different ROMs are being compared, it is to be expected that a difference will soon be found. If the ROMs are identical, up to &83FF, DAFB follows.

DAFB X = (ØØF4), and if X is positive a jump to DBØC is taken.

DAFF A = (8ØØ6), which is the type number for the selected ROM. This is stored in (Ø2A1 + X), setting up a dictionary of the ROM types available. If the type number AND &8F is zero, (Ø24B) = X. This identifies the BASIC ROM, which should be the only one which returns a type number with bit 7 = Ø. (However, it is stated that bit 1 should always be set, which from this code appears to be an error.)

DBOC X is incremented, and if the result is less than &1Ø a jump back to DABD repeats the process. Otherwise, if bit 7 of the Port B input on the internal VIA is 1, a jump to DB27 is taken. This bit senses the VSPINT line on the speech generator, and if the speech facility is not fitted the line will be high. If the line is low, (Ø27B) is decremented from Ø to &FF to show that the speech facility is present. DB19 follows.

DB19 The previous action left X = &1Ø. Now Y = &FF and subroutine EE7F is called. X is decremented, and if X ≠ Ø the routine loops to DB19. This initialises the speech generator system. Then the internal VIA T2 counter, used with speech, is zeroed by (FE48) = Ø, (FE49) = Ø.

DB27 A = (Ø28F), which holds the inversion of (ØØFC), and C3ØØ is called. This is a jump to the screen initialisation routine. Bits Ø – 3 of (Ø28F) determine the mode which is set up.

The routine continues by calling E4F1 with Y = &CA. This enters the value in the keyboard buffer. It is perhaps no coincidence that &CA is the BASIC token for 'NEW'.

Subroutine EAD9 is then called. This is a check to see whether a boot address is set up, in which case the address follows.

F14Ø is called to set up the cassette options, and (FEEØ) = &81, A = (FEEØ). If bit Ø of A = Ø, DB4D follows. There is no second processor. Otherwise, F168 is called with X = &FF to perform a ROM select function. If the return is zero, (Ø27A) is decremented from Ø to &FF to show that the TUBE is in use and that the appropriate ROM is available.

DB4D Y = &ØE, X = 1, and ROM select (F168) is again called. X is changed to 2, and F168 is called again. (Ø243) = (Ø244) = Y = &ØE. This is the 'PAGE' variable.

X = &FE, Y = (Ø27A), and F168 is again called.

If A AND (Ø267) gives a positive result, a jump to DB87 is taken. Bit 7 of (Ø267) bars the startup message if true. It may be set up by a ROM during initialisation.

DEA9 is called with Y = 2. This outputs a string starting at C3ØØ + Y + 1; "BBC Computer".

IF (Ø28D) = Ø a jump to DB82 is taken. This will be remembered as having been set to Ø, 1 or 2 according to the type of initialisation being executed. Otherwise DEA9 is called again with Y = &11 or &16 according to the contents of (Ø28E), which indicate the size of RAM.

DB82 DEA9 is called with Y = &1B, which gives two newlines.

DB87 C is set, and EAD9 is called to look for a 'booting jump', which may have been set up during ROM initialisation. Then E9D9 is called, this being OSBYTE 118, which sets up the LEDs in accordance with keyboard status. (Whereas EEEB set them according to data supplied.)

P is now pushed and A pulled. Then LSRA is called four times. This will zero bits 4 – 7, and bits Ø – 2. Bit 4, which was the sign flag, may be set. A = A EØR (Ø28F) AND 8. Bits Ø – 3 and 5 – 7 will now be zero, and bit 4 will be 1 if bit 4 of (Ø28F) = 1. This is disc drive data, and may or may not be 1.

Y = A, X = 3, and F168 (ROM select) is called. If it returns with the equal condition set, DBBE follows.

It must be assumed that this is a check for disc facilities, in view of what follows:

If Y ≠ Ø, a jump to DBB8 is taken. Otherwise F135 is called with A = &8D to set up standard cassette baud rates. X/Y are then set to EAD2, which is the address of a text string 'BOOT', and the Command Line Interpreter is called at FFF7. During the call, (Ø267) is decremented, this being the 'start-up suppression' flag, which is mainly concerned with the disc system.

If (Ø267), incremented again after return from the call, is ≠ Ø, DBBE follows.

DBB8 F137 is called with A = Ø, X = Ø, to set tape speed.

DBBE If (Ø28D) ≠ Ø (not warm restart), DBC8 follows. Otherwise, if (Ø28C) is positive (current ROM number), a jump is taken to DBE6.

DBC8 X = &ØF

DBCA A loop is entered which checks the ROM 'directory' from (Ø2A1) upwards. If bit 6 of the directory entry is 1 (ROM has a language entry), the routine jumps to DBE6. The ROMs are checked in descending order. If none of the ROMs has a language entry, A = Ø, and it bit 7 of (Ø27A) is true, DCØ8 follows, otherwise the report 'Language' is displayed. ((Ø27A) is the 'TUBE' flag, set to &FF if the TUBE is in use.)

DBE6 Carry is cleared, whereas the OSBYTE call enters with carry set.

OSBYTE 142: Enter Language ROM: DBE7

DBE7 P is pushed, and the Language ROM number is set in (Ø28C) from X. DC16 is called to select that ROM. Then DEAB is called with A = &8Ø and Y = 8 to display a text string held in the ROM at 8ØØ9. Y = &FD, and newline is called twice at FFE7. P is pulled, and A = 1. If (Ø27A) is negative (second processor fitted), a jump to 4ØØØ follows, else the language ROM is entered at 8ØØØ.

This completes the initialisation routine. Understanding of it will grow as other parts of the program are studied. Some of the functions will only be relevant to particular system configurations.

We are left with a small problem. Most of the subroutines called by initialisation will crop up in other contexts, where they can be examined more effectively, but there are some exceptions, which, for convenience, are described below. The first performs ROM selection:

DCOB X = (ØØF4), the currently selected ROM number, and (ØØF4) = Y, (FE3Ø) = Y, selecting ROM Y. Y = Ø, and A = ((ØØF6) + Y). Then;

DC16 (ØØF4) = X, (FE3Ø) = X. The routine returns.

The string output routine has three possible entry points:

DEA9 A = &C3, this being the high byte of string start.

DEAB (ØØFE) = A, (ØØFD) = Ø. This sets up a base address, to which Y + 1 is added to give the string start.

DEB1 Y is incremented, and A = ((ØØFD) + Y). OSASCI (FFE3) is called to output the character in A. If A ≠ Ø, the routine loops back to DEB1, else returns.

E6A7 is the tail end of a routine beginning at E689. It sets the serial ULA:

E6A7 (Ø282) = A, this being the RAM copy of the last output to the ULA, which is then set by (FE1Ø) = A. A = Y, X = A, the routine returns.

EAD9 looks for a link in ROM:

EAD9 IF (Ø287) ≠ &4C (jump op-code), return, else go to Ø287.

AT FØ55 there is an indirect jump to (FDFE), which is an address associated with the disc controller.

Review

The BREAK key can be very useful on occasion, but some of the consequences of its use can be annoying. Some significant chips in the peripheral system are reset, and this can be particularly annoying in the case of the User Interface, which may need several bytes of data to set it up in the required working mode.

It would be useful if a user-defined routine could be called up to rectify matters. The jump checked by EAD9 looks hopeful, but the jump is cleared to zeroes in both initial start and warm restart.

It is therefore necessary to incorporate any resetting process in the main program.

One thing we have learned about the initialisation routine is that it is authoritarian. It will brook no interference, and will deliver you into the hands of either the 'language ROM' or the 'TUBE'. Incidentally, if you are wondering whether you might fool the routine by setting (Ø27A) = &FF, and then putting your set-up routine at 4ØØØ, you should note that (Ø27A) is zeroed in all initialisation modes.

Nevertheless, our study of the initialisation procedure has brought to light a number of useful facts, though some of the facts are not, perhaps, quite as we would wish them to be.

Chapter 3
INTERRUPTS

The BBC computer makes extensive use of interrupt control in handling its numerous peripheral functions, and a close study of the interrupt routines is essential to an understanding of how these functions work.

In essence, an interrupt is a request for program service. If a peripheral device has data that it wants the program to accept, it may put up an interrupt, and the program being executed is then laid aside for the moment while the request is attended to. Sufficient data must be stored away to allow the original program to be resumed when the request has been satisfied.

In a 65Ø2 processor system, the various devices which can raise interrupt requests are connected to a common line on an open-collector basis, so that any of the devices can pull the line down. When this happens, the processor completes executing the current instruction, advances the program counter to point to the next instruction in sequence, then pushes the program counter and status register on to the stack. A jump is then performed to an address defined in locations FFFE/F in ROM. This is the entry to the interrupt handler.

To complicate matters, however, it is also the entry to the routines for handling a BRK instruction. When a zero op-code is found, the processor increases the program counter by two, having first set it to point to the byte after the BRK instruction, and pushes the result and the status register on to the stack. Bit 4 of the status register is set true to show that this is a BRK and not an interrupt.

The BRK instruction is primarily used to preface text which is to be displayed, especially error text. The text is preceded by the related error number.

The first task for the interrupt/BRK routine to perform is clearly to check whether it was called to service an interrupt or a BRK instruction:

DC1C A is saved in (ØØFC), and the stacked status word is pulled from the stack into A and pushed again. If bit 4 is true, the BRK handling routine is entered at DC27. Otherwise, an indirect jump to (Ø2Ø4) is taken. This will normally point to the interrupt handling routine at DC93, but can be changed to give access to a user-defined routine, a possibility which will be examined when the standard routine has been studied.

DC27 X is pushed on to the stack, and X = S, the stack pointer. This allows the stacked value of the program counter to be read, reduced by two, and stored in (ØØFD/E). The result points to the byte following the BRK instruction.

(Ø24A) is set from (ØØF4) to keep a record of the paged ROM in use, and X, still holding the stack pointer value, is copied to (ØØFØ).

Next, X = 6, and subroutine F168 is called to check for a paged ROM with a 'service entry', the entry being called. However, DC16 is then called with X = (Ø28C) to reselect the current ROM.

X is restored from the stack, and A from (ØØFC). The interrupt flag is cleared, and an indirect jump to (Ø2Ø2) is taken.

Initially, (Ø2Ø2) points to DC54, but a paged ROM may elect to change the link to point to a procedure of its own. For example, the BASIC ROM executes a short BASIC program held in ROM to tack a statement of the current line number on to the error text.

DC54 Subroutine DEB1 is called with Y = Ø. We have met this subroutine before, in the initialisation process. It displays text until its action is terminated by a zero byte. Note that it increments Y before picking up the first text byte, thereby skipping past the error number.

When the text has been output A = (Ø267), and the lsb is put into carry. If the bit is true, a dynamic halt follows, the instruction jumping to itself. Otherwise, two newlines are called, and the routine enters the initialisation process at DBB8.

Remember, this procedure is only used if a paged ROM has not taken over the task of interpretation.

Two short subroutines are placed before the main interrupt handler, both dealing with serial input/output. They are called from the body of the handler, and will be more readily understood in the context of the routines that call them. DC68 is called from DCCB and DCD4, and at DC78 from DC90.

DC68 C is set and (Ø24F) is rotated right to set bit 7 = 1. This indicates that the serial system is free. If the RS423 control byte, (Ø25Ø), shows bit 7 = Ø, a jump to DC78 is taken.

Otherwise E741 is called to count the current buffer, which will be that for the serial input buffer. X = Ø. If carry is set, the buffer is full to its permitted limit, and a jump to DC7A is taken.

DC78 X = &4Ø.

DC7A Go to E17A to transfer serial system input data.

The second subroutine is called from DCE9:

DC7D Y = (FEØ9), this being serial input data from the ACIA. If A AND &3F ≠ Ø, the routine jumps to DCB8.

Otherwise, X = (Ø25C), the RS423 input suppression flag. If X ≠ Ø, the routine jumps to DC92, RS423 input being ignored.

If the flag is zero, E4F3 is called to enter a byte in the buffer, then E741 is called to count the buffer. If carry is clear, a jump to DC78 is taken, otherwise the routine returns.

The main handler now begins. The first task is to ensure that all relevant data is preserved for use in continuing execution:

DC93 Clear D, because binary working is essential. Decimal working will be resumed, if appropriate, when the stored status byte is pulled. A is recovered from (ØØFC) and pushed. X and Y are pushed via A, then a link to DE82 is pushed, though the actual number set is DE81, because RTS adds 1 to the number it reads from the stack. DE82 is the address of the exit routine.

The overflow flag is cleared, because it is used in a looping situation.

Serial System Interrupts

Interrupts from the serial system are handled first.

DCA2 A = (FEØ8), reading ACIA status. If V is clear, and A is positive, indicating that there is no ACIA interrupt, a jump to DDØ6 enters the handler for the internal VIA. V set indicates that there has been a loop back from DE2E.

DCA9 X = (ØØEA), the RS423 timeout counter. X is decremented, and if that makes it negative the routine jumps to DCDE. Otherwise if V is set the routine returns directly. If V is clear the return is VIA F588, which reads the ACIA. Note that all returns are to the dummy link to the exit routine.

The two modules which follow are called from DCDE:

DCB3 Y = (FEØ9), ACIA data, and A is rotated left and arithmetically shifted left. This acts on the bit mask for the ACIA interrupt word, which has already been manipulated. The bits are now arranged in the order X 7 6 5 4 3 2 X, the X items being zeroes.

DCB8 X = A, A = Y, Y = 7, and E494 is entered to check and, if appropriate, service Event 7, RS423 disable. The exit routine follows.

The second module investigates possible data destinations:

DCBF E46Ø is called with X = 2 to read buffer 2, the RS423 output buffer. If C is clear on return, indictating that the buffer is not empty, a jump to DCD6 is taken.

Otherwise, the printer type is checked. If it is not a serial model ((Ø285) = 2), the routine jumps to DC68 to enquire further.

If a serial printer is selected, E46Ø is called with X = 3 to read the printer buffer. The buffer flag in (Ø2D2) is rotated right to pass carry into bit 7, and if carry was true (buffer empty), DC68 follows.

DCD6 (FE∅9) = A, passing either RS423 or printer data to the ACIA. The timeout counter in (∅∅EA) is set to &E7 (−25), and the exit routine follows.

A word on the timeout counter may be useful here. If it holds 1, the cassette system is using the ACIA. If it holds ∅ the system has timed out, but if it holds a negative number the RS423 system is using the serial facilities.

The main serial system handler comes next.

DCDE A = A AND (∅278). A holds the input from (FE∅8), the ACIA status register, and (∅278) is a mask determining which of the status bits are to be used. Normally, the mask is &FF, and all bits are significant. Then LSRA puts the lsb into carry. If the bit is ∅, the receive register is not full, and a jump to DCEB is taken. If V is set the routine again jumps to DCEB. Otherwise, the copy in (∅25∅) of the last control output to (FE∅8) is checked, and if it is negative the receive interrupt is enabled and the routine jumps to DC7D.

DCEB LSRA and RORA put bit 2 of the ACIA status word into carry. If the bit is set, the Data Carrier Detected condition applies, and the routine jumps to DCB3. If bit 7 (the original bit 1) is true, the transmit data register is empty, and the routine jumps to DCBF. If V is set, the exit routine follows.

DCF3 If this point is reached, the foregoing routines have achieved nothing, perhaps because some functions are masked out. The following routine is also executed if no other valid interrupt is found, in which case the source may be a special one introduced by the user. F168 is called with X = 5 to check for a paged ROM requiring a service routine call, and if the return is in the EQ state the normal exit routine follows.

Otherwise, the dummy return link is pulled from the stack, and X and Y are pulled via A. A is also pulled and set in (∅∅FC). The routine then jumps to (∅2∅6), which is normally DE89, but can be reset to enter a user-defined interrupt handler. Note that all the original register values have been restored, bar the program counter and status byte, and they will have to be saved again on entry to a user routine.

This completes the ACIA interrupt handler, which is complicated by the use of this channel for both RS423 and cassette work. The operation of the system may be more clearly understood when the other routines relevant to serial transfers are examined. Meanwhile, some interesting light has been shed on the interrupt-controlled functions.

Internal VIA Interrupt 1: Frame Sync

If there is no ACIA interrupt, DDØ6 is reached, and the VIA 1 interrupt 1 is looked for. This occurs every 2Ø mS, during vertical fly-back of the display.

DDØ6 IF (FE4D), the VIA 1 interrupt flag register, has bit 7 = Ø, there is no VIA 1 interrupt, and the routine jumps to DD47 to check for an interrupt from VIA 2, which serves the printer and user interfaces.

Otherwise, A = (FE4D) AND (FE4E) AND (Ø279). True bits in (FE4D) indicate active VIA 1 interrupts, true bits in (FE4E) indicate which VIA 1 interrupts are enabled, and (Ø279) is a mask, normally set to &FF, but which can be set to disable one or more of the VIA 1 interrupts. A is rotated right twice, putting the original bit 1 into carry, and if the bit is Ø there is no interrupt 1. The routine jumps to DD69 to look for interrupt 5. Otherwise, interrupt 1 is implemented as follows:

The frame counter in (Ø24Ø) is decremented, the change allowing animation to proceed.

If (ØØEA), the serial system timeout counter, is negative, it is incremented. Being initialised to &E7, it reaches zero in 5ØØ mS.

The colour flash counters in (Ø251/3) are then dealt with. The current count is in (Ø251), with the reset values in (Ø252) and (Ø253). If (Ø251) = Ø, the system is not in use, and the routine jumps to DD3D. Otherwise (Ø251) is decremented, and if that gives a non-zero result the routine jumps to DD3D. No further action is needed this time round.

If (Ø251) has been decremented to zero, X = (Ø252), and A = (Ø248), the copy of the last output to the video ULA, on (FE2Ø). If bit Ø of A is zero, the first colour is currently effective, and a jump to DD34 is taken. If the bit is 1, X = (Ø253).

DD34 A = (Ø248) EØR 1, reversing bit Ø, and subroutine EAØØ (see OSBYTE 154) is called to instruct a change of colour. (Ø251) = X, restarting the appropriate count-down.

DD3D E494 is called with Y = 4 to check and if appropriate implement, Event 4 (vertical sync event). A = 2, and a jump to DE6E clears interrupt 1. The exit routine follows.

External VIA Interrupt 1: Printer

If there is no VIA 1 interrupt, DD47 is reached, and a check is made for the VIA 2 interrupt 1, which relates to the printer

DD47 If bit 7 of (FE6D), the VIA 2 interrupt flag register, is zero, there is no VIA 2 interrupt, and the routine jumps to DCF3.

Otherwise, A = (FE6D) AND (FE6E) AND (Ø277). True bits in (FE6D) indicate active VIA 2 interrupts, true bits in (FE6E) indicate which VIA 2 interrupts are enabled, and (Ø277) is a mask which can be used to block a particular interrupt. A is rotated right twice, bringing the original bit 1 into carry, and if the bit is zero there is no interrupt 1. The routine jumps to DCF3. If the bit is true, the printer is serviced thus:

Y = (Ø285) − 1. If the result is non-zero, a parallel printer is not in use, and the routine jumps to DCF3. A serial printer will have been serviced by the serial system.

(FE6D) = 2 to reset the interrupt 1 flag, and (FE6E) = 2 to disable the interrupt 1. X = 3 to indicate the printer buffer, and E13A is called to output data to the parallel printer.

There are some interesting possibilities here. Calling E13A with X set to point to a different buffer would allow data to be printed from a chosen buffer. Bit 1 of (Ø277) would need to be zeroed to prevent normal print action from buffer 3, and bit 1 of (FE6D) would have to be checked to ensure that the printer was ready.

Subroutine E13A re-enables the printer interrupt.

Internal VIA Interrupt 5: Speech

If there is a VIA 1 interrupt, but it is not interrupt 1, a check is made for interrupt 5, which deals with the speech system. The entry point is at DD69.

DD69 A is rotated left four times, bringing the original bit 5 of (FE4D) to the msb position. If the bit is zero, there is no interrupt 5, and the routine jumps to DDCA to look for interrupt 6.

Otherwise (FE4D) = &2Ø, clearing the interrupt flag, and (FE49) = Ø, zeroing the high byte of the T2 timer.

DD79 X = 8, (ØØFB) = X.

DD7D Subroutine E45B is called to examine buffer X, and the resulting carry is shifted into bit 7 of (Ø2D7), the buffer flag. If the bit is 1, meaning that the buffer is empty, the routine returns.

Otherwise, the byte in the buffer (which has not been disturbed) is passed to Y. If it is zero, a jump to DD8D is taken. Otherwise, subroutine EE6D is called to control the speech chip. A return with negative set results in the routine returning.

DD8D Subroutine E46Ø is called to remove a byte from buffer X. The byte is placed in (ØØF5). This indicates a speech ROM or a file ROM. Two more bytes are read and placed in (ØØF7) and (ØØF6), giving the address to be accessed in a paged ROM for service actions, subject to later modification.

If (ØØF5) = Ø, the routine jumps to DDBB, while if (ØØF5) is greater than Ø, the jump is to DDB8.

If bit 6 of (ØØF5) = 1, the routine jumps to DDAB.

Otherwise, EEBB is called for further speech action.

DDA9 If V is clear, DDB2 follows.

DDAB The contents of (ØØF6/7) are doubled, and subroutine EE3B is called.

DDB2 & = (Ø261), and EE7F follows. (Ø261) is the speech suppression flag.

DDB8 Subroutine EE7F is called.

DDBB Y = (ØØF6), and EE7F is called. Y = (ØØF7), and EE7F is again called. (ØØFB) is shifted right logically, and if it is not zero the routine loops to DD7D. Note that (ØØFB) is set to 8 just before the loop point. If (ØØFB) is now zero, the routine returns.

As the speech facility was not fitted to the equipment on which this study was based, the implications of the above will not be examined in detail.

Internal VIA Interrupt 6: 1Ø mS Clock

If there is a VIA 1 interrupt, but it is neither 1 nor 5, a check is made for interrupt 6, which occurs every 1Ø mS.

DDCA Previous manipulations of (FE4D), held in A, have brought the original bit 6 into carry. If the bit is Ø, there is no interrupt 6, and the routine jumps to DE47 to look for interrupt 4.

Otherwise, (FE4D) = &4Ø clears interrupt 6. X = (Ø283), A = (Ø283) EOR &OF. A is pushed and copied into Y.

A word of explanation is needed here. There are two timer counters, each occupying five bytes, with the most significant byte in the lowest locations. Counter 1 occupies (Ø292/6), counter 2 occupies (Ø297/B). To ensure that the contents of one counter or the other are always valid, updating is performed by adding 1 to counter 1 and putting the result in counter 2, or vice versa, the direction of transfer being changed at every iteration. (Ø283) holds &Ø5 or &ØA, providing a displacement relative to Ø291 to the upper byte of one counter or the other.

DDD9 (Ø291 + Y) = (Ø291 + X) + C. Carry is initially true, or the jump to DE47 would have been taken, so the count is incremented. X and Y are decremented, and if neither has reached Ø the routine loops to DDD9 to deal with the next byte.

DDE7 A is pulled and copied into (Ø283). X = 5, in preparation for the loop which follows, updating the third counter. This is described as a 'countdown timer', but it is incremented like the clock timers.

DDED (Ø29B + X) is incremented. If the result is not zero, no carry is needed, and a jump to DDFA is taken. Otherwise X is decremented, and if the result is not equal to Ø the routine loops to DDED.

If all locations of (Ø29B/AØ) are zero, X reaches zero, and E494 is called with Y = 5 to process Event 5: Interval timer event.

DDFA The keyboard delay timer in (Ø2B1/2) is checked. If it does not hold zero, it is decremented.

DEØA If bit 7 of (Ø2CE) = Ø, a jump is taken to DE1A. The sound routine is being executed, and must not be called again.

Otherwise (Ø2CE) is incremented from &FF to Ø, the I flag is cleared to permit interrupts, and subroutine EB47 is called to implement the routine sound processes. On return, I is set to bar further interrupts, and (Ø2CE) is decremented from Ø to &FF.

There are a number of interesting points here. First, the sound routine is protected against a further interrupt 6, which must mean that the routine can take more than 1Ø mS to execute. This time may be broken into by other interrupts, and the other functions of interrupt 6 can be executed. However, it would seem that an interesting situation could arise if the sound routine took slightly less than 1Ø mS to execute, so that it could be called at every 1Ø mS interrupt, but would mop up nearly all computing time. Other interrupt-controlled functions would be able to force their way in, but routine processes might be rather delayed . . .

DE1A If bit 7 of (Ø2D7) = 1, the routine jumps to DE2B. The speech buffer is empty. Otherwise, EE6D is called to update the speech system variables, and then A = A EOR &AØ. If the result is equal to or greater than &6Ø, DD79 is called; this is another speech function, part of the speech interrupt process.

DE2B The V and S flags are set, and DCA2 is called. This is the loop back to check whether the ACIA requires attention.

Then A = (ØØEC) OR (ØØED) AND (Ø242). The first two locations hold the key numbers of recently-pressed keys, while (Ø242) is the keyboard semaphore, which holds zero if the keyboard is to be ignored. If A is non-zero, the keyboard routine is called at FØ65, with carry set.

DE3E E19B is called to see if there is data for the user-defined printer channel. If bit 6 of (FECØ), the A/D converter status, is true, a jump is taken to DE4A. Otherwise the routine returns.

Internal VIA Interrupt 4: End of Conversion

Having found no interrupt 1, 5 or 6, the program checks for interrupt 4. This is raised when an A/D conversion is complete.

DE47 A is rotated left to put the original bit 4 from (FE4D) into bit 7 of A. If the bit is Ø, there is no interrupt 4, and the routine jumps to DE72.

DE4A X = (Ø24C), which holds the current A/D channel number. If X = Ø, a jump to DE6C is taken. Otherwise, (Ø2B5 + X) = (FEC2), setting the lower byte of the conversion result, and (Ø2B9 + X) = (FEC1), setting the upper byte. (Ø2BE) = X to mark the last channel read.

E494 is called with Y = 3 to handle Event 3, Conversion complete.

X is decremented, and if the result is zero X = (Ø 24D), to select the next channel.

DE69 DE8F is called to start another conversion. (See OSBYTE 17)

DE6C A = &1Ø, preparing to reset interrupt 4.

DE6E (FE4D) = A. The routine returns.

Internal VIA Interrupt 0: Keyboard

With no interrupt 1, 4, 5 or 6, only interrupt Ø remains:

DE72 A is rotated left four times to put the original bit Ø in the bit 7 position. If the bit is Ø, DE7F = DCF3 follows.

Otherwise, FØ65 is called to scan the keyboard, the interrupt meaning that a key has been pressed.

A = 1 and the routine jumps to DE6E to reset the interrupt flag.

Exit Routine

The exit routine has two entries:

DE82 Y and X are pulled via A, and A is pulled and copied in (ØØFC).

DE89 A = (ØØFC), and an RTI instruction follows.

Review

One of the more difficult things to appreciate about an interrupt routine is that it can interrupt itself. An attempt to imagine the possible complications of multiple nested interrupts is enough to make the mind boggle. The point to appreciate is that at all times the intervention of an interrupt must not be allowed to disrupt the apparent continuity of the program which has been interrupted. Five bytes, plus return links, go on to the stack for each interrupt, and it is by no means impossible to reach a situation which makes the stack overflow.

For this reason, any addition to the interrupt routine must be considered with care. As matters stand, there are a hundred 1Ø mS interrupts a second, and fifty 2Ø mS interrupts. Fortunately, most are implemented fairly rapidly, but some, like the Sound function, take longer, and can rather gum up the works.

However, it is quite possible to add further interrupts to service system extensions dreamed up by the user. The first need is for a means of raising the interrupt. The user interface can raise one through VIA 2, and the 1 MHz interface provides another path, though one more difficult to implement.

There must be provision for identifying the interrupt source, unless only a single interrupt is involved. the handling routine must store away A,X and Y, restoring them before it exits. There are two obvious points of access, the indirect links to DC93 and DE89. Remember, however, that all indirect links will be reset if you press the BREAK key, and on resumption they have to be set again.

Once the system is appreciated, there are a number of possibilities arising from the interrupt handler, but full appreciation will not be possible until the associated routines have been examined.

Chapter 4
THE OSBYTE AND OSWORD CALLS

Having dealt with initialisation and interrupts, we must now turn to the OSBYTE call system, which spreads its tentacles throughout the operating system, and identifies and explains many functions.

Entry to the OSBYTE system is at FFF4, but this leads to an indirect jump to E772. Most of the system entry points are arranged on this basis, so that they need not be changed if the routine is revised. Your version may show indirection via (Ø2ØA), but (Ø2ØA) may not contain E772. It will, nevertheless, point to the OSBYTE master routine:

E772 A and P are pushed, and the I flag is set to bar interrupt. A is also saved in (ØØEF), X in (ØØFØ), and Y in (ØØF1). X = 7.

The routine then branches according to the value of A:
A = Ø - &74 (Ø - 116): Go to E7C2
A = &75 - &AØ (117 - 160): Go to E78E
A = &A1 - &A5 (161 - 165): Go to E7C8
A = &A6 - &FF (166 - 255): Continue

C is cleared.

E78A A = &A1 + C, i.e. &A6 to &FF are converted to &A1, whereas entry at E78A with carry set gives &A2.

E78E A = A − &5F. This converts &75 - AØ to &16 - &41. (22 - 65).

E791 A is doubled and C is set.

E793 (ØØF1) = Y, Y = A. If bit 7 of (Ø25E) = Ø, the routine jumps to E7A2. The variable is the flag for Econet interception, and the jump skips Econet access;

A = X. V is cleared, and (Ø224) is called, this being the Econet vector. If the return has V set, the attempt to pass an OSBYTE call to Econet is barred, and the routine jumps to E7BC. Tracing back, we find that X was set to 7, this being the code to tell Econet that an OSBYTE call is being attempted.

If Econet is not fitted, all this is skipped.

E7A2 (ØØFA/B) = (E5B3/4 + Y). This sets up an address read from a word table, a table that gives the entry point for all OSBYTE and OSWORD calls, and so provides a positive gold-mine of information on where the OSBYTE routines can be found. For convenience, the table is reproduced here, though you may need to produce a revised table for your particular version of the system.

A is now restored from (ØØEF) and Y from (ØØF1). However, if C is clear (OSBYTE &A6 - &FF), Y = Ø and A = ((ØØFØ)), i.e. the contents of the location pointed to by (ØØFØ/1).

E7B6 C is set, X = (ØØFØ), and FØ58 is called, this being in fact a call to (ØØFA/B), the address set up from the table.

E7BC On return, A is rotated right, P is pulled, and A is rotated left to bring carry into the lsb. A is then pulled, V is cleared, and the routine returns.

The above routine is not complete in itself, since it enters:

E7C2 Y = Ø. If A is less than &16, the main routine is re-entered at E791.

E7C8 P is pushed twice, to balance the stack for;

E7CA A is pulled twice, and F168 is called to offer a paged ROM service call. If the return is NE, E7D6 follows, otherwise X = (ØØØFØ) and the routine jumps to E7BC, the exit routine.

E7D6 P and A are pulled, V and S are set, and the routine returns.

For OSBYTE calls Ø -&15, &75 - &AØ, and &A6 - &FF, the above is largely irrelevant, but OSBYTE calls &16 - &74 and &A1 - &A5, which are listed as 'not used by OS 1.20', reach E7C8, where they might be expected to go directly to the exit.

The OSWORD system has much in common with the OSBYTE system, but it has a different entry at FFF1 = (Ø2ØC), and its own control routine:

E7EB A and P are pushed, and I is set to bar interrupts. As with OSBYTE, (ØØEF) = A, (ØØFØ) = X, (ØØF1) = Y. X = 8, which is the Econet code for an attempt to pass an OSWORD call.

If A exceeds &DF, the routine jumps to E78A with carry set, A = &A2, and this is converted to &43 by subtracting &5F.

If, otherwise, A exceeds &ØD, a jump to E7C8 treats the call as if it was a rejected OSBYTE call.

Barring these jumps, A = A + &44, converting Ø - &ØD to &44 - &51. A is then doubled, and the OSBYTE control routine is entered at E793.

To clarify the make-up of the table of link addresses:

Words Ø - &15:	OSBYTE Ø - &15
Words &16 - &41:	OSBYTE &75 - &AØ
Word &42:	OSBYTE &A6 - &FF
Word &43:	OSBYTE &EØ - &FF
Words &44 - 51	OSWORD Ø - & OD.

We can now take a tour of some of the OSBYTE routines, omitting those which are too lengthy to include here or which are closely related to other major functions.

OSBYTE 0 : Display OS version number: E821

This enters a text block, prefaced as usual by a BRK instruction, which displays the OS number.

OSBYTE 1: Reserved: E988
OSBYTE 3: Select Output: E997
OSBYTE 4: Reset Edit Keys: E997
OSBYTE 5: Set printer type: E976

OSBYTE 6: Suppressed printer character: E988
OSBYTE 11: Keyboard repeat delay: E995
OSBYTE 12: Keyboard repeat period: E98C
OSBYTE 166 – 255: Reset variables: E99C

All these use a common routine, beginning at E976.

E976 Clear I and set it again, to give interrupt a chance. If bit 7 of (ØØFF) = 1 (ESCAPE), return. If bit 7 of (Ø2D2) = Ø, loop to E976. Buffer 3 (printer) is not empty.

When the buffer is empty, E1A4 is called in case there is a user-defined printer routine to be taken into account. Then (ØØF1) = Y = Ø.

E988 A = A OR &FO. Go to E99A. A holds the OSBYTE number, so the result is &F5 for OSBYTE 5, &F6 for OSBYTE 6.

E98C If (ØØFØ) ≠ Ø the routine jumps to E995, but if (ØØFØ) = Ø, which means that X in the call was Ø, (Ø254) = &32 and X = 8. This resets the auto repeat delay to the standard values and prepares to perform the same service for the repeat period.

E995 A = A + &DØ. This is the entry for setting keyboard delay.

E997 A = A + &E9. This is the entry for output select and reset edit keys. (Carry is cleared before the addition.)

E99A (ØØFØ) = X.

E99C Y = A, A = (Ø19Ø + Y). This is the key to the whole thing, because the location accessed will be in page 2, and will be related to A by the addition of Ø19Ø. Next, X = A, to preserve the original value, which is returned after the call. Then A = A AND (ØØF1) EOR (ØØFØ) and (Ø19Ø + Y) = A. Y = A = (Ø191 + Y), and the routine returns.

This is a routine that needs careful study. Entry at E99C presents few problems. A will have a value between &A6 and

&FF, so the location accessed will be (Ø236) to (Ø28F). We can identify the meaning of each of these variables in terms of the OSBYTE call definition. The change to the variable will depend on the contents of (ØØFØ) and (ØØF1). A zero bit in (ØØF1) will zero the corresponding bit in the variable. A true bit in (ØØFØ) will reverse the corresponding bit of the variable. Working out the effect may involve a little head massage, but is not unduly difficult.

Entry at E997 will change A from 3 to &EC or from 4 to &ED. The location accessed will be (Ø27C) or (Ø27D). We could equally well have used OSBYTE &EC or OSBYTE &ED.

Confusion is possible over entry at E98C. This is for OSBYTE 12, and adding &DØ and &E9 will give (Ø255) as the location to be dealt with. This is Repeat period. Entry at E995, on the other hand, is for OSBYTE 11, and the location affected will be (Ø254), which holds repeat delay.

Finally, it is commonsense not to change the printer selection while printout is taking place, which explains the loop to E976.

OSBYTE 2: Select Input Devices: E6D3

This deals with the keyboard and RS423 data sources.

E6D3 A = A AND 1, and A is pushed. This isolates bit 1, which determines keyboard selection.

A = (Ø25Ø), the copy of the last ouptut to the ACIA control port. If X is greater than zero, bit 7 of A is set to 1, otherwise to Ø. If this makes A different from (Ø25Ø), the NE condition is set. P is pushed.

(Ø25Ø) and (FEØ8) are set from A, being the ACIA control input and copy. E173 is called to deal with the RS423 buffer.

P is pulled, and if the NE state is found the V and S bits are set from bits 6 and 7 of (FEØ9), the ACIA data input.

X = (Ø241), to return the old keyboard state, then A is pulled and copied into (Ø241) as the new state.

OSBYTE 7: Select Receive Baud Rate: E68B

OSBYTE 8: Select Transmit Baud Rate: E689

E689 A = &38.

E68B A = A EOR &3F. This converts &38 to &Ø7 and &Ø7 (OSBYTE 7) to &38. The result is a mask picking out either bits Ø – 2 or 3 – 5, the former applying to transmit, the latter to receive. (ØØFA) = A.

Then Y = (Ø282), the last output to the serial ULA, and if X exceeds 8 a jump to E6AD is taken: the parameter is out of range.

Otherwise, A = A AND (E9AD + X), which refers to a look-up table. The table becomes more comprehensible if it is written out in binary, when it becomes apparent that the same pattern appears in bits Ø – 2 and 3 – 5 in each byte. A is copied to (ØØFB).

Then A = Y OR (ØØFA) EOR (ØØFA), which zeroes the three bits which are set true in (ØØFA). Then A = A OR (ØØFB) OR &4Ø, setting up the data read from the look-up table plus bit 6. Finally, A = A EOR (Ø25D), which takes the Cassette/RS423 flag into account. (Ø for RS423, &4Ø for cassette. RS423 will leave A unaltered, cassette will reset bit 6.)

E6A7 (Ø282) = (FE1Ø) = A, setting up the Video ULA and its RAM copy.

E6AD A = Y

E6AE X = A. The routine returns.

OSBYTE 9: Duration of First Colour: E6BØ

OSBYTE 1Ø: Duration of Second Colour: E6B2

E6BØ Y is incremented from Ø to 1, and C is cleared.

E6B2 A = (Ø252 + Y), which is either the mark or space count source for flashing colours. (See interrupt routine.) A is pushed, and (Ø252 + Y) = X. Y is pulled, and A = (Ø251), the actual counter for colour flash control. If A is non-zero, a jump to E6D1 is taken.

Otherwise, (Ø251) = X, to initialise a new count. Then bit Ø of (Ø248) is set from carry (Ø for first colour, 1 for second), and (FE2Ø) = A to set the Video ULA.

E6D1 The routine exits via E6AD in OSBYTE 7/8.

OSBYTE 13: Disable Event: E6F9
OSBYTE 14: Enable Event: E6FA

E6F9 A = Y = Ø.

E6FA IF X exceeds 9, the routine jumps to E6AE in OSBYTE 7/8, the parameter being out of range. Otherwise, Y = (Ø2BF + X), the present event flag, and (Ø2BF + X) = A. The routine exits via E6AD in OSBYTE 7/8.

It should be noted that merely enabling an event is not enough. It is necessary to supply a user-defined routine which will implement the required response to the event.

OSBYTE 15 will be covered under 'Buffers'.

OSBYTE 16: Select A/D Channel: E7Ø6

E7Ø6 If X in the call was Ø, go to E7ØB, else call DE8C to start conversion. (OSBYTE 17, below.)

E7ØB A = (Ø24D), (Ø24D) = X. This sets the maximum A/D channel number and saves the old number in A, which is copied to X. The routine returns.

OSBYTE 17: Start Conversion: DE8C

DE8C (Ø2BE) = Y, setting 'last channel to finish conversion'.

If X is greater than 4, X = 4, avoiding out-of-range values. Then (Ø24C) = X, setting 'current A/D channel'.

Y = (Ø24E) – 1, A = Y AND 8. This handles the flags for 8 or 12 bit conversion. (Ø24E) holds Ø or &ØC for 12-bit converson, 8 for 8-bit conversion. The process here converts Ø or &ØC to 8, 8 to Ø.

A = A + (Ø24C) – 1, and the result is passed to (FECØ), the A/D control channel.

OSBYTE 18 will be covered under Command Line Interpreter.

OSBYTE 19: Wait for Animation: E9B6
OSBYTE 160: Read VDU Parameters: E9C0

E9B6 A = (0240). This location is decremented at the Frame Sync interrupt. While (0240) remains equal to A, the routine loops to E9B6. When (0240) changes:

E9C0 Y = (0301 + X), X = (0300) + X. This picks up two variables related to the VDU control system. The routine returns:

OSBYTE 20 will be covered under VDU Control.
OSBYTE 21 will be covered under Buffers.

The next call is:

OSBYTE 117: Read VDU Status: E86C

E86C X = (00D0). This is the status byte which controls VDU action. This routine is oddly appended to the sound setting routine.

OSBYTE 118 will be covered under Keyboard.
OSBYTE 119 will be covered under Files.
OSBYTE 120 will be covered under Keyboard.
OSBYTE 121 will be covered under Keyboard.
OSBYTE 122 will be covered under Keyboard.
OSBYTE 123 will be covered under Output.

OSBYTE 124: Clear Escape Condition: E673
OSBYTE 125: Set Escape Flag: E674
OSBYTE 126: Acknowledge Escape: E65C

E65C X = 0. If bit 7 of (00FF) = 0, the Escape condition is not set. The routine jumps to E673.

Otherwise, if (0276) ≠ 0 the usual responses to Escape are suppressed, the routine jumping to E671.

If (0276) = 0, the interrupt flag is cleared, (0269) = 0, resetting the line counter for paged mode, F68D (EXEC) is called to close any open EXEC file, and F0AA is called to flush buffers.

E671 X = &FF, indicating that Escape has been acknowledged.

E673 Carry is cleared.

E674 Carry will be set if OSBYTE 125 enters here. (ØØFF) is rotated right, shifting carry into bit 7.

If bit 7 of (Ø27A) = 1, there is a second processor, and the routine jumps to Ø4Ø3, otherwise returning.

OSBYTE 127: End of File check: EØ35
OSBYTE 139: File Options: EØ34

EØ34 A is doubled.

EØ35 A = A AND 1. The routine jumps to EØ31.

EØ31 is an entry to a branching routine covered under the Command Line Interpreter. OSBYTE 127 enters this with A = 1, giving a branch to F61E. OSBYTE 139 enters with A = Ø, giving F54D, the *OPT routine.

OSBYTE 128: ADVAL: E74F

E74F If the negative flag is set, the routine jumps to E732 to report on the buffer defined by X. (See below)

If the EQ flag is set, X = Ø, and the routine jumps to E75F to report on the ADC system. If X is greater than 4, the routine jumps to E729 (OSBYTE 13Ø).

Otherwise, Y = (Ø2B9 + X), the high part of the last value read from channel X, and X = (Ø2B5 + X), the low part of the value.

The routine returns.

E75F A = (FE4Ø) + 16. This brings the upper nibble of Port B of VIA 1 into the lower nibble. A = A EOR &FF, inverting the nibble. Then A = A AND 3, isolating the 'fire button' bits. Y = (Ø2BE), the number of the last ADC channel to convert, and (Ø2BE) is set from X (to Ø). X = A. The routine returns.

The following routine is given here for convenience. It is entered from ADVAL above:

E732 X = X EOR &FF. This converts the negated value used in the OSBYTE call. (To be precise, complemented, not negated.)

If X ≠ 2, carry is set.

E738 V is cleared. The routine jumps to E73E to count a buffer.

E73B V is set, selecting buffer purge.

E73E The routine jumps to (Ø22E), normally E1D1.

For futher details, see Buffers.
OSBYTE 129-131 are covered under Keyboard.
OSBYTE 132-135 are covered under VDU control.

OSBYTE 136: Execute Code via User Vector

E657 A = Ø.

E659 The routine jumps to (Ø2ØØ). If this vector has not been set, it links to 'Bad Command'.

E659 is an entry point for the *LINE function.
OSBYTE 137 is covered under Files.
OSBYTE 138 is covered under Buffers.
OSBYTE 140-141 are covered under Files.
OSBYTE 142 is covered under Initialisation.
OSBYTE 143 is covered under Files.

OSBYTE 144: Alter CRT Controller Bias: EAE3

This is equivalent to the *TV function.

EAE3 A = (Ø29Ø), (Ø29Ø) = X. This is a variable which is added to the frame sync delay setting, moving the display up and down. The X = A, A = Y AND 1, Y = (Ø291), (Ø291) = A. This variable determines the interlace setting of the display.

OSBYTE 145 is covered under Buffers.

OSBYTE 146: Read from FCØØ-FCFF: FFAA

FFAA Y = (FCØØ + X). The routine returns.

OSBYTE 147: Write to FCØØ-FCFF: EAF4

EAF4 (FCØØ + X) = Y. The routine returns.

OSBYTE 148: Read from FDØØ-FDFF: FFAE

FFAE Y = (FDØØ + X). The routine returns.

OSBYTE 149: Write to FDØØ-FDFF: EAF9

EAF9 (FDØØ + X) = Y. The routine returns.

OSBYTE 150: Read from FE00-FEFF: FFB2

FFB2 Y = (FE00 + X). The routine returns.

OSBYTE 151: Write to FE00-FEFF: EAFE

EAFE (FE00 + X) = Y. The routine returns.

OSBYTE 152-153 are covered under Buffers.

OSBYTE 154: Set Video ULA: E9FF

E9FF A = X.

EA00 The routine is entered at this point from the VDU control system. P is pushed and interrupt barred. (0248) = A, (FE20) = A. This sets the video ULA and the RAM copy of the last setting. Also, (0251) = (0253), initialising the flash counter to the space count. P is pulled, the routine returns.

OSBYTE 155: Write to Palette Register: EA10

EA10 A = X.

EA11 This entry is used by the VDU control system. A = A EOR 7, converting the RAM format to the palatte format, P is pushed and interrupt barred. (0249) = A, (FE21) = A, setting the palette register and its RAM copy. P is pulled and the routine returns.

The data set in the palette register is in two parts. The upper nibble defines a logic colour, the lower nibble defines an actual colour.

OSBYTE 156 is covered under Output.

OSBYTE 157: BPUT for TUBE: FFA7

FFA7 A = X. Go to FFD4. (OSBPUT).

This does not appear to be markedly different from OSBPUT.

OSBYTE 158, 159 are covered under Files. The remaining OSBYTE calls have been covered earlier.

OSWORD Calls

OSWORD calls assume that a block of parametric data has been set up, starting at an address defined in X/Y. Data may be set in the same block. The address is copied to (00F0/1)

OSWORD Ø: Read a Line to Memory: E9Ø2

E9Ø2 Y = 4.

E9Ø4 (Ø2B1 + Y) = ((ØØFØ) + Y). This copies the line length (Y = 2), the minimum ASCII code (Y = 3) and the maximum ASCII code (Y = 4). Y is decremented, and if the result is two or more the routine loops to E9Ø4.

Otherwise, (ØØE9) = ((ØØFØ) + Y), copying the upper byte of the address of the buffer holding the line. Y is decremented to Ø, and used to zero the paged mode line counter in (Ø269). Then (ØØE8) = ((ØØFØ) + Y), copying the lower byte of the buffer address. Interrupt is enabled, and the routine jumps to E924.

E91D This is a loop point. A = 7, the code for Bell, used as a warning that buffer length has been exceeded.

E91F Another loop point. Y is decremented.

E920 Another loop point. Y is incremented.

E921 Call FFEE (OSWRCH) to write the last character found.

E924 Call FFEO (OSRDCH) to read a character. If carry is set, the routine exits via E972. This will occur if buffer length has been exceeded, or an illegal code has been found, being determined by the nature of the looping jump.

Otherwise, X = A, and A = (Ø27C), which holds the flags determining output channels. A is rotated right twice to put the original bit 1 into carry. If the bit is 1, the VDU driver is disabled, and the routine jumps to E937. Otherwise the parameter count is checked, and if parameters are outstanding, shown by (Ø26A) ≠ Ø, the routine loops back to E921, disregarding validity checks, which do not apply to parametric data.

E937 If A ≠ &7F, the character is not deleted, and the routine jumps on to E942. Otherwise, if Y = Ø this is the first character, and delete is ignored by a jump to E924 to read the next character. Barring that, Y is decremented to mark the omitted character, and the routine loops to E921. The delete will be dealt with elsewhere.

E942 If A ≠ &15, the character is not Control U, which deletes the whole line and E953 follows. If A = &15, Y is checked. If it holds zero, the first character is being read, and the routine jumps to E924 (with carry set). Otherwise, A = &7F, delete, and:

E94B FFEE (OSWRCH) is called to perform a delete, and Y is decremented. The routine loops to E94B until Y = ∅. Since Y counts the number of characters so far copied, this deletes all those characters. The routine then jumps to E924 with carry set.

E953 ((∅∅E8) + Y) = A stores the character in the designated buffer, and if the character is &∅D the routine exits via E96C. Otherwise, loop points are seleted thus: If Y is equal to or greater than (∅2B3), the loop is to E91D, ringing the Bell. (Carry set.) If A is less than (∅2B4), the jump is to E91F. (Carry clear.) If A is equal to (∅2B5) the jump is to E92∅ with carry set, while a lesser value of A causes the same jump with carry clear. Otherwise the routine jumps to E91F with carry set.

E96C Newline is called (FFE7) and E57E = (∅224), the Econet vector, is called.

E972 A = (∅∅FF), and a rotate left puts bit 7 into carry, indicating whether Escape is active or not. The routine returns.

Some aspects of this routine will be clearer when the VDU system has been studied.

OSWORD 1: Read Clock: E8D5
OSWORD 3: Read Timer: E8D1

E8D1 X = &∅F the displacement from clock to timer in RAM, and the routine jumps to E8D8.

E8D5 X = (∅283), which indicates which of the two timers is currently selected.

E8D8 Y = 4

E8DA ((∅∅F∅) + Y) = (∅28D + X), copying the timer or clock data into the designated parameter block. X is incremented, Y is decremented, and the routine loops to E8DA until Y is negative.

E8E3 The routine returns.

OSWORD 2: Write Clock: E8E8
OSWORD 4: Write Timer: E8E4

E8E4 A = &ØF, the offset between clock and timer. E8EE follows.

E8E8 A = (Ø283) EOR &ØF. The current timer pointer is inverted to select the quiescent timer. Carry is cleared. It will be set for OSWORD 4.

E8EE A is pushed, and X = A. Y = 4

E8F2 (Ø28D + X) = ((ØØFØ) + Y) . X is incremented and Y is decremented. While Y is positive, the routine loops to E8F2, copying the parameter data to the clock or timer. A is pulled, and if carry is set the routine returns via E8E3. Otherwise (Ø283) = A, selecting the timer which has been set.

OSWORD 5: Read I/O Processor Memory: E8Ø3

E8Ø3 E815 is called to set up the address of the data block, then LDA (&F9,X) picks up a byte and the byte is stored in ((ØØFØ) + Y) . The routine returns.

OSWORD 6: Write to I/O Processor Memory: E8ØB

E8ØB E815 is called to set up the address of the data block, then A = (ØØFØ + Y), and STA (&F9,X) stores the byte. The routine returns.

E815 (ØØFA) = A. Y (initially Ø) is incremented, and (ØØFB) = ((ØØFØ) + Y). Y = 4, X = 1, the routine returns.

In the OSWORD call, X and Y define a four-byte block start. The block contains a 32-bit address. The OSWORD contol routine copies the block start address to (ØØFØ/1).

OSWORD 7, 8 are covered under Sound.

OSWORD 9-13 are covered under VDU Control.

The higher OSWORD calls are equivalent to OSBYTE 186.

The OSBYTE/OSWORD system is complex, but provides a valuable indication of some of the major entry points in the system. The key advantage of this lies in the fact that the OSBYTE and OSWORD calls have clearly defined functions, so the coding used is easier to follow. (With some notable exceptions!)

Table of OSBYTE and OSWORD Calls

OSBYTE Ø	E821	Display OS Version number
OSBYTE 1	E988	Modifies (Ø281), the 'user flag'
OSBYTE 2	E6D3	Select input stream. Modifies (Ø27C)
OSBYTE 3	E997	Select output stream. Modifies (Ø27D)
OSBYTE 4	E997	Select Cursor Editing mode. Modifies (Ø27D)
OSBYTE 5	E976	Select Printer Channel. Modifies (Ø285)
OSBYTE 6	E988	Set Printer Ignore Character. Modifies (Ø286)
OSBYTE 7	E68B	Receive Baud Rate Select
OSBYTE 8	E689	Transmit Baud Rate Select
OSBYTE 9	E6BØ	Set mark period for flashing colours
OSBYTE 1Ø	E6B2	Set space period for flashing colours
OSBYTE 11	E995	Set keyboard repeat delay
OSBYTE 12	E98C	Set keyboard repeat rate
OSBYTE 13	E6F9	Disable events
OSBYTE 14	E6FA	Enable events
OSBYTE 15	FØA8	Flush buffers
OSBYTE 16	E7Ø6	Select AD converter channels
OSBYTE 17	DE8C	Force AD conversion
OSBYTE 18	E9C8	Reset Soft Keys
OSBYTE 19	E9B6	Wait for vertical sync.
OSBYTE 2Ø	CDØ7	Explode soft characters
OSBYTE 21	FØB4	Flush specific buffer
OSBYTE 117	E86C	Read VDU Status
OSBYTE 118	E9D9	Set keyboard LEDs
OSBYTE 119	E275	Close SPOOL or EXEC files
OSBYTE 12Ø	FØ45	Write key pressed data

OSBYTE 121	FØCF	Keyboard scan
OSBYTE 122	FØCD	Keyboard scan from &1Ø
OSBYTE 123	E197	Warn printer going dormant
OSBYTE 124	E673	Clear Escape
OSBYTE 125	E674	Set Escape
OSBYTE 126	E65C	Acknowledge Escape
OSBYTE 127	EØ35	Check for end of file
OSBYTE 128	E74F	ADVAL
OSBYTE 129	E713	INKEY
OSBYTE 13Ø	E729	Read High Order Address
OSBYTE 131	FØ85	READ OSHWM
OSBYTE 132	D923	READ HIMEM
OSBYTE 133	D926	Read bottom of screen RAM
OSBYTE 134	D647	Read Text Cursor Position
OSBYTE 135	D7C2	Read Character at Text Position
OSBYTE 136	E657	Execute Code via User Vector
OSBYTE 137	E67F	Switch cassette motor relay
OSBYTE 138	E4AF	Put value in buffer
OSBYTE 139	EØ34	Select file options
OSBYTE 14Ø	F135	Select Tape filing system
OSBYTE 141	F135	Select ROM filing system
OSBYTE 142	DBE7	Enter Language ROM
OSBYTE 143	F168	Paged ROM Service Request
OSBYTE 144	EAE3	Alter CRT Controller Bias
OSBYTE 145	E46Ø	Get character from buffer
OSBYTE 146	FFAA	Read from Page &FC
OSBYTE 147	EAF4	Write to Page &FC
OSBYTE 148	FFAE	Read from Page &FD
OSBYTE 149	EAF9	Write to Page &FD
OSBYTE 15Ø	FFB2	Read from Page &FE
OSBYTE 151	EAFE	Write to Page &FE
OSBYTE 152	E45B	Examine buffer status
OSBYTE 153	E4F3	Character to input buffer, checking Escape
OSBYTE 154	E9FF	Write to Video ULA and RAM copy
OSBYTE 155	EA1Ø	Write to palette register
OSBYTE 156	E17C	Update ACIA registers and RAM copy
OSBYTE 157	FFA7	Second processor access
OSBYTE 158	EE6D	Read from Speech Processor
OSBYTE 159	EE7F	Write to Speech Processor

OSBYTE 160	E9C0	Read VDU variable
OSBYTE 166	- 255	Access variable (OSBYTE No + 0190)
OSWORD 0	E902	Read input line to memory
OSWORD 1	E8D5	Read System Clock
OSWORD 2	E8E8	Write System Clock
OSWORD 3	E8D1	Read Interval Timer
OSWORD 4	E8E4	Write Interval Timer
OSWORD 5	E803	Read I/O Processor
OSWORD 6	E80B	Write I/O Processor
OSWORD 7	E82D	Sound
OSWORD 8	E8AE	Envelope
OSWORD 9	C735	Read Pixel Colour
OSWORD 10	CBF3	Read character pattern
OSWORD 11	C748	Read Colour
OSWORD 12	C8E0	Write Colour
OSWORD 13	D5CE	Read previous and current graphic cursor positions

OSWORD 224-225 E659. Equivalent to *LINE. See OSBYTE 186.

Chapter 5
INPUT AND OUTPUT

The primary input sources are the keyboard and the RS423 system, but that is really an oversimplification. In the section on Files, it will be seen that input data can be drawn from ROMs or a cassette recorder, and in a disc system there is yet another input source.

The input and output paths are provided with buffers, so that data can be set up before it is needed. These will be dealt with in the next chapter, and a chapter on the keyboard follows. This will include an examination of the OSRDCH routine, which is the main means for obtaining input data. OSBGET, on the other hand, is covered under files.

OSWRCH, the main output routine, is a different matter. It will be dealt with here, since it is rather more complex than OSRDCH.

The starting point for the examination is OSASCI (FFE3). Unlike the other main entry points for the operating system, this does not have an immediate soft link. Instead, there is a short routine for handling Newline:

FFE3 If A ≠ &ØD, the routine jumps to FFEE. Otherwise;

FFE7 A = &ØA, and FFEE is called. Then A = &ØD, and;

FFEE The routine jumps to (Ø2ØE), here taken as EØA4.

Entry at FFE3 outputs ASCII code, the &ØD code being expanded to give line feed as well as carriage return.

Entry at FFE7 gives a new line.

FFEE is the OSWRCH entry, using the following code:

EØA4 A, X and Y are pushed, and X = S, the stack pointer. This allows A, modified in pushing X and Y, to be recovered from the stack by A = (Ø1Ø3 + X). The stack is not disturbed.

A, now holding the code to the output, is pushed.

If bit 7 of (Ø26Ø) = Ø, Econet is not involved, and the routine jumps to EØBB. Otherwise Y = A, A = 4, and a jump to (Ø224) enters the Econet routines. If the return has a carry set, the routine jumps to E1ØD. No other access is involved.

EØBB Carry is cleared, and if bit 1 of (Ø27C) = 1, the routine jumps to EØC8. The screen is disabled. Otherwise, A is pulled and pushed to restore the ASCII code, and C4CØ is called. This is the VDU control routine, and its address should be noted for future reference.

EØC8 If bit 3 of (Ø27C) = 1, the routine jumps to EØD1. The printer is enabled, even if the VDU control routine thinks it is not. Otherwise, if carry is clear the routine jumps to EØD6. This means that either the VDU control routine has not been called, or has returned with carry clear, indicating that the printer has already been served.

EØD1 A is pulled and pushed, again restoring the character code, and E114 is called to drive the printer. Then:

EØD6 If bit Ø of (Ø27C) = Ø, the routine jumps to EØF7. The RS423 driver is not enabled. Otherwise, Y = (ØØEA) − 1, and if Y is then positive the routine jumps to EØF7. The cassette system is using the RS423 facility.

Otherwise, A is pulled and pushed, and P is pushed. Interrupt is barred. X = 2, and A is pushed again. E45B is called to examine buffer X, returning with carry set if the buffer is empty. If carry is clear, the routine jumps to EØFØ, otherwise calling E17Ø, the ACIA control routine.

EØFØ A is pulled, and E1F8 is called with X = 2 to enter a character in buffer X. P is pulled.

EØF7 A = &1Ø as a mask to check bit 4 of (Ø27C). If the bit is 1 the routine jumps to E1ØD, spooled output being disabled. Otherwise, if (Ø257) = Ø there is an input file handle for SPOOL, and the routine jumps to E1ØD.

If spooling is in order, A is pulled and pushed, C is set, and (ØØEB) is rotated right to set bit 7 = 1. OSBPUT is called at FFD4, then (ØØEB) is shifted left to clear bit 7.

E1ØD A, Y, X and A are pulled. The routine returns.

The printer driver comes next. It can be called at E114 by the preceding routine, but this is essentially to start the process, which is interrupt controlled. The interrupt routine calls E13A with X = 3.

E114 If bit 6 of (Ø27C) = 1, the printer is disabled except for VDU 1 action, and the routine returns.

If A = (Ø286), the printer ignore character, the routine returns.

Otherwise, P is pushed and interrupt barred. If bit 2 of (Ø27C) = 1, the printer driver is disabled, and the routine jumps to E138 with X = A. Otherwise E1F8 is called with X = 3 to put A in the printer buffer. If the subroutine returns with carry set, the routine jumps to E138. If bit 7 of (Ø2D2) = Ø, the routine jumps to E138.

If E1F8 returns with carry clear, and the buffer is empty, E13A is called to open up the printer channel.

E138 P is pulled and the routine returns.

The buffer action is explained under Buffers.

E13A If (Ø285) = Ø, the 'printer sink' is selected, and the routine exits via E1AD to clear the printer buffer. If (Ø285) ≠ 1, the normal parallel printer interface is not in use, and the routine jumps to E164.

Otherwise, E46Ø is called to read a byte from the printer buffer. The resulting carry is copied into bit 7 of (Ø2D2): If carry is set the buffer is empty, and the routine returns via E19Ø.

Otherwise, (FE6E) = &82 enables interrupt 1 of the external VIA. (FE61) = A passes the character code to Port A, the printer interface. Then the sequence (FE6C) = (FE6C) AND &F1 OR &FC, (FE6C) =

(FE6C) OR &ØE pulses the CA2 line, generating a Strobe to the printer to advise it that data is waiting. The routine returns.

The Acknowledge returned by the printer calls interrupt 1 of the external VIA, which calls E13A to send another character. The process ends when the buffer is empty.

The serial printer interface must now be covered:

E164 A = (Ø285) from the calling routine. If A ≠ 2, the serial interface is not in use, and the routine jumps to E191.

If (ØØEA) – 1 is positive, the serial system is in use by the cassette system, and the routine jumps to E1AD to flush buffer X. Otherwise, (Ø2D2) is shifted right to clear bit 7.

E17Ø (Ø24F) is shifted right to clear bit 7, marking the serial system as busy.

E173 E741 is called to count buffer 1. If it returns with carry clear, there is no room in the buffer, and the routine returns. Otherwise, X = 2Ø, and;

E17A Y = &9F. Then:

OSBYTE 156: Update ACIA Setting and RAM Copy: E17C

E17C P is pushed and interrupt is barred. A = Y, (ØØFA) = X. Then A = A AND (Ø25Ø) EOR (ØØFA). (Ø25Ø) is the RAM copy of the last output to the ACIA on (FEØ8). Bits 5 and 6 are zeroed, bit 5 is reversed. (This sets RTS low, transmit interrupt enabled.) X = (Ø25Ø).

E189 (Ø25Ø) = A, (FEØ8) = A, resetting the ACIA. P is pulled.

E19Ø The routine returns.

If the printer is neither parallel nor serial, it must be a home-brewed type:

E191 Carry is cleared, A = 1, and E1A2 is called. Then:

OSBYTE 123: Warn Printer Going Dormant: E197

E197 (Ø2D2) is rotated right to put carry into bit 7, marking the buffer as empty for the OSBYTE entry, the carry otherwise depending on the result of E1A2.

E19A The routine returns.

The next block is entered at E19B from DE3E in interrupt.

E19B If bit 7 of (Ø2D2) = 1 (buffer empty), the routine returns via E19A. Otherwise, A = Ø, and:

E1A2 A = 3, Y = (Ø285), and E57E = (0224) is called. This is the Econet vector. The routine then returns via the user print vector (Ø222), allowing access to a special routine to suit a particular printer.

This completes the OSWRCH routine, which makes extensive use of the buffer facilities, and should be studied in connection with the interrupt handler for interrupt 1 of VIA 2.

Chapter 6
BUFFERS

The operating system implements nine buffers. These must not be confused with files, which are mainly concerned with the creation and retrieval of data blocks to be stored on tape or disc. The buffers are temporary holds for data streams, working on a first-in-first-out basis, using separate input and output pointers. A 'circular' form of buffer is used, the pointers wrapping round to the start of the storage area when they reach the end.

The buffers are:

No	**Main Use**	**Address Range**	**Flag**	**Out Pointer**	**In Pointer**
Ø	Keyboard	Ø3EØ – Ø3FF	(Ø2CF)	(Ø2D8)	(Ø2E1)
1	RS423 Input	ØAØØ – ØAFF	(Ø2DØ)	(Ø2D9)	(Ø2E2)
2	RS423 Output	Ø9ØØ – Ø9BF	(Ø2D1)	(Ø2DA)	(Ø2E3)
3	Printer	Ø88Ø – Ø8BF	(Ø2D2)	(Ø2DB)	(Ø2E4)
4	Sound Ø	Ø84Ø – Ø84F	(Ø2D3)	(Ø2DC)	(Ø2E5)
5	Sound 1	Ø85Ø – Ø85F	(Ø2D4)	(Ø2DD)	(Ø2E6)
6	Sound 2	Ø86Ø – Ø86F	(Ø2D5)	(Ø2DE)	(Ø2E7)
7	Sound 3	Ø87Ø – Ø87F	(Ø2D6)	(Ø2DF)	(Ø2E8)
8	Speech	Ø8CØ – Ø8FF	(Ø2D7)	(Ø2DF)	(Ø2E9)

Buffer 2 may be used as an extension of envelope storage. Buffers 2 and 8 may be used jointly as a cassette output buffer. Buffer 1 can serve as a cassette input buffer. (In the cassette role, the buffers become files. Confusing.)

The buffer routines can be located via OSBYTE calls:

OSBYTE 15: Flush Selected Buffer Class: FØA8
OSBYTE 21: Flush Specific Buffer: FØB4
OSBYTE 138: Put Byte in Buffer: E4AF

OSBYTE 145: Get Byte from Buffer: E46Ø
OSBYTE 152: Examine Buffer Status: E45B
OSBYTE 153: Byte to input buffer, checking Escape: E4F3

We will begin, however, with a subroutine called by the main routines.

E45Ø (ØØFA) = E43E + X), (ØØFB) = (E435 + X). This establishes a nominal base address for buffer X. However, a third table which follows those used above determines the minimum value for the pointers, which have a maximum value of &FF. The routine returns.

E45B This is the OSBYTE 152 entry. V is set, and the routine jumps to E461.

E46Ø This is the OSBYTE 145 entry. V is cleared, and;

E461 The routine jumps to (Ø22C), the buffer remove vector, which in this case points to E464.

E464 This routine will examine buffer X if V is set, the contents remaining unchanged, or will, with V clear, remove the character from the buffer. P is pushed and interrupt barred. A = (Ø2D8 + X), the output pointer for buffer X. If this is equal to (Ø2E1 + X), the input pointer, the buffer is empty. The routine exits via E4EØ, where P is pulled and carry set before return.

Otherwise, Y = A, the output pointer, and E45Ø is called to set the buffer base address. A = ((ØØFA) + Y), reading the next byte due to be output. If V is set, the routine jumps to E491 to exit with carry clear.

Otherwise, A is pushed, and the pointer in Y is incremented. If the result is non-zero, the end of the buffer has not been reached, and the routine jumps to E47E, but if the result is zero it is replaced by (E447 + X), the pointer start given in the third buffer-defining table.

E47E The pointer, whether incremented or reset, is copied back into (Ø2D8 + X). If X is less than 2 (Keyboard or RS423 input buffer) the routine jumps to E48F.

Otherwise, if the output pointer just set is equal to the input pointer in (Ø2E1 + X) E494 is called with Y = Ø to signal Event Ø: Buffer empty event.

E48F A is pulled and copied to Y.

E491 P is pulled, C is cleared, and the routine returns.

Note that a return with carry set means the buffer is empty, and that A holds the byte examined or removed. Y also holds the byte if it was removed.

As reference has just been made to the Event routine, which comes next in address sequence, it may as well be dealt with here:

E494 P is pushed and interrupt barred. A is pushed and copied into (ØØFA). Then A = (Ø2BF + Y), which is the flag for event Y. If A = Ø, the routine exits via E4DF, where A and P are pulled and carry set before the routine returns.

Otherwise, A = Y and Y = (ØØFA). Vector (Ø22Ø) is called to implement the required response to the event. A and P are pulled, and the routine returns with carry clear to indicate that action has been taken.

Vector (Ø22Ø) is normally set for an immediate return, and there is no point in enabling events unless the vector is changed to point to a suitable response routine. Note that A is saved on the stack, and need not be preserved by the response routine.

We now come to the OSBYTE 138 routine. The OSBYTE entry is at E4AF. Entry at E4A8 checks Event 2: Character entering buffer. The most common entry is at E4BØ.

E4A8 A = Y, and the event routine is called with Y = 2. On return, Y = A.

E4AF A = Y, holding the byte to be put into the buffer.

E4BØ The routine jumps to vector (Ø22A). This is usually E4B3.

E4B3 P is pushed and interrupt barred. A is pushed. Then Y = (Ø2E1 + X) + 1, the input pointer incremented. If Y = Ø, then it is reset to (E447 + X) to wrap round to the buffer start.

E4BF A = Y, and if Y = (Ø2D8 + X), the input pointer, the buffer is full. The routine jumps to E4D4.

Otherwise, (Ø2E1 + X) is picked up in Y and set from A. E45Ø is called to set the buffer base address in (ØØFA/B), A is pulled, and the byte is set in the buffer by ((ØØFA) + Y) = A. P is pulled, carry is cleared, and the routine returns.

E4D4 A is pulled, and if X is greater than 1 (not an input buffer) a jump to E4EØ is taken. Otherwise E494 is called with Y = 1 to service Event 1: Input buffer full. A is pushed to balance the subsequent pull.

E4DF A is pulled.

E4EØ P is pulled, carry is set, and the routine returns.

Skipping a check for alphabetic codes, which is covered under Keyboard, we reach OSBYTE 153, which enters at E4F3.

E4F1 X = Ø

E4F3 A = X AND (Ø245). If A ≠ Ø, the RS423 mode calls for Escape to be ignored, and X is an odd number. The routine jumps to E4AF.

Otherwise, A = Y EOR (Ø26C) OR (Ø275). The character value is compared with the current Escape code, and ORed with Escape key status (usually zero). A zero result means a genuine Escape. If A ≠ Ø, the routine jumps to E4A8 to enter the byte in the buffer.

Otherwise, A = (Ø258), the Escape/Break mode flags. If bit Ø of A = 1, the routine jumps to E513 with A = Y, escape being disabled.

Barring that, E494 is called with Y = 6 to check Event 6: Escape pressed. If it returns with carry set, E674 is called to set the Escape flag.

E513 Carry is cleared, the routine returns.

We must now turn to the buffer flushing routines.

OSBYTE 15: Flush selected buffer: FOA8
OSBYTE 21: Flush specific buffer: FOB4

FO95 X = (Ø241). This defines the input source, being Ø for the keyboard, 1 for RS423.

FO98 The routine jumps to E1AD

FOA8 If X ≠ Ø the routine jumps to FØ95. Only the input buffer is to be flushed. Otherwise, all buffers are to be flushed, and X = 8.

FOAC Interrupt is permitted briefly, then FØB4 is called. X is decremented, and the routine loops to FØAC while X is positive.

FOB4 If X is less than 9, the routine jumps to FØ98, otherwise returning.

These are just the control routines. The work is done at E1AD.

E1AD Carry is cleared

E1AE A and P are pushed, interrupt is barred. If carry is set (entry at E1AE from E843) the routine jumps to E1BB

Otherwise if (E9AD + X) is positive, the routine jumps to E1BB.

Barring that, ECA2 is called to clear sound data.

E1BB Carry is set, and (Ø2CF + X) is rotated to set bit 7, this being the buffer flag, now showing buffer empty. If X = 2 or more, the routine jumps to E1CB. (Not an input buffer.) Otherwise (Ø268), the soft key length, and (Ø26A), the VDU parameter count, are both zeroed.

E1CB E73B is called, which enters (Ø22E), the count/purge vector, with V set, calling for purge. The vector is normally E1D1.

Before continuing, it should be said that E9AD is the start of the baud rate table, but it also serves to ensure that sound data is only cleared if a sound buffer is being flushed.

E1D1 If V is clear, the routine jumps to E1DA. Otherwise the input pointer is set equal to the output pointer by (Ø2E1 + X) = (Ø2D2 + X), and the routine returns. The buffer is effectively empty.

E1DA P is pushed, interrupt is barred, and P is pushed again. A = (Ø2E1 + X) − (Ø2D8 + X), giving the difference between the input and output pointers. If a carry is generated by the subtraction, (E447 + X) is subtracted. (This may seem odd, until you note that the amount subtracted is equal to Ø1ØØ − buffer length, so in effect the buffer length is added.)

E1EA P is pulled, and if C is clear the routine jumps to E1F3. The number of entries in the buffer is the required answer. Otherwise, the space remaining is to be reported, and A = A (E447 + X). This time, the table value really is subtracted. Then A = A EOR &FF, inverting the contents of A.

E1F3 Y = Ø, X = A, P is pulled, the routine returns.

One routine remains in this group. It persistently tries to enter a byte in a buffer, if necessary waiting until there is room. It also flashes the keyboard lights, but does it too rapidly to be seen other than as a limited brilliance.

E1F8 Interrupt is barred, and E4BØ is called to enter a byte in buffer X. If the return has carry clear, the routine returns.

Otherwise E9EA is called to put the shift LEDs on, then P and A are pushed while EEEB is called to control the shift LEDs. (See Keyboard.) A negative condition produces a return, otherwise interrupt is allowed, and if carry is set the routine loops to E1F8 to try again. Barring that, the routine returns.

A negative return from E9EA indicates that Escape has been pressed. EEEB just sets the LEDs.

To complete the buffer routines, a few more modules must be covered:

E732 This is entered from OSBYTE 128 to report on the buffer defined by X complemented. X = X EOR &FF. If X is greater than 1, carry is set.

E738 V is cleared and the routine jumps to E73E to perform a count.

E73B V is set.

E73E The routine jumps to (Ø22E) = E1D1, this being the count/purge vector.

E741 This is a special check for the RS423 input buffer. X = 1, to select that buffer, and E738 is called with carry set to report on the space remaining. If Y, the high byte of the result, is 1 or more, the routine returns. Otherwise carry is set if X is equal to or greater than (Ø25B), which determines reserved space in this particular buffer.

Just one small point: E1D1 always sets Y = Ø, since none of the buffers are more than a page in length . . .

That completes the buffer routines, other than some which are specialised to functions under which they are covered.

Chapter 7
THE KEYBOARD

The keyboard uses a typical matrix connection system, each key being connected between a column wire and a row wire. There are ten columns and eight rows.

If the keyboard enable line is high, following an input of &ØB from Port B of the internal VIA, a counter runs continuously, its output being decoded to drive the column wires negative, one at a time. If any key is pressed, its row line will be driven low, and this will generate an interrupt Ø in the internal VIA to warn that keyboard service is needed.

The system responds by an output of &Ø3 to Port B of the internal VIA, and this stops the counter, which becomes a transparent latch. Outputs on bits Ø-3 of Port A of the internal VIA will then pull one column wire low. Outputs on bits 4-6 of Port A will set a data selector chip to sense one particular row wire. If the key at the intersection of the column and row wires is pressed, a high state will be input on bit 7 of Port A.

This explains the rather odd codes associated with INKEY, as tabulated in Fig. K.1. However, these codes are inverted, and the code output to sense the SHIFT key is not &FF, but Ø. The code seen on reading Port A is &8Ø if the key is pressed, so it would be more accurate to say that the code output to check a key is the code shown in the diagram AND &7F.

There are a number of entry routes to the keyboard routine, including OSBYTE 118, which sets the LEDs to reflect keyboard status, OSBYTE 12Ø, which simulates key depression, OSBYTE 121 and 122, which call up a keyboard scan, and OSBYTE 129, which reads a key with a time limit. The keyboard routines are also accessed from the handler for interrupt Ø of VIA 1.

The coding of these routines is a little difficult to trace out, because it involves some six-byte blocks alternating with character code tables. We will begin with OSBYTE 118, which starts at E9D9.

OSBYTE 118: Set LEDs to keyboard status: E9D9

E9D9 P is pushed and interrupt is barred. Then E9EA is called with A = &4Ø. The LEDs are switched on, and if Escape applies, the return is with the minus flag set, in which case the routine jumps to E9E7.

Otherwise, C and V are cleared, and the main keyboard entry at FØ68 is called. This does the actual work of setting the LEDs.

E9E7 P is pulled, A is rotated left to bring carry into bit Ø, and the routine returns.

E9EA If C is clear the routine jumps to E9F5, but for an OSBYTE call C is set. Y = 7, and (FE4Ø) = Y, setting the Shift Lock LED, then Y is decremented and (FE4Ø) = Y lights the Caps Lock LED.

E9F5 If bit 7 of (ØØFF) = 1, the minus flag is set to indicate that the Escape condition exists.

A further relevant module follows:

E9F8 P is pushed, interrupt is barred, and (FE4Ø) = A, setting Port B of VIA 1. P is pulled and the routine returns.

The next block to be considered also deals with the keyboard LEDs. It is entered at EEDA from FOOC, which will be dealt with shortly.

EEDA X = &FF and A = (ØØEC) OR (ØØED). These two variables hold the numbers of the last two keys pressed. If A = Ø no keys are outstanding, and interrupt Ø of VIA 1 is enabled to check if any further keys are pressed. X is incremented to Ø in this case.

EEE8 (Ø242), the keyboard semaphore, is set from X, being Ø if there were keys outstanding, otherwise &FF.

EEEB This is an important entry in its own right. P is pushed and A = (Ø25A), keyboard status. This has the following meanings:

Bit 3 is 1 if SHIFT is pressed
Bit 4 is Ø if Caps Lock is effective
Bit 5 is Ø if Shift Lock is effective
Bit 6 is 1 if CONTROL is pressed
Bit 7 is 1 if SHIFT is enabled.

A is shifted right, and A = A AND &18 OR &Ø6. (FE4Ø) = A. It must be remembered that only bits Ø-3 of VIA 1 Port B are outputs, so only the Caps Lock bit is significant. If it is true (Caps Lock not effective) the output is effectively &ØE, turning off the relevant LED. Otherwise, the output is &Ø6, turning the LED on.

A is again shifted right, and A = A OR 7. The Shift Lock bit is now in bit 3, and determines whether the output is &ØF or &Ø7.

F12E is then called to give (FE4Ø) = &ØB, enabling the counter scan of the keyboard columns. A is pulled, and the routine returns.

We now reach (ØØ28), here EFØ2, which is the main entry to the keyboard routines, but there are several possible paths:

EFØ2 If V is clear, the routine jumps to EFØE. Otherwise, (FE4E) = 1 disables interrupt Ø. If carry is set, the routine jumps to EF13, otherwise to FØØF.

EFØE If carry is clear, EF16 follows, otherwise FØD1.

EF13 This is reached with V and C both set. (Ø242), the keyboard semaphore, is incremented from &FF to Ø.

EF16 This is reached if V is clear and C clear. A = (Ø25A) AND &B7. This is keyboard status again, but bits 3 and 6 are zeroed, only set states being relevant, not keys currently pressed. X = Ø and FØ2A is called. This is the 'keyboard interrogate' routine, and called with X = Ø it checks the SHIFT key, returning &8Ø if the key is pressed. (ØØFA) = X to preserve this. V is cleared, and if the return from FØ2A was Ø the routine jumps to EF2A. Otherwise V and MI are set and A = A OR &Ø8, setting the shift pressed bit of keyboard status.

EF2A X is incremented to either 1 or &81 and FØ2A is again called, this time to check the CONTROL key. If carry is clear, the routine jumps to EEEB. But carry is only clear if the EF16 entry was used, and it appears that the data just obtained by FØ2A will be lost if the jump is taken.
Otherwise, if the key was not pressed the routine jumps to EF34, while if the key was pressed A = A OR &4Ø, setting the CONTROL key bit of the keyboard status word, still held in A.

EF34 A is set in (Ø25A), keyboard status. Then, if (ØØEC) = Ø, indicating no previously pressed key on record, a jump to EF4D is taken.

If (ØØEC) holds a key number, FØ2A is called with X = (ØØEC) to check whether the key is still pressed. If it is, the repeat routine is entered at EF5Ø. Otherwise, X is compared with (ØØEC).

EF42 (ØØEC) = X, and if this changes (ØØEC) the routine jumps to EF4D. Otherwise, (ØØEC) = Ø.

EF4A FØ1F is called to reset the repeat system.

EF4D The routine jumps to EFE9.

The repeat action now comes into play.

EF5Ø If X ≠ (ØØEC), the routine jumps to EF42.

Otherwise if (ØØE7) = Ø or is decremented to a non-zero value a jump to EF7B is taken. The repeat system is dormant or not at the end of its count.

Otherwise, (ØØE7) = (Ø2CA) and (Ø2CA) = (Ø255), the count source.

A = (Ø25A), keyboard status, and X = (ØØEC). If X ≠ &DØ (CAPS LOCK key) the routine jumps to EF7E.

Otherwise A = A OR &9Ø EOR &AØ. This disables SHIFT, Reverses Shift Lock, and makes Caps Lock ineffective.

EF74 (Ø25A) = A, resetting keyboard status, and (ØØE7) = Ø.

EF7B The routine jumps to EFE9.

EF7E If X ≠ &CØ (CAPS LOCK key) the routine jumps to EF91.

Otherwise, A = A OR &AØ, setting SHIFT enabled and making Shift Lock ineffective. If bit 7 of (ØØFA) = Ø, the routine jumps to EF8C. SHIFT is not pressed.

Otherwise, A = A OR EOR &8Ø. This marks SHIFT pressed, SHIFT not enabled (i.e. it will not reverse shift action).

EF8C A = A EOR &9Ø, reversing the Caps Lock and SHIFT enabled bits. The routine jumps to EF74 above.

We are now ready to discover what ASCII code is needed.

EF91 A = (EFAB + X). This is a code look-up table, which is split into ten-byte groups. (See below). If the result is non-zero, the routine jumps to EF99. A zero indicates the TAB key, which can be re-coded by OSBYTE 219, which sets (Ø26B). This is copied into A.

EF99 X = (Ø25A), the keyboard status, and (ØØFA) = X. If bit 6 of (ØØFA) = Ø (CONTROL not pressed) the routine jumps to EFA9. Otherwise, X = (ØØED).

EFA4 If NE, then EF4A. This not only relates to (ØØED), but also allows EFA4 to provide an onward jump from EFCC below. Subroutine EABF is called to implement the changes which are caused by pressing CONTROL. (The modifying subroutines are given later.)

EFA9 If bit 5 of keyboard status = 1, the routine jumps to EFB5. Shift Lock is not effective. Otherwise, subroutine EA9C is called to perform code changes appropriate to the Shift Lock condition. The routine jumps to EFC1. (The successive bits of keyboard status are checked by repeatedly rotating (ØØFA) left and looking at the sign bit.)

EFB5 If bit 4 of keyboard status = 1, the routine jumps to EFC6. Caps Lock is not effective.

Otherwise, subroutine E4E3 is called to implement the code changes appropriate to Caps Lock. It returns with C clear for alphabetic codes.

If carry is set the routine jumps to EFC6. Otherwise, subroutine EA9C is called, as for Shift Lock.

EFC1 If bit 7 of keyboard status = Ø, the routine jumps to EFD1.

EFC6 If bit 3 of keyboard status = Ø, the routine jumps to EFD1.

If (ØØED) ≠ Ø, the routine jumps to EFA4 and on to EF4A. Otherwise, subroutine EA9C is called.

EFD1 If A ≠ (Ø26C), Escape code, the routine jumps to EFDD. Otherwise, if (Ø275), Escape status, is not equal to A, the routine jumps to EFDD. Otherwise, (ØØE7) = X.

EFDD Y = A, and F129 is called to disable the keyboard, putting it into the auto-scan counting mode. If (Ø25) ≠ Ø (Disable keyboard) the routine jumps to EFE9, otherwise calling E4F1. (OSBYTE 153, character to input buffer.)

EFE9 X = (ØØED). If X = Ø, EFF8 follows, otherwise FØ2A is called to interrogate the key indicated. This is the second key in a two-key rollover. (ØØED) = X, and if FØ2A returned with negative set, the routine jumps to EFF8 (Key still pressed). Otherwise X = Ø, (ØØED) = X.

EFF8 X = (ØØED). If X ≠ Ø the routine jumps to FØ12. Otherwise Y = &EC and subroutine FØCC is called. If the routine shows negative, the routine jumps to FØØC. Otherwise, (ØØED) = (ØØEC), the first key becoming the second.

FØØ7 (ØØEC) = X. Subroutine FØ1F is called.

FØØC The routine loops to EEDA.

Subsidiary routines follow:

FØØF On entry, X is set to a key number. FO2A is called to check whether the key is pressed.

FØ12 A = (ØØEC). If A ≠ Ø then FØØC. Otherwise, FØCC is called with Y = &ED. If the return is negative, FØØC follows, else FØØ7.

FØ1F (ØØE7) = 1. (Ø2CA) = (Ø254), the routine returns. This sets the delay period for keyboard repeat.

FØ2A The interrogate routine. (FE4Ø) = 3, stopping auto-scan. Then (FE43) = &7F, setting Port A of VIA 1 to output on bits Ø-6, input on bit 7. (FE4F) = X, which is an output of Port A selecting a key. X = (FE4F), an input from port A with bit 7 true if the key is pressed. The routine returns.

FØ3B The first code data block, for X = &9Ø to &99:

	71	33	34	35	84	38	87	2D	5E	8C
Key:	q	3	4	5	F4	8	F7	–	∧	→

OSBYTE 120 : Write Key Pressed Data: F045

FØ45 (ØØEC) = Y, (ØØED) = X. The routine returns.

FØ4B The second code data block, for X = &AØ to &A9:

	8Ø	77	65	74	37	69	39	3Ø	5F	8E
Key:	FØ	w	e	t	7	i	9	Ø	—	←

FØ55 Jump to (FEFE)

FØ58 Jump to (ØØFA)

FØ5B The third code data block, for X = &BØ to &B9:

	31	32	64	72	36	75	6F	7Ø	5B	8F
Key:	1	2	d	r	6	u	o	p	[	↓

Next, the main entry to the keyboard routines:

FØ65 The V and MI flags are set.

FØ68 The routine jumps to (Ø228) = EFØ2.

FØ6B The fourth code data block, for X = &CØ to &C9:

	01	61	78	66	79	6A	6B	40	3A	OD
Key:	CL	a	x	f	y	j	k	@	:	Ret

CL = Caps Lock.

FØ75 ØØ FF Ø1 Ø2 Ø9 ØA: Speech routine data. See files.

FØ7B The fifth code data block, for X = &DØ to &D9:

	02	73	63	67	68	6E	6C	3B	5D	7F
Key:	SL	s	c	g	h	n	l	;	]	Del

SL = Shift Lock.

OSBYTE 131: Read OSHWM: FØ85

FØ85 Y = (Ø244), X = Ø, the routine returns.

FØ8B The sixth code data block, for X = &EØ to &E9:

	ØØ	7A	2Ø	76	62	6D	2C	2E	2F	8B
Key:	TAB	Z	Space	V	b	m	,	.	/	COPY

FØ95 X = (Ø241), and the routine jumps to E1AD (Flush current buffer).

FØ9B The seventh code data block, for X = &FØ to &F9:

	1B	81	82	83	85	86	88	89	5C	8D
Key:	Esc	F1	F2	F3	F5	F6	F8	F9	/	→

Code not relevant to keyboard action intervenes, then;

OSBYTE 121: Keyboard Scan: FØCF
OSBYTE 122: Keyboard Scan from &1Ø: FØCD

Entry at FØCC is from EFFE and F≠18 above, while entry at FØD1 is from EF1Ø.

FØCC Carry is cleared.

FØCD X = &1Ø.

FØCF If carry is set, as it will be for an OSBYTE call, go to FØ68. As carry will be set and V clear, the routine will jump to FØD1, the next location! However, this may not be the case if (Ø228) is changed to access a different keyboard routine.

FØD1 A = X. If X is positive, the routine jumps to FØD9. Otherwise the interrogate routine FØ2A is called. If carry is set, the routine then jumps to F12E to select auto scan.

FØD9 P is pushed, and if carry is clear the routine jumps to FØDE. Otherwise, Y = &EE.

FØDE (Ø2DF + Y) = A. This may access (Ø2CB), (Ø2CC) or (Ø2CD), which are holds for two-key rollover processing. The value of Y is in some cases determined before calling FØØC. X = 9.

FØE3 This is a major loop point. F129 is called to select auto scan, allow an interrupt, and then select auto scan again. (FE43) = &7F, setting Port A of VIA 1 for output on bits Ø-6, input on bit 7. (FE4Ø) = 3, stopping auto scan. (FE4F) = &ØF, an output on Port A which selects a non-existent keyboard column.

Then (FE4D) = 1, cancelling interrupt Ø. (FE4F) = X, an output to Port A. If bit 7 of (FE4D) = Ø, there is no VIA 1 interrupt, and the routine jumps to F123. Otherwise, A = X.

F1Ø3 This is another loop point. If A is less than (Ø1DF + Y), the routine jumps to F11E. Otherwise (FE4F) = A, and if bit 7 of (FE4F) = Ø the routine jumps to F11E.

Otherwise, P is pulled and pushed again, and if carry is set the routine jumps to F127. Barring that, A is pushed, and A = A EOR (ØØØØ + Y). This may seem odd, but remember that Y may hold &EC to &EE, so one of the key number holds will be accessed. A is shifted left logical, and if A is equal to or greater than 1 carry is set. This implies that A was not equal to the number hold. A is pulled, and if carry is set the routine jumps to F127.

F11E A = A + &1Ø. If the result is positive, the routine jumps to F1Ø3.

F123 X is decremented, and if the result is positive, the routine jumps to FØE3. A = X.

F127 X = A. P is pulled.

F129 F12E is called as a subroutine, selecting auto scan. Then interrupt is allowed briefly, and F12E is reached again.

F12E (FE4Ø) = &ØB, selecting auto scan. A = X. The routine returns.

Of all the variations of the keyboard routine, this is perhaps the most difficult to follow, and needs to be traced out with pencil and paper.

We have reached the end of the main block of keyboard routines, but it is now necessary to pick up the code-modifying routines which cropped up earlier.

The first returns with carry clear if A on input holds an alphabetic code. A is preserved:

E4E3 A is pushed, and A = A AND &DF. This zeroes bit 6, converting lower case codes to upper case. If A is less than &41 (code for A), the routine jumps to E4EE. If A is less than &5B (one more than the code for Z), the routine jumps to E4EF (with carry clear).

E4EE Carry is set.

E4EF A is pulled, and the routine returns.

The second code modifier is more complex. It implements Shift Lock or SHIFT:

EA9C If A = &3Ø, the routine jumps to EABE. (Zero code)
If A = &4Ø, the routine jumps to EABE. (Code for @)
If A is less than £40, the routine jumps to EAB8.
If A = &7F, the routine jumps to EABE. (Delete)
If A is greater than &7F, the routine jumps to EABC.

Codes unaffected by shift are untouched, since EABE = RETURN. EAAC is reached for codes &41 to &7E, the codes directly affected by SHIFT.

EAAC A = A EOR &3Ø, reversing bits 4 and 5. If A = &6F (previously &5F), the routine jumps to EAB6. If A ≠ &5Ø (previously &6Ø), the routine jumps to EAB8.

EAB6 A = A EOR &1F, changing &6F to &7Ø, overall &5F to &7Ø, and &5Ø to &4F, overall &6Ø to &4F. (But wait . . .)

EAB8 If A is less than &21, the routine jumps to EABE.

EABC A = A EOR &1Ø, reversing bit 4.

EABE The routine returns.

*Codes &ØØ-&2Ø are unaffected.
*Codes &21-&3F have bit 4 reversed, interchanging &21-&2f with &31-&3F.
*Code &4Ø is unchanged.
*Codes &41-&5E have bit 5 reversed (upper case to lower).
*Code &5F becomes &6Ø.
*Code &6Ø becomes &5F.
*Codes &61-&7E have bit 5 reversed (lower case to upper).
*Code &7F is unchanged.
*Codes &8Ø up have bit 4 changed.

The third routine implements CONTROL:

EABF If A = &7F, the routine returns via EAD1.
If A exceeds &7F, the routine jumps to EAAC in the previous block.
If A ≠ &6Ø the routine jumps to EACB. Otherwise A = &5F.

EACB If A is less than &4Ø, the routine jumps to EAD1. Otherwise, A = A and &1F, zeroing bits 5-7.

EAD1 Return.

Mercifully simpler than the SHIFT routine.

It will be appreciated that there are other routines which are broadly associated with the keyboard. There has been no mention of 'soft keys'. They are dealt with elsewhere. On the other hand, there are OSBYTE routines that must be included here.

OSBYTE 129: Read Key With Time Limit: E713
OSBYTE 13Ø : Read Higher Order Address: E729

E713 A = Y. If A is negative then go to E721, this being the case with Y = &FF, and X holding an INKEY value.

Otherwise, X/Y is taken as holding a time in hundredths of a second. Interrupt is permitted, being essential to the count, and DEBB is called (below). If it returns with carry set, the routine jumps to E71F. Otherwise X = A, A = Ø.

E71F Y = A. The routine returns.

E721 X = X EOR &7F. This converts the INKEY value to a keyboard input. The main keyboard routine is called at FØ68. When it returns, A is rotated left to put bit 7 in carry.

E729 X = Y = &FF. If carry is set a jump to E731 preserves these values to show the key was pressed. Otherwise X and Y are incremented to Ø.

E731 The routine returns.

As a means of reading high order address, OSBYTE 13Ø pays mere lip service.

The actual timed routine is:

DEBB (Ø2B1/2) = X/Y. This sets up the time, and the two RAM locations are thereafter decremented by each 1Ø mS interrupt, providing they do not hold zero. A = &FF, and the OSRDCH routine is entered at DEC7. The OSRDCH entry is at DEC5.

DEC5 A = Ø

DEC7 (ØØE6) = A. X and Y are pushed via A. Y = (Ø256), which is the EXEC file handle. If it is Ø, the routine jumps to DEE6. There is no need to deal with a file.

Otherwise, bit 7 of (ØØEB) is set. This warns against a clash between the cassette filing system and a BGET or BPUT. OSBGET is called at FFD7, and then bit 7 is shifted out of (ØØEB), but not into carry, which is preserved.

If OSBGET returned with carry clear, the routine jumps to DFØ3 to exit with character found. Otherwise, the EXEC file is closed by calling OSFIND with A = Ø and Y holding the file handle. (Ø256) = Ø, clearing the EXEC file handle.

The above is not directly relevant to the timed keyboard check, and will usually be skipped.

DEE6 If bit 7 of (ØØFF) = 1, Escape has been pressed, and the routine exits with data = &1B via DFØØ.

Otherwise, E577 is called to get a byte or string from the keyboard buffer. If successful, it returns with carry clear, and the routine exits via DFØ3, with the code byte as data.

Otherwise, (Ø2B1/2) is checked, and if the count has not reached zero the routine loops to DEE6 to try again. If (Ø2B1/2) = ØØØØ, and carry is set, the routine jumps to DFØ5 to register failure to find an input.

DFØØ Carry is set, and A = &1B, the standard Escape code.

DFØ3 (ØØE6) = A, registering the code found.

DFØ5 Y and X are pulled, A = (ØØE6), the routine returns.

The next routine is entered at E577. It takes a byte from the keyboard buffer, and — if necessary — interprets it.

E515 This point is reached with A = (Ø27D), the cursor/edit flags, if A is non-zero, which means that cursor editing is disabled. RORA puts bit Ø of A into carry. It will be 1 if the cursor keys are to generate codes &87 to &8B, Ø if they are to be 'soft keys'. A is pulled, which sets it to the relevant code, and if carry is set the routine returns.

E519 The cursor keys are to be 'soft keys'. This point is also reached for the function keys. A = Y restores the original key code.

Then A is divided by sixteen and bit 2 is reversed. The result is copied to Y to allow A = (Ø265 + Y). This reads from a conversion table which returns 1 for Y = 8, &DØ for Y = 9, and other values if special characters have been set up. If there are no special characters for the given code, the result is Ø.

If the result is 1, the routine jumps to E594 to call up a key string. Otherwise A is pulled. If carry is clear the routine jumps to E539 to get another code from the buffer. This is a consequence of the result of A = (Ø265 + Y) returning zero, and the subsequent comparison with 1.

Otherwise A = A AND &ØF + (Ø265 + Y). C is cleared, and the routine returns.

E534 This point is reached if an error is made in using Edit. E86F is called to produce a 'Bell'. X is pulled, this being the buffer number, and;

E539 E46Ø is called to get a byte from buffer X. If carry is set the buffer is empty, and the routine exits via E593.

Otherwise A is pushed to save the code obtained, and if X = 1 (RS423 buffer) E173 is called to execute part of OSWRCH. Carry is set.

E549 A is pulled. If carry is clear the routine jumps to E551. Otherwise if (Ø245) ≠ Ø the RS423 mode bars soft keys, Escape, etc., and a jump to E592 gives a return with carry clear.

E551 Y = A, saving the code obtained. If A is positive, the routine exits via E592 with carry clear. This is a simple code. Otherwise, a code in the &8Ø-&FF range is involved, and that will need treatment.

A = A AND &OF. If A is less than &OB, the routine jumps to E519. A function key or special code is identified. Otherwise A = A + &7C, which converts codes &8B-&8F to &87-&8B. (Note that carry is set when the addition is called.) A is pushed.

A = (Ø27D), the cursor/edit status, and if A is non-zero the routine jumps back to E515.

Otherwise, A = (Ø27C), the character destination status. Two rotate rights put bit 1 into carry. A is pulled, and if carry is set the routine jumps to E539. The display is disabled.

If the screen is enabled, and A = &87, COPY, the routine jumps to E5A6. For other key codes, X is pushed, Y = A, and D8CE is called to execute Edit action. X is pulled.

For straightforward characters, the routine returns, but in the case of Edit action the process returns to the starting point:

E577 If bit 7 of (Ø25F), the Econet status byte, is Ø, the routine jumps to E581. Otherwise, A = 6, the Econet code asking for a data byte, and;

E57E The routine jumps to (Ø224), the Econet vector.

E581 If a character string was invoked by the previous code, the length of the string is held in (Ø268). If that location holds zero, the routine jumps to E539 to get a character from the buffer.

Otherwise Y = (Ø2C9), which holds the index to the start of the key string required, and A = (ØBØ1 + Y), reading a byte from the string. (Ø2C9) is incremented and (Ø268) is decremented, advancing the pointer and reducing the length count.

E592 Carry is cleared.

E593 The routine returns.

The next routine is entered if a key string is to be set up:

E594 A is pulled, restoring the original code. Then Y = A AND &ØF, obtaining the key string number. E3A8 is called to set up the string length (See CLI). This is copied from A into (Ø268), and (Ø2C9) is set from (ØBØØ + Y), the string start displacement. The routine jumps to E577 to deal with the string output.

The next routine responds to COPY:

E5A6 X is pushed, and D9Ø5 is called to read a character from the screen. Y = A. If A = Ø, the routine jumps to

E534, giving a warning beep. Otherwise X is pulled, A = Y, and the routine returns with carry clear.

The above routines involve action described under CLI and VDU control, to which reference should be made.

Keyboard Matrix

ESCAPE &FØ −113	**F1** &F1 −114	**F2** &F2 −115	**F3** &F3 −116	**F5** &F4 −117	**F6** &F5 −118	**F8** &F6 −119	**F9** &F7 −12Ø	\ &F8 −121	→ &F9 −122
Q &8Ø −17	**3** &91 −18	**4** &92 −19	**5** &93 −20	**F4** &94 −21	**8** &95 −22	**F7** &96 −23	– &97 −24	Λ &98 −25	← &99 −26
FØ &AØ −33	**W** &A1 −34	**E** &A2 −35	**T** &A3 −36	**7** &A4 −37	**I** &A5 −38	**9** &A6 −39	**Ø** &A7 −4Ø	— &A8 −41	↓ &A9 −42
1 &BØ −49	**2** &B1 −50	**D** &B2 −51	**R** &B3 −52	**6** &B4 −53	**U** &B5 −54	**O** &B6 −55	**P** &B7 −56	[&B8 −57	↑ &B9 −58
CAPS LOCK &CØ −65	**A** &C1 −66	**X** &C2 −67	**F** &C3 −68	**Y** &C4 −69	**J** &C5 −7Ø	**K** &C6 −71	@ &C7 −72	: &C8 −73	**RETURN** &C9 −74
SHIFT LOCK &DØ −81	**S** &D1 −82	**C** &D2 −83	**G** &D3 −84	**H** &D4 −85	**N** &D5 −86	**L** &D6 −87	; &D7 −88	] &D8 −89	**DELETE** &D9 −9Ø
TAB &EØ −97	**Z** &E1 −98	**Space** &E2 −99	**V** &E3 −1ØØ	**B** &E4 −1Ø1	**M** &E5 −1Ø2	, &E6 −1Ø3	. &E7 −1Ø4	/ &E8 −1Ø5	**COPY** &E9 −1Ø6
SHIFT &8Ø −1	**CONTROL** &81 −2	**LINK8** &82 −3	**LINK7** &83 −4	**LINK6** &84 −5	**LINK5** &85 −6	**LINK4** &86 −7	**LINK3** &87 −8	**LINK2** &88 −9	**LINK1** &89 −1Ø

Figure K.1

The hexadecimal numbers are the codes returned for key pressed.

The interrogating bytes have bit 7 = Ø.

The decimal numbers are the 'internal key numbers'.

Chapter 8
COMMAND LINE INTERPRETER

The Command Line Interpreter (CLI) is entered at FFF7 = (Ø2Ø8), which in this case leads to DF89. The CLI is used to read and interpret command lines starting at an address identified by X/Y on entry to the routine. The line must be terminated by &ØD. The asterisk prefix normally shown in defining the relevant command words is for the benefit of BASIC, and is ignored by the actual CLI routine.

Immediately before the entry point at DF89 there is a table which links the command words to addresses and qualifying bytes:

DF1Ø	2E EØ 31 Ø5		EØ31	Ø5	(F32B)
DF14	46 58 E3 43 FF	FX	E342	FF	(OSBYTE)
DF19	42 41 53 49 43 EØ 18 ØØ	BASIC	EØ18	ØØ	
DF21	43 41 54 EØ 31 Ø5	CAT	EØ31	Ø5	(F32B)
DF27	43 4F 44 45 E3 48 88	CODE	E348	88	(OSBYTE 136)
DF2E	45 58 45 43 F6 8D ØØ	EXEC	F68D	ØØ	
DF35	48 45 4C 5Ø FØ B9 FF	HELP	FØB9	FF	
DF3C	4B 45 59 E3 27 FF	KEY	E327	FF	
DF42	4C 4F 41 44 E2 3C ØØ	LOAD	E23C	ØØ	
DF49	4C 49 4E 45 E6 59 Ø1	LINE	E659	Ø1	
DF5Ø	4D 4F 54 4F 52 E3 48 89	MOTOR	E348	89	(OSBYTE 137)

DF58	4F 5Ø 54 E3 48 8B	OPT	E348	8B	(OSBYTE 139)
DF5E	52 55 4E EØ 31 Ø4	RUN	EØ31	Ø4	(F3Ø5)
DF64	52 4F 4D E3 48 8D	ROM	E348	8D	(OSBYTE 141)
DF6A	53 41 56 45 E2 3E ØØ	SAVE	E23E	ØØ	
DF71	53 50 4F 4F 4C E2 81 ØØ	SPOOL	E281	ØØ	
DF79	54 41 50 45 E3 48 8C	TAPE	E348	8C	(OSBYTE 14Ø)
DF8Ø	54 56 E3 48 9Ø	TV	E348	9Ø	(OSBYTE 144)
DF85	EØ 31 Ø3	Default	EØ31	Ø3	
DF88	Ø	Terminator			

The command word need not be given in full if the shortened form is followed by a full stop, and there are enough letters to prevent ambiguity. R. will give RUN, and RO. is required for ROM. A simple full stop gives CAT.

For the implementation of *SPOOL, *RUN, *CAT, *OPT and *EXEC, see under Files.

Commands with the link address E348 are OSBYTE commands, the qualifying byte giving the OSBYTE number. Commands with the link address EØ31 branch to the addresses noted in brackets.

For a number of these commands, subsequent text is required, and that is read by the relevant routine.

The first step in the CLI routine is to check that the text line is correctly terminated by &ØD and does not exceed 255 bytes in length.

DF89 The text start address is copied from X/Y into (ØØF2/3), and EØ31 is called with A = 8. This accesses a branching routine at F1B1, to be described later. The index A is rejected as being out of range, so no action is taken. Y is then zeroed as a pointer to the text, relative to (ØØF2/3), and;

DF94 A = ((ØØF2) + Y), reading a byte from text. If A = &ØD, the routine jumps on to DF9E. Otherwise, Y is incremented, and the routine loops to DF94 unless Y = Ø, in which case the routine returns.

DF9E This point is only reached if the line is correctly terminated within the maximum length. Y = &FF, again as a displacement pointer.

DFAØ EØ39 is called to increment Y, read byte Y in the text, and skip on a byte if space code is found. If the byte is &ØD, the subroutine returns with EQ set, in which case the main routine returns.

If, otherwise, the byte is &2A (*), the routine jumps back to DFAØ to start again.

EØ3A is called, this being EØ39 without the initial increment of Y, setting A to the byte it already holds. Again, the routine returns if the byte is &ØD. If, otherwise, the byte is &7C (vertical divider) the routine returns, while for other bytes not equal to &2F (/), a jump to DFBE is taken.

If &2F is found, Y is incremented, EØØ9 is called, then the routine jumps to EØ31 with A = 2, entering the RUN function.

This raises two problems. The combination */(filename) is not well documented, but is equivalent to *RUN (filename). A more difficult point is that EØØ9 does not appear exactly suitable to implement the function (see below).

DFBE (ØØE6) = Y, storing the pointer to the effective text start, X = Ø, and the routine jumps to DFD7.

DFC4 This is a loop point. A = A EOR (DF1Ø– X) AND &DF. A is compared with a byte from the table, bit 5 being zeroed to make upper and lower case letter codes equivalent (but see below). If A = Ø, the text and table bytes match, and the routine jumps to DFE2. Otherwise Y is incremented, carry is cleared, and;

DFCD If carry is set, the routine jumps to DFF4. Otherwise X is incremented, and A = (ØØF2) + Y) reads the next text byte. E4E3 is called to return with carry set if the code is not upper case alpha. If carry is clear, the routine loops to DFC4. Otherwise;

DFD7 If (DF1Ø + X) is negative, the routine jumps to DFF2. The upper byte of a link address has been reached.

Otherwise the byte is read again, and if it is &2E (.) the routine jumps to DFE6, the byte-by-byte comparison being abandoned. Otherwise;

DFE2 Carry is cleared, and Y = (ØØE6) − 1, preparing to scan the text command again.

DFE6 X and Y are incremented.

DFE8 X is incremented. If (DFØE + X) = Ø the routine jumps to EØ21. If (DFØE + X) is otherwise positive the routine jumps to DFE8. If (DFØE + X) is negative, DFCD follows. (Note the use of a different base, where DF1Ø is used elsewhere.)

This routine is tortuous, but can be followed through with pencil and paper. A jump to DFF2 indicates that an address has been reached with the preceding text matched, while a jump to DFF4 indicates that a qualifying byte has been reached with text matched.

DFF2 X = X + 2.

DFF4 X = X − 2. For either entry, X now points to the first byte of a link address. A holds (DF1Ø + X), the first address byte. This is pushed, then (DF11 + X), the second address byte, is pushed, forming an artificial return link on the stack.

Then EØ3A is called to set A = ((ØØF2) + Y), returning EQ if the byte is &ØD. Carry is cleared, P is pushed, and EØØ4 is called to set up a pointer to the start of the text following the command word. An RTI instruction pulls P and jumps to the link address.

EØØ4 A = (DF12 + X). This is the last byte of the line in the data block. If the byte is negative, the routine returns. Otherwise;

EØØ9 A = Y, Y = (DF12 + X), again reading the last byte. At least, that is true if the routine was entered at EØØ4, but when EØØ9 is called in response to &2F, X is still set to the lower byte of the text start address, which makes no sense. Perhaps, however, it is irrelevant.

EØØD A = A + (ØØF2), adding the last value of pointer Y to the low byte of the text start address. This is passed to X, and A is reset from Y. Then Y = (ØØF3), and is incremented if the earlier addition generated a carry. X/Y hold the address of the qualifying text start.

E017 The routine returns.

Note that if the last byte is negative, Y is preserved for use as a pointer. We now reach the first functional module, that for BASIC.

*BASIC: E018: &00

E018 X = (024B), the number of the BASIC ROM. If there is no BASIC ROM, X is negative, and the routine jumps to E021. Otherwise the routine jumps to DBE7 in initialise, with carry set.

E021 Y = (00E6), the pointer to the effective start of the text line, and F168 is called with X = 4. Another ROM may understand the command. If F168 returns with EQ set, the routine returns. Otherwise, A = (00E6), and E00D is called to set X/Y = (00FD/3) + A. A = 3, and E031 follows.

*. : E031: 05
*CAT : E031: 05
*RUN : E031: 04
Default: E031: 03

E031 The routine jumps to (021E) = F1B1, examined later.

Next come some text scanning routines:

E039 Y is incremented.

E03A A = ((00F2) + Y) If A = &20 the routine loops to E039, else;

E040 A is compared with &0D. The routine returns.

E043 If carry is clear, the routine jumps to E03A, else;

E045 E03A is called. If A ≠ 2C (,) the routine jumps to E040. Otherwise Y is incremented and the routine returns. (This skips commas.)

A general purpose routine for converting ASCII decimal numerics to binary comes next:

E04E E03A is called to skip any spaces, and then E07D is called. It reads the next text byte, and if the code is not numeric, returns with carry clear, in which case the routine exits via E080.

If EØ7D returns with carry set, A holds the equivalent of the numeric in binary form. Then;

EØ56 (ØØE6) = A. EØ7C is again called to read the next byte, the routine returning via EØ76 if EØ7C returns with carry clear.

Otherwise, A = A * 1Ø, a check for overflow being made at each step, the routine dropping out via EØ8D if the number created is too large. (The process involves A * 2, A * 2, A + (ØØE6), A * 2).

X is then added to A, the routine again dropping out via EØ8D if the result overflows a single byte. Otherwise, the routine loops to EØ56 to look for another digit.

EØ76 X = (ØØE6). A is compared with &ØD. The routine returns with carry set.

EØ7C Y is incremented.

EØ7D A = ((ØØF2) + Y). If A is less than &3Ø or more than &39, the routine jumps to EØ8D. Otherwise A = A AND &ØF, and the routine returns with carry set, due to the second comparison check.

EØ8A This is an entry from the routine which follows. EØ45 is called to skip commas and check for &ØD.

EØ8D Carry is cleared to indicate an invalid result.

EØ8E The routine returns.

The next block deals with hexadecimal codes:

EØ8F EØ7D is called. If it returns with carry set (Ø + 9), the routine jumps to EØA2. Otherwise A = A AND &DF to convert lower case to upper case, and if A exceeds &46 (F) or is less than &41 (A), a jump to EØ8A is taken. Otherwise carry is set and P is pushed. A = A = &37, converting hex to binary, and P is pulled.

EØA2 Y is incremented, the routine returns.

To be strictly correct, the above routine is nothing to do with CLI, except that it is used by SAVE/LOAD to set up a file block, but it is more easily dealt with here. A number of routines which deal with other matters follow, and CLI is resumed with:

E31Ø "Bad Command"

E31D "Bad Key".

*KEY : E327: &FF

E327 EØ4E is called to set up the key number in A. If a valid number is not found, or the number in A exceeds 15, the routine jumps to E31D to report "Bad Key".

Otherwise, EØ45 is called to skip commas and check for newline. The resulting status byte is pushed for future reference. (If newline is found, the instruction is to clear the key string, there being no defining text.)

Next, X = (ØB1Ø), the pointer to the top of the existing key strings. Y is pushed to preserve the text read pointer, and E3D1 is called. Y and P are pulled, and if EØ45 returned NE the routine jumps to E377 to set up a new string. Otherwise, the routine returns, having set a null string.

A word about the string storage system is necessary here. It uses the whole of page &ØB. Locations &ØØ to &1Ø define the positions of the strings, the start of string n being at ØBØ1 + (ØBØØ + n), and the end of string n being at ØBØØ + (ØBØ1 + n). The actual strings are stored in locations &11 – &FF.

The method used to index the strings implies that the same byte defines the end of string n and the start of string n + 1. When a new string is inserted, the old string for that key (if any) must be erased, and the new string must be put into its correct place. This involves some rather complex processing, which is best understood by tracing through some changes with pencil and paper. The result can be checked by dumping page &ØB. An alternative approach is to transcribe the relevant routines into BASIC, which allows each stage in the process to be examined.

However, we have only found the main routine, and other matters have to be dealt with before we reach the subsidiaries.

*FX : E342 : &FF
*CODE : E348 : &88
*MOTOR : E348 : &89
*OPT : E348 : &8B

*ROM : E348 : &8D
*TAPE : E348 : &8C
*TV : E348 : &90

E342 EØ4E is called to convert the number following *FX to binary. A return with carry clear causes a jump to E31Ø to report "Bad Command". Otherwise A = X, and;

E348 A is pushed, and (ØØE4/5) = Ø. EØ43 is called to skip comma and check for newline. If newline is found the routine jumps to E36C.
Otherwise, EØ4E is called to convert a parameter to binary, "Bad Command" being again reported following a return with carry clear. (ØØE5) takes the result.

EØ45 is called to skip comma and check for newline. If newline is found, the routine jumps to E36C, otherwise another parameter is picked up in the same way, this time in (ØØE4). Then a newline is required, lacking which the report "Bad Command" is given.

E36C Y = (ØØE4), as the third OSBYTE parameter. X = (ØØE5), as the second OSBYTE parameter. A is pulled, as the first OSBYTE parameter. OSBYTE is called at FFF4. If the return has V set, "Bad Command" is reported. The routine returns.

We now return to the KEY function:

E377 EA1E is called with carry set to look for a &22 code ("). If one is found, bit 7 of (ØØE4) = 1. In any case, bit 6 of (ØØE4) = 1.

E37B EA2F is called to read and check a character code. If the end of text has been reached, it returns with carry set, and the routine jumps to E388.

Otherwise, X is incremented. (X is initially (ØB1Ø), pointer to the end of existing strings.) If X reaches Ø, "Bad Key" is reported, as there is insufficient room in the storage area. Note that the new string is inserted above the others.

If space is available, (ØBØØ + X) = A copies the character to store. The routine loops to E37B.

E388 If NE is set, a jump to E31D reports "Bad Key". The line was incorrectly terminated (e.g. a missing "). Otherwise P is pushed and interrupt barred. E3D1 is called to move the string. X = &1Ø.

E391 If X = (ØØE6), the routine jumps to E3A3 (the nominated key number). If (ØBØØ + X) ≠ (ØBØØ + Y) the routine jumps to E3A3. Otherwise, (ØBØØ + /x) = (ØB1Ø).

E3A3 X is decremented, and if it is still positive the routine loops to E391. P is pulled and the routine returns.

The next block is called by E3D1 to set up string lengths:

E3A8 P is pushed and interrupt barred. (ØØFB) = (ØB1Ø) – (ØBØØ + Y), giving the number of bytes in strings above the end of string Y. X is pushed and X = &1Ø.

E3B7 A = (ØBØØ + X) – (ØBØØ + Y). If there is no carry, or A = Ø or A is equal to or greater than (ØØFB), the routine jumps to E3C8. Otherwise (ØØFB) = A.

E3C8 X is decremented, and if it is still positive the routine loops to E3B7, else X is pulled, A = (ØØFB), P is pulled, the routine returns.

E3D1 P is pushed and interrupt barred. X is pushed. Then E3A8 is called with Y = (ØØE6), the key number, to set up (ØØFB). A = (ØBØØ + Y). Y = A, A = A + (ØØFB), X = A, (ØØFA) = A. If (Ø268), soft key length, is not zero, "Key in Use" is reported, otherwise E3F6 follows.

E3F6 The string consistency flag in (Ø284) is decremented to &FF to warn that the strings are being modified. A is pulled, and (ØØFA) = A – (ØØFA). If (ØØFA) = Ø, the routine jumps to E4ØD, else:

E4Ø1 (ØBØ1 + Y) = (ØBØ1 + X). X and Y are incremented, (ØØFA) is decremented. If (ØØFA) ≠ Ø the routine jumps to E4Ø1, else;

E4ØD Y is pushed and Y = (ØØE6), the key number. X = &1Ø.

E413 A = (ØBØØ + X). If A is less than (ØBØØ + Y), the routine jumps to E422. Otherwise, (ØBØØ + X) = A – (ØØFB).

E422 X is decremented, and if the result is positive the routine loops to E413, else (ØBØØ + Y) = (ØB1Ø), A is pulled and (ØB1Ø) = A (the value pushed from Y at E4ØD) X = A, (Ø284) is incremented back to zero. P is pulled, the routine returns.

OSBYTE 18: Reset Function Keys: E9C8

E9C8 A = &1Ø. (Ø284) = A, setting the consistency flag. X = Ø.

E9CF (ØBØØ + X) = A. X is incremented. If it is non-zero, the routine loops to E9CF. Otherwise (Ø284) = X = Ø. The routine returns.

GSINIT: EA1D
GSREAD: EA1E

GSINIT prepares for interpretation of text by GSREAD:

EA1D Carry is cleared.

EA1E Rotate right moves carry to bit Y of (ØØE4). EØ3A is called to get a character from the text. When it returns, Y is incremented, as the text pointer. If A = &22 ("), the routine jumps to EA2A with carry set. Otherwise, Y is decremented and carry is cleared.

EA2A Another rotate right of (ØØE4) moves bit 7 to bit 6 and bit 7 is set from carry. A is compared with &ØD. The routine returns.

EA2F A = Ø

EA31 (ØØE5) = A. A = ((ØØF2) + Y), reading a character from text. If A ≠ &ØD, the routine jumps to E3AF.

If A = &ØD: If bit 7 of (ØØE4) = 1 the " code found earlier has not been balanced, and EA8F follows, reporting "Bad String". Otherwise the routine jumps to EA5A.

EA3F If A is less than &2Ø, EA8F follows to report "Bad String", and if A is otherwise not equal to &2Ø the routine jumps to EA4B.

If A = &2Ø, then if bit 7 of (ØØE4) = 1, EA89 follows. If bit 6 of (ØØE4) is otherwise equal to Ø, EA5A follows, else;

EA4B If A ≠ &22, the routine jumps to EA5F.

If A = &22 ("), and bit 7 of (ØØE4) = Ø, EA89 follows. Otherwise, Y is incremented, and the next byte is read from text. If that is also &22, the routine jumps to EA89, else;

EA5A EØ3A is called to read a byte from text. The routine returns with carry set.

EA5F If A ≠ &7C (vertical divider) the routine jumps to EA89.

If A = &7C, Y is incremented, and another byte is read from text. If A then holds &7C or &22 the routine jumps to EA89. If A ≠ &21, the routine jumps to EA77.

If A = &21, Y is incremented, A = &8Ø, and the routine loops back to EA31. Bit 7 will be added to the character following '!'.

EA77 If A is less than &2Ø, a jump to EA8F reports "Bad String". Otherwise, if A = &3F (?) the routine jumps to EA87. Barring that, EABF is called to modify the code in A as if it had been keyed in with CONTROL pressed. If V is set, the routine jumps to EA8A.

EA87 A = &7F

EA89 V is cleared.

EA8A Y is incremented. A = A OR (ØØE5). The routine returns with carry clear.

EA8F "Bad String"

All that remains of the CLI routines is the branching system entered via EØ31 = (Ø21E) = F1B1:

F1B1 If A is greater than 6, the routine returns via F1A2. Only indices Ø – 6 are allowed.

Otherwise, (ØØBC) = X, as a temporary hold, A is doubled, X = A, and (F1A4 + X) and (F1A3 + X) are pushed on to the stack as an artificial return link. As a normal return instruction is to be used, the address pushed is one less than that required. X = (ØØBC), and the return instruction jumps to the link address + 1.

The actual entry points are:

A = Ø:	*OPT	F54D
A = 1:	EOF	F61E
A = 2	*RUN	F3Ø5
A = 3:	Bad Command	E310
A = 4:	*RUN	F3Ø5
A = 5:	*CAT	F32B
A = 6:	Close files	E275.

The routine called are covered under Files.

Chapter 9
VDU CONTROL

The VDU Control Routine handles all outputs to the display. These may be character codes, control codes, or parameters qualifying control codes. The actions taken are conditioned by mode, cursor type, window settings and other factors, some of whch are expressed by the VDU status byte, held in (ØØDØ):

Bit Ø = 1:	Printer enabled by VDU2
Bit 1 = 1:	Scrolling barred
Bit 2 = 1:	Paged mode
Bit 3 = 1:	Text window, with software scrolling
Bit 4 = 1:	Not used
Bit 5 = 1:	Graphics cursor selected
Bit 6 = 1:	Twin cursors for Edit
Bit 7 = 1:	Display disabled by VDU21.

The VDU control routines are long and complex. They begin with an analysis section, which calls up functional routines by reference to a pair of link tables. The first table gives the lower byte of the link address in all cases. If the item from the second table exceeds &7F, it gives the upper byte of the link address, and no parameters are required. If the second table item is less than &8Ø however, the lower nibble is ORed with &FØ to form a negation of the number of parameters required, this being set in (Ø26A). The upper nibble is then added to &C3 to give the upper byte of the link address.

To clarify this, the data for the 1.2Ø cassette operating system are tabulated here.

The large number of page three variables used by VDU control are also tabulated. It should be noted that some are also used for transient workspace.

The entry point to the VDU control system can be found by reference to the OSWRCH routine. In this case, the entry point is C4CØ.

VDU Function Link Table

VDU	Table 1	Table 2	Link	Parameters	Function
Ø	&11	&C5	C511	Ø	Does nothing
1	&3B	&2F	C53B	1	Next character to printer
2	&96	&C5	C596	Ø	Enable Printer
3	&A1	&C5	C5A1	Ø	Disable Printer
4	&AD	&C5	C5AD	Ø	Select Text Cursor
5	&B9	&C5	C5B9	Ø	Select Graphics Cursor
6	&11	&C5	C511	Ø	Enable Display
7	&6F	&E8	E86F	Ø	Beep (See Sound)
8	&C5	&C5	C5C5	Ø	Cursor Left
9	&64	&C6	C664	Ø	Cursor Right
1Ø	&FØ	&C6	C6FØ	Ø	Cursor Down
11	&5B	&C6	C65B	Ø	Cursor Up
12	&59	&C7	C759	Ø	Clear Text Screen
13	&AF	&C7	C7AF	Ø	Newline
14	&8D	&C5	C58D	Ø	Select Paged Mode
15	&A6	&C5	C5A6	Ø	Cancel Paged Mode
16	&CØ	&C7	C7CØ	Ø	Clear Graphics Screen
17	&F9	&4F	C7F9	1	Define Text Colour
18	&FD	&4E	C7FD	2	Define Graphics Colour
19	&92	&5B	C892	5	Define Logic Colour
2Ø	&39	&C8	C839	Ø	Set Default Logic Colours
21	&9B	&C5	C59B	Ø	Disable Display
22	&EB	&5F	C8EB	1	Select Mode
23	&F1	&57	C8F1	9	Define Character
24	&39	&78	CA39	8	Define Graphics Window
25	&8C	&6B	C98C	5	Plot
26	&BD	&C9	C9BD	Ø	Set Default Windows
27	&11	&C5	C511	Ø	Does nothing
28	&FA	&3C	C6FA	4	Define Text Window
29	&A2	&7C	CAA2	4	Set Graphics Origin
30	&79	&C7	C779	Ø	Home Cursor
31	&87	&4E	C787	2	Position Text Cursor
32	&AC	&CA	CAAC	Ø	Delete (Code &7F)

Page 3 Variables for VDU Control

Ø3ØØ/1	Graphics Window, Left
Ø3Ø2/3	Graphics Window, Bottom
Ø3Ø4/5	Graphics Window, Right
Ø3Ø6/7	Graphics Window, Top
Ø3Ø8	Text Window, Left
Ø3Ø9	Text Window, Bottom
Ø3ØA	Text Window, Right
Ø3ØB	Text Window, Top
Ø3ØC/D	Graphics Origin, Horizontal (External Values)
Ø3ØE/F	Graphics Origin, Vertical (External Values)
Ø31Ø/1	Current Graphics Cursor, Horizontal (External Values)
Ø312/3	Current Graphics Cursor, Vertical (External Values
Ø314/5	Last Graphics Cursor, Horizontal (Internal Values
Ø316/7	Last Graphics Cursor, Vertical (Internal Values)
Ø318	Text Column
Ø319	Text Line
Ø31A	Graphics scan line, expressed as line of character.
Ø31B-Ø323	VDU parameters, last parameter in (Ø323)
Ø324/5	Current Graphics Cursor, Horizontal (Internal Values)
Ø326/7	Current Graphics Cursor, Vertical (Internal Values)
Ø328-Ø349	General Workspace
Ø34A/B	Text Cursor Address to CRT Controller
Ø34C/D	Width of text window in bytes
Ø34E	High byte of address of screen RAM start
Ø34F	Bytes per character.
Ø35Ø/1	Address of window area start
Ø352/3	Bytes per Character Row
Ø354	High byte of Screen RAM size
Ø355	Mode
Ø356	Memory map type
Ø357-Ø35A	Current colours
Ø35B/C	Graphics plot mode
Ø35D/E	Jump vector

Ø35F	Last setting of CRT Controller Cursor Start Register
Ø36Ø	Number of logic colours available, less one
Ø361	Pixels per byte (Zero if graphics not available)
Ø362/3	Colour masks
Ø364/5	X/Y for Text Input Cursor
Ø366	Output Cursor Character for Mode 7
Ø367	Font flag
Ø368/E	Font location bytes
Ø36F-Ø37E	Colour palette

Reference to internal and external values relates to the fact that graphics co-ordinates are scaled for internal use, the scale factor depending on current mode.

Character Analysis

The VDU Control routine begins by analysing the code held in A to determine whether it is printable, a control code, or a parameter:

C4CØ If (Ø26A) ≠ Ø, one or more parameters are expected, and the routine jumps to C515. Otherwise, if bit 6 of (ØØDØ) = Ø, there is only one cursor, and C4D8 follows.

If bit 6 of (ØØDØ) = 1, there are two cursors, one for read and one for write, and C568 is called to exchange cursor values, CD6A then setting up the special write cursor, as used in Edit. If the display is disabled, C4D8 follows, otherwise if A = &ØD subroutine D918 is called to terminate Edit.

Note that even if the screen is disabled the routine must continue, in case VDU6 is being called to enable screen.

C4D8 If A = &7F the routine jumps to C4ED, where A = &2Ø, and the routine handling control codes is entered. If A = Ø – &1F, the control code routine is entered at C4EF.

If screen is disabled, with bit 7 of (ØØDØ) = 1, the routine exits via C55E. Otherwise CFB7 is called to display a character and C664 is called to perform cursor right, before C55E is reached.

The next block reads the link addresses and number of parameters:

C4ED A = &2∅, replacing &7F, the Delete code.

C4EF Y = A, and (∅35D) = (C333 + Y) sets up the low byte of the link address to the required function routine. Then A = (C354 + Y). If A is negative, the upper byte is given explicitly, and there are no parameters: the routine jumps to C545.

Otherwise, (∅26A) = A OR &F∅, setting up the negated parameter count, and (∅35E) = A ÷ 16 + &C3, setting the upper byte of the link. If bit 6 of (∅∅D∅) = 1, the routine jumps to C52F, as the earlier exchange of pointers must be balanced. Otherwise carry is cleared, and;

C511 The routine returns.

Reference to the OSWRCH routine will show that a return from the VDU routine with carry clear indicates that no printer action is required.

The next block is entered with X = (∅26A) if X ≠ ∅, showing that parameters are outstanding:

C512 (∅224 + X) = A, setting the new input as a parameter. Since the last parameter is set with X = &FF, it will go into (∅323), the previous parameter will go in (∅322), and so on.

(∅26A) = X + 1, incrementing the negated count, and if (∅26A) ≠ ∅ the routine exits via C532. There are still parameters to come.

If the parameters are complete, the routine jumps to C534 if bit 7 of (∅∅D∅) = 1 (Display disabled), or to C526 if bit 6 of (∅∅D∅) = 1, showing that two cursors are in use. Otherwise CCF5 is called to execute the required function, and the routine returns with carry clear.

C526 C568 and CD6A are called here, instead of at the start of the routine, then CCF5 is called to execute the function.

C52F C565 is called to balance the earlier pointer exchange, and;

C532 The routine returns with carry clear.

Now we reach the first executive routine, also entered from above.

VDU1: Next Character to Printer: C53B: 1 Parameter

C534 If (Ø35E), the upper byte of the link address, is not &C5, the printer is not interested, and the routine exits via C532.

C53B If bit Ø of (ØØDØ) = Ø, the printer is not enabled, and the routine returns. Otherwise, the routine jumps to E11E in the printer driver. Note that A holds the last parameter read, which — in relation to the VDU code — is the 'next character'.

We now return to the overall control routine, the next block being entered if an explicit link address is found. The routine leads on directly into the main exit sequence at C55E:

C545 (Ø35E) = A, setting the upper byte of the link address. The A is restored from Y, to which it was copied earlier. If A holds less than 8, the routine jumps to C553 with carry clear. Otherwise, C is set if A exceeds &ØD.

C553 If bit 7 of (ØØDØ) = 1, display is disabled, and the routine jumps to C58Ø to check for VDU6, otherwise P is pushed while CCF5 is called to execute the control function. If carry is clear, then C561 follows.

C55E This is the start of the main exit routine. Carry is set if the printer is enabled, i.e. if bit Ø of (ØØDØ) = 1. An exit by this routine requires printer action later.

C561 If bit 6 of (ØØDØ) = Ø, there being a single cursor, the routine returns via C511. Otherwise, balancing actions are needed.

C565 CD7A is called to restore the normal write cursor.

C568 P and A are pushed, and CDDE is called with X = &18, Y = &64 to exchange (Ø318/9) with (Ø364/5), these being the two cursor position definitions. CFØ6 is then called to set up a display address, CAØ2 sets the cursor position, bit 1 of (ØØDØ) is toggled to allow scroll or bar it, A and P are pulled, and the routine returns.

C58Ø If A ≠ 6, the routine returns via C58C. Otherwise, the routine exits via C5A8 with A = &7F, which zeroes bit 7 of (ØDØØ). (This jump on CC is always executed, since carry is cleared for A holding less than 8.)

C588 This is a much-used module. It sets A from bit 5 of (ØØDØ), giving a zero for a text cursor.

C58C The routine returns.

The smaller and simpler executive modules now begin.

VDU14: Set Paged Mode: C58D

C58D The paged mode counter in (Ø269) is zeroed, and the routine jumps to C59D with A = 4, which sets bit 2 of (ØØDØ).

VDU2: Printer On: C596: No Parameters
VDU21: Disable Display: C59B: No Parameters

C596 E1A2 in the printer routine is called, and A = &94.

C59B This is entered with A = &15, the VDU number. A = A EOR &95, which converts &94 to &Ø1, for setting bit Ø of (ØØDØ), while &15 becomes &8Ø, for setting bit 7.

C59D A = A OR (ØØDØ), and C5AA follows.

VDU3: Printer off: C5A1: No Parameters
VDU15: Cancel Paged Mode: C5A6: No Parameters

C5A1 E1A2 is called, and A = &ØA

C5A6 This is entered with A = &ØF. A = A EOR &F4 converts &ØA to &FE, clearing bit Ø of (ØDØØ), while &ØF becomes &FB, clearing bit 2.

C5A8 A = A AND (ØØDØ)

C5AA (ØØDØ) = A

C5AC The routine returns.

VDU4: Select Text Cursor: C5AD: No Parameters

C5AD If (Ø261) = Ø, there are no graphics in the current mode, and the routine returns. Otherwise C951 is called to set the CRT controller for a text type of cursor, A = &DF, to clear bit 5 of (ØØDØ), which is done by an exit via C5A8.

VDU5: Select Graphics Cursor: C5B9: No Parameters

C5B9 If (Ø261) = Ø, there are no graphics in the current mode, and the routine returns. Otherwise C954 is called with A = &2Ø to set up a graphics type cursor in the CRT Controller, the contents of A being used to set bit 5 of (ØØDØ) by an exit via C59D.

More complex routines follow, to deal with cursor movements. In a number of instances one routine may call another. For example, a cursor right which goes outside the window area calls up a cursor down action, the column count being zeroed. There are also a number of general purpose subroutines which are invoked.

VDU8: Cursor Left: C5C5

C5C5 C588 is called, returning with A = Ø if the text cursor is in use. If A ≠ Ø, a jump to C61F enters the graphics version of the cursor left routine.

Otherwise, (Ø318), the text column count, is decremented. If it is then less than (Ø3Ø8), the left margin column, the routine jumps to C5EE to execute a move to the right of the next line up. Otherwise, X/A is set to (Ø34A/B) – (Ø34F), which is the text cursor address less the number of bytes in a character. If A, the upper byte, is less than (Ø34E), the upper byte of screen RAM start, (Ø354), the number of pages in screen RAM, is added to wrap round to the bottom of the screen. Y = A, and the routine jumps to C9F6 to set up the new cursor address.

The next routine executes the wrapround action indicated above, and is also entered at C5F4 for the cursor up function with text cursor.

C5EE (Ø318) = (Ø3ØA) sets the column count to the right margin.

C5F4 The paged mode line count in (Ø269) is decremented, since the cursor is moving up a line.

However, if this takes (Ø269) below zero it is incremented again. X = (Ø319), the line count, and if X = (Ø3ØB), the top text margin, the routine jumps to C6ØA. Otherwise, (Ø319) is decremented, and the routine jumps to C6AF to complete cursor resetting.

The next block is entered if the cursor is on the top line.

C6ØA Carry is cleared, and CD3F is called to check window violation. If bit 3 of (ØØDØ) = 1, the routine jumps to C619, otherwise C994 is called to adjust screen RAM address, and C61C follows.

C619 For a text window, CDA4 is called in place of C994, and;

C61C The routine exits via C6AC.

The next routine deals with cursor left and down, with graphics cursor in use. C61F is the entry for cursor left, C621 is the entry for cursor down. The difference lies in the value of X, which is used as a displacement to select either vertical or horizontal data.

C61F X = Ø, selecting horizontal parameters.

C621 Entry at this point is with X = 2, selecting vertical parameters. X is saved in (ØØDB) while D1ØD is called to check for window violations, setting bits in (ØØDA) if any are present.

(Ø324/5 + X), the current graphics cursor co-ordinate (horizontal or vertical), is reduced by 8. If (ØØDA) ≠ Ø, the routine jumps to C658. Otherwise D1ØD is called again to assess the new position, and this time the routine jumps to C658 if (ØØDA) = Ø.

Otherwise A = (Ø3Ø4 + X), the low byte of the right or top margin of the graphics window. If X = Ø, A = A – 7. Then (Ø324/5 + X) is set from A/(Ø3Ø5 + X). In effect, (Ø326/7 = (Ø3Ø6/7) , or (Ø324/5) = (Ø3Ø4/5) – 7.

If X = Ø, the routine jumps to C66Ø to execute graphics cursor up.

C658 The routine exits to D1B8, which sets up external co-ordinate values from internal values.

VDU11: Cursor Up: C65B: No Parameters

C65B If bit 5 of (ØØDØ) = Ø, the text cursor is in use, and the routine jumps to C5F4. Otherwise the routine jumps to C6B6 with X = 2.

VDU9: Cursor Right: C664: No Parameters

C664 If bit 5 of (ØØDØ) = 1, the graphics cursor is in use, and the routine jumps to C6B4. Otherwise X = (Ø318), the column count. If X exceeds (Ø3ØA), the right margin, a jump to C684 implements a return to the left margin and a cursor down.

Otherwise, (Ø318) is incremented, A/X = (Ø34A/B) + (Ø34F), the sum of the RAM address plus bytes per character. The routine jumps to C9F6 to reset and, if necessary, adjust screen address.

The next block is entered from above at C684, or from text cursor down at C68A:

C684 (Ø318) = (Ø3Ø8), setting column count to left margin.

C68A Carry is cleared, and CAE3 is called to check bottom margin, holding up action if paged mode is selected and the bottom line has been reached, unless SHIFT is pressed.

When CAE3 returns, X = (Ø319), the line count. If X matches or exceeds (Ø3Ø9), the bottom margin, the routine jumps to C69B. Otherwise (Ø319) is incremented, and the routine exits to C6AF to set screen addresses.

C69B CD3F is called to check for margin violations. When it returns, if bit 3 of (ØØDØ) = 1, the routine jumps to C6A9. Software scrolling is selected. Otherwise C9A4 is called, and C6AC follows.

C6A9 CDFF is called.

C6AC CEAC is called.

C6AF CFØ6 is called, and the routine exits via CAØ2.

The numerous subroutines are best studied separately, but in general C9A4 handles 'hardware scrolling', CDFF handles 'software scrolling', CEAC clears a line, and CFØ6 calculates a screen RAM address from column and line data. CAØ2 sets up the CRT controller.

The next block serves graphic cursor right and up. Cursor right enters at C6B4, cursor up at C6B6, with X = 2.

C6B4 X = Ø

C6B6 (ØØDB) = X while D1ØD is called to check margins and set bits in (ØØDA) if there are any violations.

(Ø324/5 + X) is increased by 8. If (ØØDA) ≠ Ø, the routine jumps to C658. Otherwise D1ØD is called again, and if it returns with (ØØDA) = Ø the routine jumps to C658.

Otherwise, if X = Ø, (Ø324/5) = (Ø3ØØ/1), while if X = 2, (Ø326/7) = (Ø3Ø2/3) + 7. (Compare with the routine at C61F.)

If X = Ø, the routine jumps to C6F5 to perform cursor down. Otherwise the routine exits via D1B8, which sets up external co-ordinate values from internal values.

VDU1Ø1 : Cursor Down: C6F0: No Parameters

C6FØ If bit 5 (ØØDØ) = Ø, the routine jumps to C68A to deal with text cursor mode. Otherwise;

C6F5 The routine jumps to C621 with X = 2.

That completes the main cursor routines, and we now move on to the relatively simple window-setting routine.

VDU28: Define Text Window: C6FA: 4 Parameters

The parameters are set up thus:

(Ø32Ø)	P1	Left Margin
(Ø321)	P2	Bottom Margin
(Ø322)	P3	Right Margin
(Ø323)	P4	Top Margin

C6FA X = (Ø355), the current mode number. Several validity checks are then made. The routine returns if P2 is less than P4, or if P2 exceeds (C3E7 + X), the maximum window height for the current mode. It returns if P3 exceeds (C3EF + X), the maximum window width for the current mode. It returns if P1 exceeds P3. (All these are reasonable criteria, but the user is not told his command has been ignored.)

If all the checks are passed, Y = P3 − P1, and CA88 is called to calculate the number of bytes in a line, within the window. Bit 3 of (ØØDØ) is set to indicate that a text window is set.

Then (Ø3Ø8/B) = (Ø32Ø/3), copying the parameters to the margin variables. CEE8 is called to set up a screen address. If it returns with carry set the routine exits to C779 to home the cursor within the window. Otherwise;

C732 The routine exits to CAØ2.

We now have some stray OSWORD functions:

OSWORD 9: Read a Pixel: C735

C735 Y = 3

C737 (Ø328 + Y) = ((ØØFØ) + Y). Y is decremented, and if it remains positive the routine loops to C737. This copies the parameter block into VDU control workspace. D839 is called with A = &28 to check window boundaries, returning with A = &FF if they are violated, else with A holding a logic colour for the specified pixel. This is set in the fifth location of the parameter block by a jump to C75Ø with Y = 4.

OSWORD 11: Read Palette: C748

C748 X = A AND (Ø36Ø), limiting A to the colour range available in the current mode. Then A = (Ø36F + X), picking up the actual colour number for logic colour X.

C74F Y is incremented, being zero at entry.

C75Ø ((ØØFØ) + Y) = A. A = Ø. If Y ≠ 4, the routine loops to C74F.

C758 The routine returns.

A five-byte parameter block is used, with the logic colour number in the first byte, the value of the other bytes irrelevant. On return, the actual colour is set in the second byte.

The three functions which follow are linked in the text mode, each entering the next.

VDU12: Clear Screen: C759: No Parameters
VDU3Ø : Home Cursor: C779: No Parameters

VDU31: Position Text Cursor: C787: Two Parameters

C759 If bit 5 of (ØØDØ) = 1, the graphics cursor is in use, and the routine jumps to C7BD. If bit 3 of (ØØDØ) = 1, a text window is set, and the routine jumps to C767. Otherwise the routine jumps to CBC1 to implement a simple clearance.

For a text window:

C7C7 X = (Ø3ØB), the top margin.

C76A (Ø319) = X, this being the line count. CEAC is called to clear a line, and then X = (Ø319) + 1. If X is less than (Ø3Ø9), the bottom margin, the routine loops to C76A to clear the next line. Otherwise Home Cursor is performed.

C779 If bit 5 of (ØØDØ) ≠ Ø, the graphics cursor is in use, and the routine jumps to CFA6, else;

C781 (Ø322) = (Ø323) = Ø. These are the parameters for Position Text Cursor, setting the Home position. The routine runs on into;

C787 If bit 5 of (ØØDØ) = 1, the graphics cursor is selected, and the command is illegal. The routine returns via C758.

Otherwise, C7A8 exchanges (Ø318/9) and (Ø328/9), saving the line/column pointers in workspace. Then (Ø318) = (Ø322) + (Ø3Ø8), setting column to the sum of parameter 1 and left hand margin. (Ø319) = (Ø323) + (Ø3ØB) similarly sets line to the sum of parameter 2 and top margin.

CEE8 is called to set up screen address, and if it returns with carry clear the routine exits via CAØ2 to set up the CRT controller, else;

C7A8 CDDE is called with X = &18, Y = &28 to exchange (Ø318/9) with (Ø328/9), restoring the original line and column settings, as the command called up an off-screen position. The routine returns.

VDU13: Newline: C7AF: No Parameters

C7AF If bit 5 of (ØØDØ) = 1, the routine jumps to C7B7, as the graphics cursor is in use. Otherwise, the routine jumps to CFAD.

C7B7 The graphics cursor newline is performed by CE6E, the routine then returning via C6AF to set up screen address and CRT controller.

VDU16: Clear Graphics Screen: C7CØ: No Parameters

The entry at C7BD is used if VDU 12 is called with graphics cursor in use. Note that the text cursor must be selected before the text screen can be cleared.

C7BD CFA6 is called to copy (Ø326/7) = (Ø3Ø6/7) and (Ø324/5) = (Ø3ØØ/1). This sets the current graphics cursor position from the left and top graphics margins.

C7CØ If (Ø361) = Ø, the current mode has no graphics, and the routine returns.

X = (Ø35A), the current graphics background colour, and Y = (Ø35C), the GCOL background colour. DØB3 is called to set (ØØD4/5) as a colour mask. D47C is called with X = 0, Y = &28 to set (Ø328/F) from (Ø3ØØ/7), copying the graphics window data to workspace. A is then set to (Ø3Ø6) – (Ø3Ø2), these being the low bytes of the top and bottom graphics margins. (Ø33Ø) = A + 1, this being used as a line count.

C7E1 D6A6 is called with X = &2C, Y = &28 to handle the actual clearance. Then (Ø32E/F), the window height in pixels, is decremented, and so is (Ø33Ø). If (Ø33Ø) ≠ Ø, the routine loops to C7E1, otherwise returning.

Like many of the graphics routines, this one is very complex, and a fully detailed study would be long and repetitive. The best way to understand the routines is to work them through for various given values.

VDU17: Define Text Colour: C7F9: One Parameter

VDU18: Define Graphics Colour: C7FD: Two Parameters

These calls correspond to COLOUR and GCOL:

C7F9 The routine jumps to C7FF with Y = Ø

C7FD Y = 2

C7FF A = (Ø323), the last parameter input. If A is negative, the value given is for background, and Y is incremented. Then A = A AND (Ø36Ø), limiting the value to an available colour (and removing the sign bit.) (ØØDA) = A. If (Ø36Ø) = Ø, the routine returns. .

Then X = (Ø36Ø) AND 7 + (ØØDA), forming a pointer to a reference table, for: (Ø357 + Y) = (C423 + X), which copies from the table to the current colour block at a point determined by Y.

If Y = 2 or 3, a graphics colour is involved, and the routine jumps to C82C. Otherwise, (ØØD2) = ((Ø357) EOR &FF) EOR (Ø358), establishing a background colour mask.

C82B The routine returns.

C82C (Ø359 + Y) = (Ø322), copying the second parameter in VDU 18 to the GCOL colour setting.

At this point, a word of explanation about colour representation in the screen RAM is desirable. This can conveniently be investigated by dumping the start of screen RAM in hex, using the program given in the Appendix.

For Mode Ø, the dump is:

3ØØØ	3C 66 ØC 1C Ø6 66 3C ØØ	Pattern for '3'
3ØØ8	3C 66 6E 7E 76 66 3C ØØ	Pattern for 'Ø'
3Ø1Ø	3C 66 6E 7E 76 66 3C ØØ	Pattern for 'Ø'
etc.		

There are no colours, only black and white, so the pattern bytes are stored unchanged. They are not read in address sequence. First bytes 3ØØØ, 3ØØ8, 3Ø1Ø and so on are read to establish the top line of all the characters in a line. Then 3ØØ1, 3ØØ9, 3Ø11 etc. are read to establish the second line of the characters, and so on.

A similar result is obtained with Mode 3 (starting at 4ØØØ), Mode 4 (starting at 58ØØ) and Mode 6 (starting at 6ØØØ). For Mode 1, however, the pattern changes:

```
3ØØØ   33 66 ØØ 11 ØØ 66 33 ØØ
3ØØ8   CC 66 CC CC 66 66 CC ØØ     Pattern for '3
3Ø1Ø   33 66 66 77 77 66 33 ØØ
3Ø11   CC 66 EE EE 66 66 CC ØØ     Pattern for 'Ø'
etc.
```

What has happened is that each pattern byte has been split into two nibbles, each of which has, in this instance, been multiplied by &11, a factor which calls up a white display. The multiplier might have been Ø for black, or 1 or &1Ø for the other two colours available. In the case shown, the background is black. If it were not, the complement of the nibble would be multiplied by the appropriate colour factor and ORed with the normal nibble.

The bytes are read in the same order as that used for Mode Ø, but each only defines half of one line of a character pattern, so only half the number of characters appear in a line. Mode 5 is similar, but with a start address of 58ØØ.

Mode 2, with sixteen colours, works on a similar principle, but the pattern bytes are divided into four bit-pairs, each of which is multiplied by a colour factor, which may be defined as XØXØXØXØ, where the X bits may be Ø or 1. Four bytes are required to define one pattern line.

Mode 7 is totally different. Each byte holds a character code, and the Teletext chip derives the required pattern bytes, setting up colours in response to control bytes.

Returning to the VDU control routines:

VDU 20: Default Colours: C839: No Parameters

C839 Locations (Ø357) to (Ø35C), holding current colour data, are cleared to zero. If (Ø36Ø) = Ø, Mode 7 is selected, and (Ø358) = &2Ø, after which the routine returns.

Otherwise, A = &3F, but if (Ø36Ø) = &ØF there are sixteen colours, and A = &FF. (Ø357) = (Ø359) = A, setting the text and graphics foreground numbers. Then A is inverted, and the result is set in (ØØD2) and (ØØD3).

(Ø31F) = (Ø36Ø), setting the first parameter of five to the number of available colours less one. If (Ø36Ø) = 3, there are four colours, and the routine jumps to C874. If (Ø36Ø) is less than 3, there are two colours, and the routine jumps to C885. Otherwise, there are sixteen colours, and the routine continues with;

(Ø32Ø) = (Ø36Ø), setting the second parameter of five, and;

C868 C892 is called to execute VDU 19, using the parameters set above. Both parameters are decremented, and if the one in (Ø31F) is positive the routine loops to C868, otherwise returning.

C874 For a four colour mode, (Ø32Ø) = 7 to set the second parameter.

C879 C892 is called to execute VDU 19. (Ø32Ø) is halved, (Ø31F) is decremented, and while (Ø31F) is positive the routine loops to C879, otherwise returning.

C885 For two-colour modes, X = 7, and C88F is called, executing VDU 19 with (Ø32Ø) = X. Then X = Ø, (Ø31F) = X, and;

C88F (Ø32Ø) = X. The routine then runs on into VDU 19.

VDU 19: Define Logic Colours: C892: Five parameters

Only the first two parameters, set in (Ø31F) and (Ø32Ø), are in fact used, though all five must be input to reduce (Ø26A) to zero and allow action to proceed:

C892 P is pushed and interrupt barred. X = (Ø31F) AND (Ø36Ø), giving parameter one limited by the number of available colours, less one. A = (Ø32Ø) picks up the second parameter.

C89E A = A AND &ØF, limiting parameter two to a valid range. Then (Ø36F + X) = A sets an entry in the colour palette. Y = A.

A = (Ø36Ø), and (ØØFA) = A. If A = 3, the EQ condition is set. P is pushed, and A = X.

C8AD A and (ØØFA) are rotated right, and if carry is set the routine loops to C8AD. This shifts the relevant bits of A into (ØØFA). For example, in a four colour mode (ØØFA) = 3. If A = 2, the process sets (ØØFA) = &4Ø. One shift too many has been performed, so (ØØFA) is doubled, and A = Y OR (ØØFA). X = A, Y = Ø.

C8BA P is pulled and pushed. If NE is set (A was not equal to 3 earlier) the routine jumps to C8CC.

Otherwise, A = A AND &6Ø. If this gives Ø or &6Ø, bits 5 and 6 are in the same state. The routine jumps to C8CB. Otherwise, X = A, and A = A EOR &6Ø, and C8CC follows.

C8CB X = A

C8CC EA11 (OSBYTE 155) is called to set (Ø249) and (FE21) from A EOR 7. This passes data to the palette register in the Video ULA.

Then Y = Y + (Ø36Ø), X = X +&1Ø. If Y is less than &1Ø, the routine loops to C8BA, setting another byte in the ULA.

Otherwise, P is pulled twice, and the routine returns.

OSWORD 12: Write Palette: C8EO

C8EO P is pushed. X = A AND (Ø36Ø), limiting A to valid values, Y is incremented from Ø to 1, and A = ((ØØFØ)

+ Y). The routine jumps to C89E to execute VDU 19, with the equivalent of parameter 1 in X, and parameter 2 in A.

VDU 22: Select Mode: C8EB: One Parameter

C8EB The routine jumps to CB33 with A = (Ø323), the parameter.

VDU 23: Define Characters: C8F1: Nine Parameters

The first parameter is set in (Ø31B), and the other eight are set in subsequent locations up to (Ø323):

C8F1 A = (Ø31B), the first parameter. If it is less than &2Ø, it means that the call is an instruction to set the CRT controller, and a jump to C93F is taken.

Otherwise A is pushed, and X = INT(A + 32). Then, using a look-up table, A = &8Ø ÷ 2^X. If A AND (Ø367) ≠ Ø the routine jumps to C927, as the necessary storage area is already established.

Otherwise, (Ø367) = (Ø367) OR A, setting the bit that was found to be zero. (ØØDF) = (X AND 3) + &BF, which sets a page within the standard character pattern area. (CØØØ – C2FF). (ØØDD) = (Ø367 + X), which reads a page reserved for special patterns. (ØØDC) = (ØØDE) = Y, which at this point holds Ø.

C920 ((ØØDC) + Y) = ((ØØDE) + Y), Y is decremented, and if Y ≠ Ø the routine loops to C92Ø. This copies a page of standard patterns into a special pattern page (overwriting any patterns already set there).

C927 A is pulled, and DØ3E is called to set up the address of the start of the required pattern in (ØØDE/F). Y = 7.

C92D ((ØØDE) + Y) = (Ø31C + Y), Y is decremented, and if Y is positive the routine loops to C92D. Otherwise the routine returns, the last eight parameters having been set in the pattern area.

This routine should be studied in relation to those at CDØ7 (OSBYTE 2Ø) and DØ3E.

The next small block appears to be a vestigial remnant, as no entry at C936 has been found, though C937 is used:

C936 Pull A.

C937 Return.

We then reach the access to the 'VDU Extension' function, which jumps to (Ø226) with carry clear and A = (Ø31F):

C938 A = (Ø31F), the fifth VDU 23 parameter. Carry is cleared.

C93C The routine jumps to (Ø226), the 'VDU Extension' vector, which normally links to a return instruction.

The next routine, part of VDU 23, but also used in other ways, sets the CRT controller, and also accesses the routine above:

C93F A holds the first parameter for VDU 23. If the parameter is less than 1 the routine jumps to C958 to set a CRT controller register. If the parameter is not 1, the routine jumps to C936 above. Otherwise, A = &2Ø, Y = (Ø31C), the second VDU 23 parameter, and if Y = Ø the routine jumps to C954.

C951 A = (Ø35F), the last setting of the CRT controller cursor start.

C954 Y = &ØA, and the routine jumps to C985 to set register Y to A.

C958 A = (Ø31D), the third parameter, Y = (Ø31C), the second parameter.

C95E If Y is less than 7, no adjustment is needed, and the routine jumps to C985. If Y = 7, A = A (Ø29Ø), adding the adjustment set up by *TV to move the display vertically. If Y = 8, A = A EOR (Ø291), modifying the setting of skew and interlace. If Y = &ØA, (Ø35F) = A to note the value used at C951, and if bit 5 of (ØØDØ) = 1 the graphics cursor is in use, and the routine jumps to C98B. Register 1Ø must not be set in these circumstances. Otherwise:

C985 (FEØØ) = Y, selecting a CRT Controller register, and (FEØ1) = A, setting the chosen register.

C98B The routine returns.

The settings of the CRT controller are too closely interrelated to make casual change possible, but some interesting effects can be produced if the component is studied carefully.

The VDU method of setting needs to be used with care. VDU 23, Ø, R, X, Ø, Ø, Ø, Ø, Ø, Ø will set register R to X. VDU 23, 1, Ø, Ø, Ø, Ø, Ø, Ø, Ø, Ø sets register 1Ø to &2Ø, and so on. With a first parameter 2 to &1F the VDU Extension link is accessed.

VDU 25: Plot: C98C: Five Parameters

C98C If (Ø361) = Ø, there are no graphics available, and the routine jumps to C938, accessing the VDU Extension routine (which seems a little odd . . .). Otherwise, the plot routine proper is entered a DØ6Ø.

The next routine is entered at C994 from C614, and at C9A4 from C6A4. It is used to adjust screen RAM addresses:

C994 X/A = (Ø35Ø/1), the address of the window area start: CCF8 is called to subtract (Ø352/3), the number of bytes per line, from this value. If the result leaves A (the high byte) less than (Ø34E), the first screen RAM page, A = A + (Ø354), the high byte of screen RAM size. This produces a wraparound from the top of the window to the bottom.

In any case, C9B3 follows:

C9A4 X/A = (Ø35Ø/1), the address of the window area start, and CAD4 is called to add (Ø352/3), the number of bytes in a line, to this value. If the result leaves A greater than &7F, (Ø354), the high byte of screen RAM size, is subtracted from A. Then:

C9B3 (Ø35Ø/1) = X/A. Y = &ØC, and CAØE is entered to set the CRT controller.

The actions above should be examined with care. The entry at C994 is from cursor up, and (Ø35Ø/1) is reduced by the number of bytes in a line, moving the start point of the CRT controller scan to the same point in the previous line. If this runs outside the screen RAM area, wraparound to the bottom line occurs.

The effect is to alter the relationship between RAM address and screen position, but although this appears to be regarded as 'hardware scrolling', it is not precisely what that term would lead one to expect.

VDU 26: Set Default Windows: C9BD: No Parameters

C9BD Locations (Ø3ØØ) to (Ø32C) are set to zero, clearing window data, cursor origin, current and last graphics cursor, column and line counts, the graphics scan line, the parameter block, and part of workspace.

Then X = (Ø355), the current mode number, and Y = (C3EF + X), the corresponding maximum window width. (Ø3ØA) = Y sets up the right margin. CA88 is called to set (Ø34C/D), window width in bytes, to Y + 1 multiplied by bytes per character from (Ø34F).

Next, Y = (C3E7 + X), the maximum window height, and (Ø3Ø9) = Y sets the bottom margin.

Now VDU 24 is brought into play to set up the graphics window. (Ø323) = 3 sets parameter 8, (Ø321) = 4 sets parameter 6, then (Ø322) and (Ø32Ø) are decremented from Ø to &FF. This sets up the parameters as: Ø; Ø; Ø4FF; Ø3FF, or Ø;Ø;1279;1Ø23 in decimal. CA39 is then called to set up the windows.

C5A8 is then called with A = &F7 to clear bit 3 of (ØØDØ), and the routine runs on into a screen address adjustment process with X/A = (Ø35Ø/1).

C9F6 (Ø34A/B) = X/A, setting up the cursor address for the CRT controller. If A exceeds &7F, A = A – (Ø354), the number of pages in screen RAM.

CAØ2 (ØØD8/9) = X/A, and X/A = (Ø34A/B). Y = &ØE.

CAØE If mode 7 is selected (Ø355) = 7), the routine jumps to CA27. Otherwise, X/A is divided by 8, and CA2B follows.

CA27 A = A – &74, A = A EOR &2Ø. This appears to be an address conversion for Mode 7.

CA2B (FEØØ) = Y, selecting register 14 in the CRT controller, and (FEØ1) = A sets data in that register. Y is incremented, and (FEØØ) = Y selects register 15, in which data is set by (FEØ1) = X. The routine returns.

VDU 24: Define Graphics Window: CA39: Eight Parameters

The eight parameters are set up as follows:

(Ø31C/D): Left margin
(Ø31E/F): Bottom margin
(Ø32Ø/1): Right margin
(Ø322/3): Top margin.

As usual, the low bytes come first:

CA39 CA81 is called to exchange (Ø31Ø/3) with (Ø328/B), saving the current graphics cursor position in workspace, for later restoration.

Then D411 is called with X = &1C, Y = &2C to calculate:
(Ø32C/D) = (Ø32Ø1) − (Ø31C/D) Width = Right − Left
(Ø32E/F) = (Ø322/3) − (Ø31E/F) Height = Top − Bottom

If either result shows negative, the routine exits via CA81, balancing the earlier exchange.

D149 is called twice, first with X = &2Ø, then with X = &1C, to scale pointers. If (Ø31F) or (Ø31D) is then found negative, the routine exits via CA81.

X = (Ø355), the current mode, and A/(ØØDA) = (Ø32Ø/1). A/(ØØDA) is halved, and (ØØDA) is halved again. If (ØØDA) ≠ Ø, the routine exits via CA81. Otherwise the process of halving A/(ØØDA) a second time is completed, and then A is halved. It now contains one eighth of the Right Margin parameter. If it is greater than (C3EF + X), the maximum window width (in bytes), the routine exits via CA81.

Otherwise D47C is called with Y = Ø and X = &1C to copy the parameters to (Ø3ØØ/7).

CA81 CDE6 is called with X = &1Ø and Y = &28 to exchange (Ø31Ø/3) with (Ø328/B), balancing the earlier exchange.

The next block performs a calculation:

CA88 Y, set to the window width limit on entry, is incremented and passed to A. Y = Ø. (Ø34C/D) =

A/Y. A = (Ø34F), bytes per character. A is divided by two, and if the result is zero the routine returns. Mode 7 is in use. Otherwise:

CA98 (Ø34C/D) is doubled, AND A is halved. If carry is clear, the routine loops to CA98. Otherwise:

CAA1 The routine returns.

This gives (Ø34C/D) = (Ø34F) * (Y + 1)

VDU 29: Set Graphics Origin: CAA2: Four Parameters

The X parameter is set in (Ø32Ø/1), the Y parameter in (Ø322/3), low byte first, as usual.

CAA2 D48A is called with X = &2Ø, Y = &ØC to copy the parameters to (Ø3ØC/F). The routine exits via D1B8, to reset co-ordinates.

VDU 32: (&7F): Delete: CAAC: No Parameters

CAAC C5C5 is called to perform a cursor left. C588 is then called to check cursor type. If it returns non-zero, the graphics cursor is in use, and the routine jumps to CAC7.

Otherwise, X = (Ø36Ø), the colour mask, and if X = Ø Mode 7 is in use, and the routine jumps to CAC2.

Otherwise, (ØØDE/F) = &C3ØØ, the address of the character pattern for space. The routine returns via CFBF, which displays a space.

CAC2 The routine returns via CFDC with A = &2Ø, to display a space.

CAC7 For the graphics cursor, DØ3E is called with A = &7F to calculate the pattern address for delete code, which consists of seven &FF bytes. X = (Ø35A), the graphics background colour, and Y = Ø. The routine exits via CF63 to display an inversion of the pattern data.

The next block adds (Ø352/3), the number of bytes in a line, to X/A (called from C9AA and CEØB):

CAD4 A is pushed so that it can be used in calculating X = X + (Ø352). Then A is pulled, and A = A + (Ø353) + carry. The routine returns.

Now comes a routine to control scrolling in paged mode:

CAEØ CB14 is called to zero (Ø269), the paged mode line counter.

CAE3 OSBYTE 118 is called to check keyboard status and set the keyboard LEDs. If it returns with carry clear, the routine jumps to CAEA. If otherwise, the minus condition is set, the routine loops to CAEØ. (For details of this OSBYTE call, see Keyboard.)

CAEA If (ØØDØ) shows scrolling barred, paged mode not selected, or twin cursors in use, the routine returns via CB1C.

Otherwise, if (Ø269), the paged mode counter, holds a negative number the routine returns via CB1C.

Otherwise, if (Ø319), the line count, is less than (Ø3Ø9), the bottom margin, the routine jumps to CB19 to increment (Ø269) and return.

Otherwise, carry is cleared, and;

CBØE OSBYTE 118 is again called, and carry is set. If the positive condition is returned the routine loops to CBØE, waiting for Shift to be pressed. Otherwise:

CB14 (Ø269) = &FF

CB19 (Ø269) is incremented.

CB1C The routine returns.

The next routine is called by initialisation via C3ØØ, and it initialises a number of screen variables. It then runs on into the Mode setting routine at CB33, and that in turn runs on into the basic screen clear routine at CBC1. Both these points are used as entries in their own right.

CB1D A, which holds data including the initial mode required, is pushed. X = &7F, and (ØØDØ) = Ø.

CB24 (Ø2FF + X) = A = Ø. X is decremented, and if it is not zero the routine loops to CB24. This clears the lower half of page three, which contains the VDU variables. CDØ7 is then called to 'implode Characters', A is pulled and (Ø366) = &7F defines the character to be used as the write cursor in mode 7.

CB33 Mode setting begins by checking the machine type, in terms of avaialable RAM size. If bit 7 of (Ø28E) = Ø, 16K of RAM is present, and A = A OR 4, ensuring that modes 4-7 will be set up, not modes Ø-3. X = A AND 7, and (Ø355) = X to set mode.

The colour mask in (Ø36Ø) is then set from (C414 + X), and bytes per character is set by (Ø34F) = (C3FF + X). The graphics variable 'pixels per byte' is set by (Ø361) = (C43A + X).

If (Ø361) = Ø, A = 7, otherwise A = (Ø361). A is doubled, and Y = A. (Ø363), a colour mask, is set from (C4Ø6 + Y).

CB5E A is doubled, and if the result is positive the routine loops to CB5E. When A becomes negative, (Ø362) = A.

Then (Ø356) = (C44Ø + X), this being the memory map type.

Next, E9F8 is called with A = (C44F + Y), and is then called again with A = (C44B + Y). These calls set outputs to Port B of the internal VIA, and determine the conditions for hardware scrolling.

The number of pages in screen RAM is set by (Ø354) = (C459 + Y), and the page of screen RAM start is set by (Ø34E) = (C45E + Y).

Then A = (Y + 2) EOR 7. A is divided by two and set in X. (ØØEØ) = (C466 + X), (ØØE1) = &C3. This sets up a pointer to one or other of two tables giving the displacement of line start addresses.

Bytes per line is set by (Ø352) = (C463 + X), (Ø353) = X.

EAØØ is then called with A = (C3F7 + X). This sets up the Video ULA, using OSBYTE 154.

Now P is pushed and interrupt barred. X = (C469 + Y), Y = &ØB.

CBBØ A = (C46E + X), and C95E is called to set register Y of the CRT controller. X and Y are decremented, and if Y is positive the routine loops to CBBØ.

P is pulled, C839 is called to set default colours, and C9BD to set default windows.

This completes the mode-setting procedure. It is so complex that it would be wise to check values by dumping for each mode in turn. The CRT controller settings, however, cannot be dumped, and must be deduced from the fixed data.

CBC1 X = Ø, A = (Ø34E), the page in which screen RAM starts. The window area start address is set by (Ø35Ø/1) = X/A. C9F6 is called to set the CRT controller accordingly. CA2B is called with Y = &ØC to set registers 12 and 13 in the controller.

Next, A = (Ø358), the text background colour, X = (Ø356), the memory map type, and Y = (C454 + X). Then (Ø35D) = Y, (Ø35E) = &CC, setting up a link address in (Ø35D/E).

(Ø269) = (Ø318) = (Ø319) = X = Ø, clearing the paged mode counter, the line and column counts. The routine jumps to (Ø35D).

Before we can discover the significance of this, we have to deal with:

OSWORD 10: Read Character Definition: CBF3

CBF3 DØ3E is called to find the address of the start of the pattern for the code in A. Y = Ø. (The address is in (ØØDE/F.)

CBF8 A = ((ØØDE) + Y), Y is incremented, and ((ØØFØ) + Y) = A. If Y is not equal to 8, the routine loops to CBF8, otherwise returning.

The pattern definition is copied into the OSWORD parameter block.

The actual screen clearance routine follows. It will be much abbreviated here, but the principle is clear enough:

CCØ2 This is the entry point of modes Ø, 1 and 2. The routine consists of (3ØØØ + X) = A, (31ØØ + X) = A, and so on, to:

CC32 This is the entry point for mode 3. The sequence continues, with (4ØØØ+ X) = A, (41ØØ+ X) = A, etc.

CC7A This is the entry point for modes 4 and 5. (58ØØ + X) = A, and so on.

CC92 This is the entry point for mode 6. (6ØØØ+ X) = A, and so on.

CCE6 This is the entry point for mode 7. (7CØØ + X) = A, (7DØØ + X) = A, (7EØØ + X) = A, (7FØØ + X) = A. X is then incremented, and the routine returns if X = Ø, otherwise:

CCF5 The routine jumps to (Ø35D).

Note that A holds background colour data, which is set in every screen RAM location.

The next block subtracts bytes per line from X/A:

CCF8 A is pushed, and X = X − (Ø352), then A is pulled and A = A − (Ø353) − C. The routine returns with flags set on A compared with (Ø34E), the start page for screen RAM.

OSBYTE 20: Explode Characters: CDØ7

CDØ7 (Ø367) = &ØF. This is the key to established character pattern pages, and the bits set true indicate that four pages are allocated. These are &CØ, &C1 and &C2 in ROM and &ØC in RAM. All the locations (Ø368) to (Ø36E), which indicate available RAM pages, are set to &ØC. The X parameter of the call is limited to the range Ø-6, and — contrary to what is said in the User Manual — indicates how many extra pages are required. (Ø246) = X, as a temporary hold. Then A = (Ø243), the upper byte of OSHWM, and X = Ø.

CD24 If X = (Ø246), the routine jumps to CD34. Otherwise Y = (C4BA + X), which is a page displacement, and (Ø368 + Y) = A. This sets up a new page for use in character definition. A and X are incremented, and the routine loops to CD24.

CD34 When the required number of pages have been set, (Ø224) = A, this being the new OSHWM high byte. Y = A, and if EQ is set the routine returns via CDØ6. Since this implies that A could equal zero, an error must be assumed. Otherwise, F168 is entered with X = &11.

This is an unsatisfactory routine in a number of ways. It does not set bits of (Ø367) to indicate available pages, and will reset bits which have been set by VDU 23. This can result in defined patterns being overwritten.

A major problem, however, is that the pattern pages eat into BASIC RAM, and this means that the start of a program must be moved, or it will be overwritten. Experiment in this area will bring some surprises, not all of them welcome.

The next group of routines are concerned with the read and write text cursors:

CD3F If bit 1 of (ØØDØ) = Ø and bit 6 is also Ø, the routine returns. Scrolling is not barred, and a single cursor is in use. Otherwise:

CD47 A = (Ø3Ø9), the bottom margin for text, but if carry is set this is changed to A = (Ø3ØB), the top margin for text. Carry is determined by the calling routine. (See C6ØB, C69B.)

CD4F If bit 6 of (ØØDØ) = 1, the routine jumps to CD59 to deal with the read cursor. Otherwise, the line count is set by (Ø319) = A. Then the return link is pulled off the stack, and the routine jumps to C6AF.

CD59 P is pushed, and if A = (Ø365), the line count for the read cursor, the routine returns via CD78, where P is pulled.

Otherwise, P is pulled, and if carry is clear a jump to CD66 is taken.

Otherwise, (Ø365) is decremented, and the routine returns.

CD66 (Ø365) is incremented, and the routine returns.

Next there are more routines associated with the double cursor mode.

CD6A P and A are pushed, and Y = (Ø34F) − 1. If Y = Ø, Mode 7 is in use, and the routine continues, otherwise jumping to CD8F to deal with other modes. ((Ø34F) holds bytes per character)

((ØØD8) + Y) = (Ø338) picks up the Mode 7 write cursor character (&7F), and places it in the write cursor position. A and P are pulled, the routine returns.

CD7A This is the reverse process. If mode 7 is in use, the write cursor character is transferred back to (Ø338). Otherwise, CD8F is entered.

CD8F A = &FF, except in mode 2, for which Y = &1F, in which case A = &3F. (ØØDA) = A, this being a display mask.

CD99 ((ØØD8 + Y) = ((ØØD8 + Y) EOR (ØØDA), which converts a space into the white block code for the write cursor. Y is decremented, and if it is positive the routine loops to CD99 to convert another line of the pattern.

Otherwise A and P are pulled, and the routine returns.

The next block is concerned with screen address management, and is complicated by the use of subroutines:

CDA4 CE5B is called to exchange the line and column counters with their copies in workspace, check window height, and react accordingly. Then (Ø319) = (Ø3Ø9) sets line = bottom margin, and CFØ6 is called to set up the screen address.

CDBØ CCF8 is called to subract bytes/line from X/A, which was set up by CFØ6, and if the result is below the start of screen RAM (Ø354), pages per screen, is added.

(ØØDA/B) = X/A, (ØØDC) = A. If C is set, there was no addition of (Ø354), and the routine jumps to CDC6. Otherwise;

CDCØ CE73 is called to copy a line to a new position, using (ØØDA/B) as a basis for reading, and (ØØD8/9) as a basis for writing. The routine jumps to CDCE.

CDC6 CCF8 is called to subract bytes/line from X/A, and this time a result outside screen RAM produces a jump to CDCØ. Otherwise CE38 is called to perform a copy. Then;

CDCE A = (ØØDC), X = (ØØDA), then (ØØD8/9) = X/A, the write pointer being set from the read pointer. (ØØDE), which holds the window height, is decremented, and if it is not zero the routine loops to CDBØ. Otherwise;

CDDA CDE8 is called with X = &28, Y =&18, A = 2 to exchange (Ø318/9) with (Ø328/9), these being the text column and line and their copies in workspace.

The exchange routine used at CDDA follows. Various entry points are used in different cases:

CDE2 X = &24. One exchange base will be Ø324.

CDE4 Y = &14. The other base will be Ø314.

CDE6 A = 4. Four bytes will be exchanged.

CDE8 (ØØDA) = A

CDEA Exchange (Ø3ØØ + X) with (Ø3ØØ + Y). Increment X and Y, and decrement (ØØDA). If (ØØDA) ≠ Ø, loop to CDEA, else the routine returns.

The next routine is called with cursor down to execute an upward scroll. It should be compared with the routine beginning at CDA4.

CDFF CE5B is called to exchange pointers, check window height, etc. (Ø319) = (Ø3ØB) sets line count = top margin. CFØ6 is called to set up screen address.

CEØB CAD4 is called to add bytes/line to X/A, pages/sceen being subtracted if necessary to keep within the screen RAM area. Then (ØØDA/B) = X/A, (ØØDC) = A. If no subtraction was needed, the routine jumps to CE22, else;

CE1C CE73 is called to copy a line, and the routine exits to CE2A.

CE22 CAD4 is called to add bytes/line to X/A, the routine jumping to CE38 if the result is above the top of screen RAM.

CE2A A = (ØØDC), X = (ØØDA). (ØØD8/9) = X/A. (ØØDE) is decremented, and if the result is not zero the routine jumps to CEØB, else to CDDA.

Now we reach the actual copy routines:

CE38 X = (Ø34D), the number of bytes in window width (high byte). If X = Ø, the routine jumps to CE4D. There are no more than 256 bytes to be copied. Otherwise, Y = Ø, and;

CE3F (ØØD8) + Y) = ((ØØDA) + Y), Y is incremented, and if Y ≠ Ø the routine loops to CE3F. This copies 256 bytes. (ØØD9) and (ØØDB), the upper bytes of the pointers, are incremented, and X is decremented, the routine looping to CE3F if X ≠ Ø. Otherwise;

CE4D Y = (Ø34C), the low byte of the number of bytes in window width, and if Y = Ø the routine jumps to CE5A, else:

CE52 Y is decremented, and ((ØØD8) + Y) = ((ØØDA + Y). If Y ≠ Ø the routine loops to CE52, otherwise;

CE5A The routine returns.

Note that only the part of the line within the window is copied. If there were no windows, the routines would be much simpler.

Before the second copy routine, the section called at the start of CDA4 and CDFF:

CE5B CDDA is called to exchange (Ø318/9) with (Ø328/9). Then A = (Ø309) − (Ø30B), bottom margin − top margin. (ØØDE) = A. If A ≠ Ø (which may be the case) the routine jumps to CE6E. Otherwise the return link is pulled off the stack and the routine jumps to CDDA to balance the exchange.

CE6E A = (Ø3Ø8), left margin, and CEE3 follows to set (Ø318), the column count, from A and return.

The second copy routine uses window width directly, rather than bytes in window width:

CE73 A = (ØØDA), and A is pushed, so that it can be used in (ØØDF) = (Ø3ØA) − (Ø3Ø8), right margin − left margin.

CE7F Y = (Ø34F), bytes per character, and Y is decremented.

CE83 ((ØØD8) + Y) = ((ØØDA) + Y), Y is decremented, and if Y is positive the routine loops to CE83. X = 2.

CE8C (ØØD8/9) + X) = (ØØD8/9 + X) + (Ø34F), bytes/character. If this goes beyond the bounds of screen RAM, (ØØD9 + X) = (ØØD9 + X) − (Ø354), the familiar correction by subtracting the number of pages in screen RAM. Then X = X − 2, and if X = Ø the routine loops to CE8C to adjust the second pair of pointers. (ØØDA/B on the first pass, ØØD8/9 on the second. Economical coding indeed.)

When the loop has been executed twice, (ØØDF) is decremented, and if it is positive the routine loops to CE7F. Otherwise A is pulled, (ØØDA) = A, and the routine returns.

The next routine clears a line, which is useful after a scroll, since the last line and the penultimate line are the same, and the last line needs to be cleared:

CEAC A = (Ø318), the column count, and A is pushed. CE6E is called to set (Ø318) = (Ø3Ø8), column count = left margin. CFØ6 is called to set screen address. (ØØDC) = (Ø3ØA) − (Ø3Ø8), right margin less left margin.

CEBF A = (Ø358), the text background colour, Y = (Ø34F), bytes per character.

CEC5 Y is decremented, and ((ØØD8) + Y) = A. If Y ≠ Ø, the routine loops to CEC5. Otherwise, X/A = X/(ØØD9) + (Ø34F), with the usual correction for overspill. (ØØD8/9) = X/A.

(ØØDC) is decremented, and if it is positive the routine loops to CEBF. Otherwise, A is pulled, (Ø318) = A, restoring the column setting, carry is set and the routine returns.

The next two routines are best covered in term of the effect of their actions, which are achieved in a complex manner:

CEE8 If (Ø318), the column count, is less than (Ø3Ø8), left margin, or greater than (Ø3ØA), right margin, the routine returns with carry set. The same result is produced if (Ø319), the line count, is less than (Ø3ØB), top margin, or greater than (Ø3Ø9), bottom margin. Otherwise, the routine runs on into:

CFØ6 This block calculates a number appropriate to each mode:
Mode Ø: (Ø319) * 64Ø + (Ø318) * 8
Mode 1: (Ø319) * 64Ø + (Ø318) * 16
Mode 2: (Ø319) * 64Ø + (Ø318) * 32

Mode 3: (Ø319) * 64Ø + (Ø318) * 8
Mode 4: (Ø319) * 32Ø + (Ø318) * 8
Mode 5: (Ø319) * 32Ø + (Ø318) * 16
Mode 6: (Ø319) * 32Ø + (Ø318) * 8
Mode 7: (Ø319) * 4Ø + (Ø318).

This gives a displacement position within screen RAM relative to the start adress, which is added to the calculated number, the result being stored in (Ø34A/B). If the result is less than 8ØØØ, the top of screen RAM, it is copied into X/A and (ØØD8/9). If the result is greater than 7FFF, the usual correction is made by subtracting (Ø354) from the upper byte before X/A and (ØØD8/9)are set.

Next comes the graphic cursor display routine:

C5DF X = (Ø359), graphics foreground colour, Y = (Ø35B), the GCOL foreground colour.

CF63 DØB3 is called to set colour masks in (ØØD4/5), the D486 copies (Ø324/7), graphics cursor, internal, to (Ø328/B) in workspace. Y = Ø.

CF6B (ØØDC) = Y. Y = (ØØDC). A = ((ØØDE) + Y). If A = Ø, the routine jumps to CF86. (ØØDD) = A.

CF75 If A is positive, the routine loops to CF7A, otherwise DØE3 is called to display a pixel.

C7FA (Ø324/5), the horizontal graphics cursor, is incremented, (ØØDD) is doubled, and if (ØØDD) ≠ Ø the routine loops to CF75.

CF86 D482 is called with X = &28, Y = &24 to set (Ø324/5) = (Ø328/9), restoring the original horizontal graphics cursor coordinate. (Ø326/7) is decremented, to select the next line of the character. Then Y = (ØØDC) + 1. If Y is not equal to 8 the routine loops to CF6B.

Otherwise, D48A is called with X = &28, Y = &24 to set (Ø324/5) = (Ø328/B) and return.

Each individual pixel is attended to separately. The pattern bytes are picked up by reference to (ØØDE/F), and the bits of each byte are examined in turn to see if a pixel is to be set. The position of the dot is determined by (Ø324/5) horizontally, and by (Ø326/7) vertically. Finally, the original pointer values are restored, since a cursor right will follow.

The next module homes the graphics cursor:

CFA6 (Ø326/7) = (Ø3Ø6/7), setting graphics line to top margin. (Ø324/5) = (Ø3ØØ/1), setting graphics column to left margin. Then D1B8 is entered to set up corresponding external coordinate values.

The text display routine, initially common with the graphics routine, comes next:

CFB7 X = (Ø36Ø), a colour mask. (Number of colours available, less 1.) If X = Ø, mode 7 is in use, and the routine jumps to CFDC. Otherwise, DØ3E is called to calculate the pattern address, which is set in (ØØDE/F). X is again set from (Ø36Ø).

If bit 5 of (ØØDØ) = 1, the graphics cursor is in use, and the routine jumps to CF5D. Otherwise, Y = 7. If X = 3 the routine jumps to CFEE to handle four-colour modes, while if X is greater than 3 DØ1E is entered to deal with sixteen colours. Otherwise:

CFDØ A = ((ØØDE) + Y), the pattern byte, and then A = A OR (ØØD2) EOR (ØØD3). ((ØØD8) + Y) + A passes the result to screen RAM. Y is decremented, and if Y is positive the routine loops to CFDØ, otherwise returning.

The routine for mode 7 is only concerned with recoding three characters, £, -, and #. The code for £ is &23, not &6Ø; the code for - is &60, not &5F; and hash is &5F, not &23.

CFDC Y = 2.

CFDE If A = (C4B6), the routine jumps to CFE9 to recode the character, otherwise Y is decremented, and if Y is then positive the routine loops to CFDE, else;

CFE6 ((ØØD8) + X) = A stores the character code in screen RAM (X = Ø).

CFE9 If one of the three character codes has been recognised, it is converted by A = (C4B7 + Y), and the routine jumps to CFE6.

The table used is:

C4B6 &23
C4B7 &5F

C4B8 &60
C4B9 &23

Next comes the routine for the four-colour modes. The pattern byte has to be split into two, each nibble being coded for colour:

CFEE A = ((ØØDE) + Y) = A picks up a pattern byte. A is pushed, and a division by 16 moves the upper nibble to the lower nibble position. Then A is multiplied by &11, using a look-up table, and the current colour data is set by A = A OR (ØØD2) EOR (ØØD3). The result is set in screen RAM by ((ØØD8) + Y) = A.

Y = Y + 8, moving the screen RAM pointer eight bytes, and A is pulled. A = A AND &ØF zeroes the upper nibble, and the multiplication by &11 and the setting of colour factors is repeated. Then Y = Y – 9, to point to the next pattern byte, and if Y is positive the routine loops to CFEE to deal with that byte, otherwise returning.

The routine for sixteen colours is, unexpectedly, little more complex. It is entered at DØ1E, DØ18 being a loop point:

DØ18 Y = Y – &21, and if Y is negative the routine returns, else;

DØ1E A = ((ØØDE) + Y) picks up a pattern byte, and (ØØDC) = A. Carry is set.

DØ23 A = Ø. Then (ØØDC) is rotated left. The first rotate will move the true bit from the carry into bit Ø of (ØØDC), and even if the pattern byte holds zero (ØØDC) will be non-zero until that bit has been shifted out into carry again. When (ØØDC) = Ø, the routine jumps to DØ18 to deal with the next pattern byte.

A is rotated left to transfer the bit shifted out of bit 7 of (ØØDC) into bit Ø of A, and then ASL (ØØDC) and another rotate left of A moves the new bit 7 of (ØØDC) to bit Ø of A, which then holds two successive bits of the pattern byte. This is multiplied by &55, using a look-up table, and the colour factors are set by A = A OR (ØØD2) EOR (ØØD3). ((ØØD8) + Y) = A sets the byte in screen RAM.

Y = Y + 8, moving the screen RAM pointer on by eight bytes, and the routine loops to DØ23 to deal with the next bit pair.

Next comes the routine that calculates the pattern address for a given character code. It will be assumed that the code held in A on entry is abcdefg:

DØ3E The sequence ASLA, ROLA, ROLA, sets A = defghxab, with carry holding C. (ØØDE) = A saves this. Then A = A AND 3 and ROLA sets A = ØØØØØabc. X = A. Y = A AND 3 + &BF. This sets a tentative page number in Y, since the patterns for the regular characters are held in CØØØ – C2FF.

However, A = &8Ø ÷ 2^X, and if (Ø367) AND A is non-zero, Y = (Ø367 + X). (Ø367) holds true bits for valid pages of character patterns, and the locations which follow it hold the page numbers of those pages.

(ØØDF) = Y, and (ØØDE) = (ØØDE) AND, &F8, which is defghØØØ, the address within the page indicated by Y. (ØØDE/F) is thus the address of the first byte of the pattern for the code in A on entry.

Reference should be made to the VDU 23 routine to relate the above to the definition of special characters.

We now approach, with some misgivings, the extremely complex Plot routines. These have so many possible variations, and so many modes, that full explanation is not feasible. Working through a given mode with pencil and paper is the only course.

The Plot routines are entered at DØ6Ø, the parameters set as follows:

(Ø31F): Parameter 1: Plot type
(Ø32Ø/1): Parameters 2/3: X coordinate
(Ø322/3): Parameters 4/5: Y coordinate

DØ6Ø D14D is called with X = &2Ø to translate the coordinates, in accordance with the choice of absolute or relative definitions.

If (Ø31F) = 4, the routine jumps to DØD9, to perform move absolute.

Y = 5. If A AND 3 = Ø, the routine jumps to DØ8Ø. The plot type is Ø, 8, 12, 16, etc, and is therefore a move, not a draw.

If bit Ø of (Ø31F) = 1, the routine jumps to DØ78 with A holding in bit Ø a copy of bit 1 of (Ø31F), the other bits of A being zero. A graphics colour is required. If A = Ø, it is the foreground colour, if A = 1 it is the background colour.

Otherwise, the routine jumps to DØ8Ø with Y = 4. Logic inverse colour is required.

DØ78 Y = (Ø35B + A), X = (Ø359 + A), setting up the graphic colours.

DØ8Ø DØB3 is called to set up colour masks in (ØØD4/5). Analysis of the plot type then proceeds.

If (Ø31F) is negative, its value is 128 – 255, and these types are not implemented. The routine jumps to DØAB.

If bit 6 of (Ø31F) = Ø, the plot type is Ø – 63. The routine jumpsto DØC6 to analyse the type further.

If (Ø31F) = Ø1ØØØXXX, the type if 64 – 71, single point plot. The routine jumps to DØD6.

If (Ø31F) = Ø1Ø1ØXXX, the type is 8Ø – 87, Fill Triangle. The routine jumps to DØA8.

At this point DØDC is called to copy (Ø32Ø/3) to (Ø324/7), setting the X/Y coordinates in the current graphics cursor locations.

If (Ø31F) = Ø1ØØ1XXX, the type is 72 – 79, Lteral Fill. (Not mentioned in the User Guide.) The routine jumps to DØAE.

If (Ø31F) = Ø1Ø11XXX, the type is 88 – 95, Horizontal line blanking. (Not mentioned in User Manual.) The routine jumps to D5Ø6 with (ØØDC) = A = 2.

Otherwise, the type is not implemented, and the routine jumps tọ DØAB.

DØA8 The routine jumps on to D5EA (Fill triangle).

DØAB The routine jumps to C938, the 'VDU extension' access.

DØAE (ØØDC) = A = Ø, the routine jumps to D4BF.

The colour masks are set by:

DØB3 (ØØD4) = X OR (C41C + Y) EOR (C41D + Y). (ØØD5) = X OR (C41B + Y) EOR (C42Ø + Y). The routine returns.

Analysis of the first parameter for the Ø − 63 range now continues:

DØC6 If (Ø31F) = ØØ1XXXXX, the type is 32 − 63, not implemented. The routine jumps to DØAB.

If (Ø31F) = ØØØXØXXX, the type is Ø − 7, or 16 − 23. The routine jumps to DØDØ. Otherwise, DØEB is called to display a point.

DØDØ D1ED is called to perform strategic calculations, and DØD9 follows.

DØD6 This is the entry for single point plot. DØEB is called to display a point.

DØD9 CDE2 is called to exchange (Ø314/7) and (Ø324/7), these being the current and last graphics cursor position (internal values).

DØDC Y = &24.

DØDE D48A is called with X = &2Ø to copy the parameters to (Ø3ØØ/3 + Y). The routine returns via D48A.

Display routines follow. Note that it is necessary to read an existing byte before replacing it.

DØE3 X = &24, and D85F is called to calculate position. If it returns with A = Ø, the routine jumps to DØFØ, otherwise returning.

DØEB D85D is called to calculate a position. If it returns with A ≠ Ø, the routine returns.

DØFØ Y = (Ø31A), the graphics scan line.

DØF3 (ØØDA) = (ØØD1) AND (ØØD4) OR ((ØØD6) + Y). This picks up and modifies a screen RAM byte, which is then set back in the same position by ((ØØD6) + Y) =

(ØØD5) and (ØØD1) EOR (ØØDA). The routine returns.

A simpler form of the above follows:

D1Ø4 ((ØØD6) + Y) = ((ØØD6) + Y) OR (ØØD4) EOR (ØØD5). The routine returns.

Now comes a routine which has been called several times by earlier routines to check window limits:

D1ØD X = &24.

D1ØF Y = Ø. (ØØDA) = Y. D128 is called with Y = 2. This pass will deal with (Ø326/7), current vertical graphics cursor position, and (Ø3Ø2/3), (Ø3Ø6/7), the bottom and top graphics margins.

(ØØDA) = (ØØDA) * 4. Data is set in bits Ø,1, and is shifted left to free these bits for the second pass.

X = X – 2, and Y = Ø. D128 is again called, and this time will deal with (Ø324/5), current horizontal graphics cursor position, and (Ø3ØØ/1), (Ø3Ø4/5), the left and right graphics margins.

X = X + 2, A = (ØØDA), and the routine returns.

D128 If (Ø302/3 + X) is less than (Ø3ØØ/1 + Y), the routine jumps to D146. There is a window violation. If (Ø3Ø2/3 + X) is less than (Ø3Ø4/5 + Y), the routine jumps to D148. There is no window violation. Otherwise, (ØØ DA) is incremented.

D146 (ØØDA) is incremented.

D148 The routine returns.

For the first violation, (ØØDA) = 1. For the second violation, it holds 2.

Now comes the routine which sets up and adjusts positional data. There are entries D149 and D14D:

D149 A = &FF. The routine jumps to D15Ø.

D14D A = (Ø31F), the first parameter in plot.

D15Ø (ØØDA) = A, as an indication of whether absolute or relative coordinates are in use, bit 2 being true for absolute coordinates.

Then D176 is called with Y = 2 to set up the vertical coordinates, the result being divided by two. D1AD is then called to divide by two again, so producing the standard vertical scaling for all modes, which converts an input of Ø – 1Ø23 to Ø – 255 for internal use.

Y = Ø, X = X − 2, and D176 is called again to deal with the horizontal coordinate. This time, the scaling process is more complicated. D176 divides the coordinate by two, which gives the required scaling for mode Ø. (128Ø to 64Ø). For other modes, D1AD is called to perform further divisions by two. These are based initially on the contents of (Ø361), pixels per byte. For modes 1 and 5, this holds 3, and a jump to D16D is taken. For modes Ø and 4, (Ø361) holds 7, and the routine jumps to D17Ø. Otherwise, D1AD is called.

D16D D1AD is called.

D17Ø If (Ø356) ≠ Ø, i.e. for modes 3 - 7, D1AD is called. The routine returns.

The overall result is that:

For mode Ø, one division is performed. 128Ø becomes 64Ø.

For mode 1, two divisions are performed. 128Ø becomes 32Ø

For mode 2, three divisions are performed. 128Ø becomes 16Ø

For mode 4, two divisions are performed. 128Ø becomes 32Ø

For mode 5, three divisions are performed. 128Ø becomes 16Ø.

D176 If bit 2 of (ØØDA) = Ø then the routine jumps to D186 to calculate relative coordinates.

Otherwise, A = (Ø3Ø2 + X) and is pushed. Then the routine jumps to D194 with A = (Ø3Ø3 + X).

D186 A = (Ø3Ø2 + X) + (Ø31Ø + Y). A is pushed, and A = (Ø311 + Y) + (Ø3Ø3 + X). The new data is added to the old cursor coordinates.

D194 (Ø311 + Y) = A. (Ø3Ø3 + X) = (Ø311 + Y) + (Ø3ØD + Y). A is pulled, and (Ø31Ø + Y) = A, (Ø3Ø2 + X) = (Ø31Ø + Y) + (Ø3ØX + Y). If carry is set, (Ø3Ø3 + X) is incremented.

D1AD (Ø3Ø2/3 + X) is halved. The routine returns.

The above routine is normally executed with X = &2∅ or X = &1E. Taking the first value, for absolute coordinates:

(∅312/3) = (∅322/3)
(∅322/3) = (∅312/3) + (∅3∅E/F).

The new vertical data is copied to the current graphics cursor (external), and the new data is then increased by the vertical origin coordinate.

For relative working, the equations become:

(∅312/3) = (∅312/3) + (∅322/3)
(∅322/3) = (∅312/3) + (∅3∅E/F)

Instead of copying the new data into (∅312/3), the routine now adds the new data.

Where the above routines produce internal coordinate values from external values, the next block reverses the process.

D1B8 D488 is called with Y = &1∅ to copy (∅324/7), the current graphics cursor position, to (∅31∅/3), the position in external values. D1D5 is then called with X = 2, Y = 2 to multiply (∅312/3) by four and subtract the origin coordinate in (∅3∅E/F).

Then X = ∅, Y = 4, A = (∅361), pixels per byte.

D1CB Y is decremented, and A is shifted right logically. If A ≠ ∅, the routine loops to D1CB. Otherwise, if (∅356) ≠ ∅, Y is incremented. (Compare this with the process in D15∅.)

D1D5 (∅31∅/1) is doubled, and Y is decremented. If Y ≠ ∅, the routine loops to D1D5. D1E3 is otherwise called with carry set, and X is incremented.

D1E3 (∅31∅ + X) = (∅31∅ + X) – (∅3∅C + X). The routine returns.

The overall effect is the reverse of that performed by D15∅.

The next routine deals with the strategy of plot. This is where pencil and paper become essential to a full understanding.

In broad terms, the X and Y spans of the plot motion are calculated and compared. To obtain a satisfactory line, points must be plotted throughout the greater span, with a proportional change in the direction of the lesser span. The choice of one span or the other is the basis of plot strategy.

D1ED D4ØD is called to set the X and Y spans in workspace at (Ø328/9), (Ø32A/B). A = (Ø32B) EOR (Ø329). If the spans differ in sign, A will be negative, and the routine jumps to D2Ø7.

Otherwise, A is set to the upper byte of the difference in the spans, and D214 follows.

D2Ø7 A is set to the upper byte of the sum of the spans.

D214 A is rotated right, X = Ø, and A = A EOR (Ø32B). If the result is negative, X = 2. (ØØDE) = X. A link address is then set up in (Ø35D/E) according to the value of X. If X = Ø, the link is D386, if X = 2, the link is D37E. This determines the sequence of actions at a later stage.

A = (Ø329 + X), the upper byte of one of the spans, and if A is positive the routine jumps to D235. Otherwise, X = &24, and D237 follows.

D235 X = &2Ø

D237 (ØØDF) = X. D48A is called with Y = &2C to set (Ø32C/F) = (Ø3ØØ/3 + X). This will pick up either the X coordinate data or the horizontal coordinate of the current graphics cursor.

A = (ØØDF) EOR 4, converting &2Ø to &24 or vice versa. (ØØDD) = A. A = A EOR (ØØDE). D48Ø is called with X = A to copy (Ø33Ø/1) in workspace from (Ø3ØØ/1 + X).

Bit 4 of plot type is then checked. If it is true, (ØØDB) = &8Ø, else (ØØDB) = Ø. D1ØF is called with X = &2C to check for window violations. If one is found, (ØØ DB) = (ØØDB) OR &4Ø.

X = (ØØDD) and D1ØF is again called to check window violations. If bit 7 of (ØØDC) = Ø, the routine jumps to D26D, otherwise returns.

D26D X = (ØØDE). If X = Ø, the routine jumps to D273. A = A + 4.

D273 A = A AND 2. If A = Ø, then D27E follows. Otherwise, X = X OR 4 and D48Ø is called to set (Ø33Ø/1) = (Ø3ØØ/1 + X).

D27E D42C is called to perform further calculations. Then A = (ØØDE) EOR 2. X = A, Y = A.

Then A = (Ø329) EOR (Ø32B), again comparing the upper bytes of the spans. If the signs differ, A is negative, and X is incremented.

Next, a second link address is set in (Ø332/3). If X = Ø, the link is D36A. If X = 1, the link is D374. If X = 2, the link is D342, and if X = 3 the link is D34B. (Ø334) = &7F.

If bit 6 of (ØØDB) = 1, the routine jumps to D2CE.

Otherwise, X = (C447 + X), A = (Ø3ØØ + X) − (Ø32D + Y), (ØØDA) = A. X = A, and if A is negative, D49B is called to negate Y/A. X = A, and Y/X is incremented. X = A, and if A ≠ Ø then Y = Ø. (ØØDF) = Y, and the routine jumps to D2D7.

D2CE A = X, and A is divided by four. Then A = A OR 2 EOR (ØØDE). (ØØDE) = A.

D2D7 D864 is called with X = &2C. X = (ØØDC). If X = Ø, (ØØDD) is decremented. X is decremented.

D2E3 If (ØØDB) = Ø, the routine jumps to D3Ø6. If (ØØDB) is positive, the routine jumps to D2F9. If bit 7 of (Ø334) = Ø the routine jumps to D2F3. Otherwise, (Ø334) is decremented, and if it is still non-zero the routine jumps to D316.

D2F3 (Ø334) is incremented, and A is doubled. If A is then positive, the routine jumps to D3Ø6, else;

D2F9 (ØØDC) = X, X = &2C, and D85F is called to calculate a screen position. X = (ØØDC), and if X ≠ Ø the routine jumps to D316.

D3Ø6 (ØØDA) = (ØØD1) AND (ØØD4) OR ((ØØD6) + Y). Then ((ØØD6) + X) = (ØØD1) AND (ØØD5) EOR (ØØDA).

D316 (Ø337) is subtracted from (Ø335), and A = (Ø336) − (Ø338). If this sets carry, the routine jumps to D339.

Otherwise, (ØØDA) = A, (Ø335) = (Ø335) + (Ø339), A = (ØØDA) + (Ø33A). Carry is cleared.

D339 (Ø336) = A. P is pushed. If carry is set the routine jumps to (Ø35D) via D438, otherwise to (Ø332). (This allows six possible jump destinations.)

The next block is accessed by (Ø332/3):

D342 Y is decremented, and if it is positive the routine jumps to (Ø35D) via D438. Otherwise D3D3 is called to advance pointers, and;

D348 The routine jumps to (Ø35D).

The next block is again accessed by (Ø332/3):

D34B Y is incremented, and if it is not equal to 8 the routine jumps to (Ø35D). Otherwise (Ø352/3), bytes per line, is added to (ØØD6/7). If the result is negative (above screen RAM), (Ø354) is subtracted to wrap round to screen top.

D363 Y = Ø, and the routine jumps to (Ø35D).

The next block is again accessed by (Ø332/3):

D36A (ØØD1) is shifted right logically, and if carry is clear the routine jumps to (Ø35D). Otherwise, D3ED is called to reset pointers, and the routine jumps to (Ø35D).

The next block is again accessed by (Ø332/3):

D374 (ØØD1) is shifted left logically, and if carry is clear the routine jumps to (Ø35D). Otherwise D3FD is called to reset pointers, and the routine jumps to (Ø35D).

The four modules above are alternatives. The first two perform vertical scans, the second two perform horizontal scans.

The next two routines are accessed via (Ø35D), and therefore follow the four above in execution sequence:

D37E Y is decremented, and if it is positive the routine jumps to D38D. Otherwise D3D3 is called to advance pointers, and D38D follows.

D386 (ØØD1) is shifted right logically, and if carry is clear the routine jumps to D38D, else D3ED is called to reset pointers.

D38D (From this point, the two routines accessed via (Ø35D) are common).

P is pulled (see push at D33C), and X is incremented. If X ≠ Ø, the routine jumps to D395, else (ØØDD) is incremented, and if it is then zero the routine jumps to D39F.

D395 If bit 6 of (ØØDB) = 1, the routine jumps to D3AØ. Otherwise, if carry is set the routine jumps to D2E3 via D3DØ, else (ØØDF) is decremented, and if it is then non-zero the routine jumps to D2E3.

D39F The routine returns.

The next block is an alternative ending to the one above:

D3AØ A = (ØØDE), (ØØDC) = X, X = A AND 2. If carry is set, the routine jumps to D3C2. If bit 7 of (ØØDE) = 1, the routine jumps to D3B7.

Otherwise, (Ø32C/D + X) is incremented, and if carry is clear the routine jumps to D3C2.

D3B7 (Ø32C/D + X) is decremented.

D3C2 X = X EOR 2. (Ø32C/D + X) is incremented. X = (ØØDC), and:

D3DØ The routine loops back to D2E3.

A number of subroutines used above come next;

D3D3 (Ø352/3), bytes per line, is subtracted from (ØØD6/7), and if this puts the pointer outside screen RAM (Ø354), pages per screen, is added to wrap round. Y = 7. The routine returns. (This moves the display point up a line.)

D3ED (ØØD1) = (Ø362), the colour mask, and 7 is added to (ØØD6/7). The routine returns.

D3FD (ØØD1) = (Ø363), the second colour mask, and 9 is subtracted from (ØØD6/7). The routine returns.

The next block is a general-purpose subtraction:

D4ØD X = &28, Y = &2Ø.

D411 D418 is called. X = X + 2, Y = Y + 2.

D418 (Ø3ØØ/1 + Y) = (Ø3Ø4/5) + X) – (Ø3ØØ/1 + X). The routine returns.

Another plot calculation comes next. It is called from D27E:

D42C If (ØØDE) ≠ Ø, the routine jumps to D437.

Otherwise, CDDE is called with X = &28, Y = &2A to exchange (Ø328/9) with (Ø32A/B), the X and Y spans.

D437 D48A is called with X = &28, Y = &37 to copy (Ø337/A) = (Ø328/B), transferring the X and Y spans. X = (ØØDE), and Y/A = (Ø33Ø/1)– (Ø32C/D + X). If A is negative, the routine jumps to D453, else D49B is called to negate Y/A.

D453 (ØØDC/D) = Y/A. X = &35.

D459 D467 (below) is called. (Ø3ØØ/1 + X) = Y/A + 2. X – X – 2.

D467 Y/A = (Ø3Ø4/5) + X). If A is positive, the routine returns. Otherwise, D49B is called to negate Y/A, and (Ø3Ø4/5 + X) = Y/A. The routine returns.

Another general purpose routine now intervenes:

D47C A = 8, and D48C follows. (Eight bytes to copy)

D48Ø Y = &3Ø. (Destination Ø33Ø onwards)

D482 A = 2, and D48C follows. (Copy two bytes)

D486 Y = &28. (Destination Ø328 onwards)

D488 X = &24. (Source Ø324 onwards)

D48A A = 4. (Four bytes to copy)

D48C (ØØDA) = A.

D48E (Ø3ØØ + Y) = (Ø3ØØ + X). X and Y are incremented, (ØØDA) is decremented, and if (ØØDA) ≠ Ø the routine loops to D48E, otherwise returning.

The negation routine for Y/A follows:

D49B Y = Y EOR &FF. A = A EOR &FF. Y is incremented, and if Y = Ø A is also incremented. The routine returns.

Another subroutine follows:

D4AA D85D is called to check window boundaries and set up a screen pointer. If it returns with A non-zero, the routine jumps to D4B7. Otherwise, (ØØDA) = A = ((ØØD6) + Y) EOR (Ø35A), comparing a screen byte with the current background colour. The routine returns.

D4B7 The return link is pulled from the stack.

D4B9 (Ø326), the current graphics cursor vertical

coordinate low byte, is incremented. The routine jumps to D545.

Next comes the Lateral Fill routine, which implements a function not described in the User Guide. Given that the X/Y data defines a point lying horizontally between two points already plotted, this function draws a line between those two points. The function may fail if the bounding points are doubled on the same scan line, as may happen if they are parts of diagonal lines.

D4BF D4AA is called to check the present screen state at ((ØØD6) + Y). If A AND (ØØD1) ≠ Ø, the routine jumps to D4B9. A plotted point has been found.

Otherwise, D592 is called with X = Ø to update pointers. If it returns with A = Ø, the routine jumps to D4FA. Otherwise, Y = (Ø31A), the graphics scan line, and (ØØD1) is shifted left arithmetically. If carry is then set, the routine jumps to D4D9. Otherwise, D574 is called, and if it returns with carry clear the routine jumps to D4FA.

D4D9 D3FD is called to pick up the colour multiplier in (ØØD1), and (ØØDA) = ((ØØD6) + Y) EOR (Ø35A), checking the pixel for graphic background. If (ØØDA) ≠ Ø, the routine jumps to D4F7.

Otherwise, A = X + (Ø361), and if carry is clear the routine jumps to D4FØ. Otherwise, (ØØDB) is incremented, and if the result is positive the routine jumps to D4F7.

D4FØ X = A, and D1Ø4 is called to display a pixel. Carry is set, and the routine loops to D4D9.

D4F7 D574 is called.

D4FA D5AC is called with Y = Ø, then CDE6 is called with Y = &20, X = &24 to exchange (Ø32Ø/3) with (Ø324/7). D4AA is called to check a screen pixel, and D592 is called with X = 4. If it returns with X = Ø, (ØØDB) is decremented. In any case, X is decremented.

D514 D54B is called. If it returns with carry clear, D54Ø follows.

D519 D3ED is called to update pointers, and (ØØDA) =

((ØØD6) + Y) EOR (Ø35A), another check on background colour. If (ØØDC) ≠ Ø, the routine loops to D536, else if (ØØDA) ≠ Ø D53D follows, else A = X + (Ø361). If carry is clear, the routine jumps to D536, else (ØØDB) is incremented, and it it is then positive the routine jumps to D53D.

D536 D1Ø4 is called with X = A to display a point, carry is set, and the routine loops to D519.

D53D D54B is called.

D54Ø D5AC is called with Y = 4.

D545 DØD9 is called, and the routine jumps to D1B8 to scale pointers.

D54B A = (ØØD1), and A is pushed. Carry is cleared, and D56Ø follows.

D551 A is pulled, X is incremented, and if X ≠ Ø the routine jumps to D559, otherwise (ØØDB) is incremented, and if the result is positive the routine jumps to D56F, else;

D559 (ØØD1) is shifted right logically, and if this sets carry D56F follows, else A = A OR (ØØD1), and A is pushed.

D56Ø A = (ØØD1), and BIT (ØØDA) sets MI and V from bits 7 and 6 of (ØØDA), and sets EQ if (ØØD1) AND (ØØDA) = Ø. The status register contents are then modified by P = P EOR (ØØDC). If EQ is set, D551 follows, else A is pulled and A = A EOR (ØØD1).

D56F DØFØ is entered with (ØØD1) = A, to display a pixel. D574ØA = Ø, carry is cleared, and D583 follows.

D574 A = Ø, carry is cleared, and D583 follows.

D579 X is incremented, and if the result is non-zero D58Ø follows, else (ØØDB) is incremented, and if the result is positive D56F follows, else:

D58Ø A is shifted left logically, and if carry is set D58E follows.

D583 A = A OR (ØØD1), and BIT (ØØDA) sets V and MI from bits 6 and 7 of (ØØDA) and sets EQ if A AND (ØØDA) = Ø. If EQ is set, the routine jumps to D579.

Otherwise A = A EOR (ØØD1), A is shifted right logical, and if carry is clear D56F follows.

D58E A is rotated right, carry is set, and D56F follows.

The next two routines are broadly complementary, and are simpler than they look:

D592 Y/A = (Ø3ØØ/1 + X) – (Ø32Ø/1). If A is positive, D49B is called to negate Y/A.

D5A5 (ØØDB) = A, X = Y, A = Y OR (ØØDB). The routine returns.

D5AC (ØØDA) = Y, A = X, Y = A. If (ØØDB) is positive, A = Ø.

D5B6 X = (ØØDA), and if X = Ø D49B is called to negate Y/A. Then (Ø32Ø/1) = (Ø3ØØ/1 + X) + Y/A.

OSWORD 13: Read last two graphic cursor positions: D5CE

D5CE D5D5 is called with A = 3. Then A = 7.

D5D5 A is pushed, and CDE2 is called to exchange (Ø314/7), the last graphic cursor coordinates, with (Ø324/7), the current coordinates. D1B8 is then called to convert the current coordinates to external values in (Ø31Ø/3). X = 3, and A is pulled and copied to Y.

D5EØ ((ØØFØ) + Y) = (Ø31Ø + X). X and Y are decremented, and if X is positive the routine loops to D5EØ, otherwise returning.

At each pass of D5D5, the contents of (Ø31Ø/3) are copied to the OSWORD parameter block. On the first pass the last cursor is copied, using external values, and on the second pass the present cursor is copied, again in external values.

We now return to plot, with the ‘fill triangle’ routine:

D5EA D47C is called with X = &2Ø, Y = &3E to copy (Ø32Ø/7) to (Ø33E/45). This covers the X/Y data parameters and the current graphics cursor position, the copy being in workspace. D632 is then called to exchange (Ø32Ø/3) with (Ø324/7) if (Ø316/7) is not greater than (Ø322/3). The X/Y data parameters are exchanged with the last cursor position if the last vertical position is not higher than the new vertical data.

D636 is then called with X = &14, Y = &24 to perform a similar exchange. (Ø314/7) being exchanged with (Ø324/7) if (Ø326/7) is not greater than (Ø316/7).

D532 is then called again, in case the situation has changed.

D411 is then called with X = &2Ø, Y = &2A, to calculate (Ø32A/B) = (Ø324/5) – (Ø32Ø/1) and (Ø23C/D) = (Ø326/7) – (Ø322/3). These are the X and Y spans between the current graphics position and the new data.

(Ø322) = (Ø32B), and D459 is called with X = &28 to set pointers.

DØDE is called with Y = &2E to copy (Ø32Ø/3), the new data, to (Ø32E/31).

CDE2 is called to exchange (Ø314/7) with (Ø324/7). Then CDE4 is called with X = &2Ø to exchange (Ø314/7) with (Ø32Ø/3).

Carry is set, and D658 is called to execute the fill process. Then D47C is called with X = &3E, Y = &2Ø to set (Ø32Ø/7) = (Ø332/45), and the routine exits to DØD9 for finaly tidying up.

The confusing exchanges, some conditional, need to be worked out for given cases. The conditional exchange subroutine follows:

D632 X = &2Ø, Y = &14.

D636 If (Ø3Ø2/3 + Y) is greater than (Ø3Ø2/3) + X, the routine returns, else an exit via CDE6 exchanges (Ø3ØØ3 + X) with (Ø3ØØ/3 + Y).

OSBYTE 134: Read Cursor Position: D647

D647 X = (Ø318) – (Ø3Ø8), column less left margin (text). Then Y = (Ø319) – (Ø3ØB), line less top margin (text).

D657 The routine returns.

After that intrusion, which is not even relevant to graphics, the triangle fill routine is resumed:

D658 P is pushed, and D411 is called with X = &2Ø, Y = &35 to set (Ø335/6) = (Ø324/5) – (Ø32Ø/1), (Ø337/8) = (Ø326/7) – (Ø322/3).

(Ø33D) = (Ø336), and D459 is called with X = &33 to set pointers.

DØDE, called with Y = &39, sets (Ø339/C) = (Ø32Ø/3).

(Ø31B/C) = (Ø322/3) – (Ø326/7). If (Ø31B/C) = Ø, the routine jumps to D69F, else;

D688 D6A2 is called to display a line. Then D744 is called with X = &33, and again with X = &28, to update pointers. (Ø31B/C) is incremented, and if the result is non-zero the routine loops to D688.

D69F P is pulled, and if carry is clear the routine returns via D657.

D6A2 X = &39, Y = &2E.

D6A6 (ØØDE) = X. If (Ø3ØØ/1 + X) is less than (Ø3ØØ/1 + Y), the routine jumps to D6BC.

A = Y, Y = (ØØDE), X = A. (ØØDE) = X.

D6BC (ØØDF) = Y. A = (Ø3ØØ + Y), and A is pushed. A = (Ø3Ø1 + Y), and A is pushed. X = (ØØDF).

D6DA D864 is called to set a screen address, X = (ØØDE), and D1ØF is called to check window violations. A is shifted right logically, and if A is non-zero the routine jumps to D7ØE to exit.

Otherwise, if carry is clear the routine jumps to D6E9. X = Ø.

D6E9 Y = (ØØDF). (ØØDC/D) = (Ø3ØØ/1 + Y) – (Ø3ØØ/1 + X). A = Ø.

D6FE A is shifted left arithmetically, and A = A OR (ØØD1). Y = (ØØDC), and if Y ≠ Ø the routine jumps to D719. (ØØDD) is decremented, and if it is positive the routine jumps to D719.

Otherwise, (ØØD1) = A, and DØFØ is called to display a point.

D7ØE X = (ØØDF), A is pulled, and (Ø3Ø1 + X) = A, A is pulled and (Ø3ØØ + X) = A. The routine returns.

D719 (ØØDC) is decremented, and X = A. If A is positive, the routine loops to D6FE. Otherwise, (ØØD1) = A, and DØFØ is called to display a point. X = (ØØDC) + 1. If X ≠ Ø the routine jumps to D72A, else (ØØDD) is incremented.

D72A A = X, and A is pushed. (ØØDD) is shifted right logically, and A is rotated right, halving A/(ØØDD), which is (ØØDC/D) incremented. Y = (Ø361). If Y = 3, the mode is 1 or 5, and a jump to D73B follows. If Y is less than 3, the mode is 2, and a jump to D73E is taken.

A/(ØØDD) is halved.

D73B A/(ØØDD) is halved.

D73E Y = (Ø31A), the graphics scan line. X = A. If A = Ø, the routine jumps to D753.

D744 Y = Y − 8. If carry is clear, (ØØD7) is decremented.

D1Ø4 is called to display a point, X is decremented, and if X ≠ Ø the routine loops to D744.

D753 A is pulled, and A = A AND (Ø361). If A = Ø, the routine exits via D7ØE. X = A, A = Ø.

D75C A is doubled, and A = A OR (Ø363), the colour multiplier, X is decremented, and if X ≠ Ø the routine loops to D75C. (ØØD1) = A (bits to be set in screen RAM). Y = Y − 8. If carry is clear, then (ØØD7) is decremented. DØF3 is called to display a point. The routine exits via D7ØE.

D774 (Ø3Ø8/9 + X) is incremented. (Ø3ØØ/1 + X) = (Ø3ØØ/1 + X) − (Ø3Ø2/3 + X). If (Ø3Ø1 + X) is positive, the routine returns via D7C1.

D791 If (Ø3ØA + X) is negative, the routine jumps to D7A1, otherwise (Ø3Ø6/7 + X) is incremented, and D7AC follows.

D7A1 (Ø3Ø6/7 + X) is decremented.

D7AC (Ø3ØØ/1 + X) = (Ø3ØØ/1 + X) + (Ø3Ø4/5 + X). If (Ø3Ø5 + X) is negative, the routine jumps back to D791. Otherwise;

D7C1 The routine returns.

And that more or less completes the plot routines, though there are still some subroutines used by plot. We now move on to a key routine, which reads characters from screen RAM, a process essential to the edit system, and one which calls for a certain amount of ingenuity.

OSBYTE 135: Read character at text cursor position: D7C2

D7C2 Y = (Ø36Ø), and if Y ≠ Ø the current mode is not 7. The routine jumps to D7DC.

Otherwise, A = ((ØØD8) + Y), and then Y = 2.

D7CB If A ≠ (C4B7 + Y) the routine jumps to D7D4, else A = (C4B6 + Y) and Y is decremented.

D7D4 Y is decremented again, and if it is still positive the routine loops to D7CB, else;

D7D7 Y = (Ø355), mode. X = A, and the routine returns.

This performs the code conversions necessary to translate mode 7 codes to the codes used elsewhere.

D7DC D8Ø8 is called to set up a copy of the pattern bytes at the text cursor. X = &2Ø.

D7E1 A = X, and A is pushed.

D7E3 DØ3E is called to set up the pattern address for the code in A. A is pulled, and X = A.

D7E8 Y = 7.

D7EA A = (Ø328 + Y), this being a byte in the pattern copy. If A ≠ ((ØØDE) + Y), the byte from the pattern source, the routine jumps to D7F9. Otherwise Y is decremented, and if Y is positive the routine loops to D7EA to check the next byte. A = X, and if X ≠ &7F the routine exits via D7D7. (Delete is not passed to the screen.)

D7F9 X is incremented, (ØØDE) is increased by 8 to point to the next block of pattern bytes, and if (ØØDE) ≠ Ø the routine loops to D7E8 to check the next character. A = X, and if X ≠ Ø the routine jumps back to D7E1 to start a fresh pattern page. Otherwise, the routine exits via D7D7 with A = Ø.

The routine for setting up the pattern copy comes next. It has to take the current screen mode into account, since the colour element of the character must be removed:

D8Ø8 Y = 7.

D8ØA (ØØDA) = Y, A = 1, (ØØDB) = 1.

D81Ø (ØØDC) = (Ø362), the first colour mask. A = ((ØØD8) + Y) EOR (Ø358), current background colour. (Text.) Carry is cleared.

D81B If A and (ØØDC) ≠ Ø, carry is set.

D82Ø (ØØDB) is rotated left, taking carry into bit Ø and putting bit 7 into carry. If carry is set, the bit originally set by (ØØDB) = 1 has emerged from bit 7, and the pattern is complete. The routine jumps to D82E. (ØØDC) is shifted right logically, and if carry is clear the routine loops to D81B. Otherwise, Y = Y + 7, and if carry is clear the routine loops to D81Ø. (This is an absolute jump.)

D82E Y = (ØØDA), A = (ØØDB). (Ø328 + Y) = A sets up a copy byte, and Y is decremented. If Y is positive, the routine loops to D8ØA, otherwise returning.

The next routine is called from C741 in OSWORD 9 (Read a pixel):

D839 A is pushed, and X = A. D149 is called to set up positional data. A is pulled, and X = A. D85F is called to set a screen address, first checking for window violations. If A ≠ Ø, the routine jumps to D95A to return with A = &FF. Otherwise, A = ((ØØD6) + Y) reads a byte from screen.

D847 A is shifted left arithmetically, and (ØØDA) is rotated left, then (ØØD1) is shifted left arithmetically. P is pushed. If carry is set, the routine jumps to D851, otherwise (ØØDA) is shifted right logically.

D851 P is pulled, and if EQ is not set the routine loops to D847. Otherwise, A = (ØØDA) AND (Ø36Ø), the colour mask. The routine returns.

D85A A = &FF.

D85C The routine returns.

The next routine is the final flourish of plot, being used to check for window violations and to set up a screen address:

D85D X = &2Ø.

D85F D1ØF is called, and if it returns with A ≠ Ø there is a window violation. The routine returns.

D864 A = (Ø3Ø2 + X) EOR & FF. Y = A, (Ø31A) = A AND 7, setting up the graphics scan line variable.

A = Y, then A = the integer value of A ÷ 8. This is doubled and passed to Y. A = ((ØØEØ) + Y), which picks up the high byte of the offset from screen RAM start for the start of the current line. (ØØDA) = A.

Y is incremented, and A = ((ØØEØ) + Y) picks up the low byte of the offset.

Y = (Ø356), the memory map type. If Y = Ø (Modes Ø, 1, 2) the routine jumps to D884, otherwise A/(ØØDA) is halved.

D884 (ØØD6/7) = A/(ØØDA) + (Ø35Ø/1), adding the start of screen RAM.

A = (Ø3ØØ + X), and is pushed. Then A = A AND (Ø361), pixels per byte minus one. Y = A + (Ø361). A = &8Ø ÷ 2^Y, using a look-up table. (ØØD1) = A. This identifies a pixel within the scan line of the given character.

A is pulled, and Y = (Ø361). If Y = 3 (Modes 1, 5) the routine jumps to D8B2. If Y is greater than 3 (Modes 1, 4), the routine jumps to D8B5. Otherwise A/(ØØDA) is doubled.

D8B2 A/(ØØDA) is doubled.

D8B5 A = A AND &F8, making A a multiple of 8. (ØØD6/7) = (ØØD6/7) + A/(ØØDA). If (ØØD7) is negative, (Ø354) is subtracted from it to wrap round to screen start. Y = (Ø31A).

D8CB A = Ø, the routine returns.

Next, for variety, another part of the edit system, called from E572:

D8CE A is pushed. If (Ø26A) ≠ Ø there are VDU parameters outstanding, and the routine jumps to D916. If bit 7 of (ØØDØ) = 1, the screen is disabled, and the routine jumps to D916. If bit 6 of (ØØDØ) = 1, the double cursor condition is already selected, and the routine jumps to D8F5.

If all these hurdles are passed, A = (Ø35F) AND &9F OR &4Ø, which is a modification of the last cursor size setting. C954 is called to change to the write cursor format.

D482 is then called with X = &18, Y = &64 to set (Ø364/5) = (Ø318/9), setting the text input cursor from the text output cursor. CD7A is called to modify the character at the cursor position.

Bit 1 of (ØØDØ) = 1, to bar scrolling.

D8F5 Bit 6 of (ØØDØ) = Ø. A is pulled, and A = A AND &7F. C4CØ is called, this being the entire VDU routine. Bit 6 of (ØØDØ) = 1, and the routine returns.

Another fragment of the edit system follows, called from E5A8:

D9Ø5 A = &2Ø. If bit 6 of (ØØDØ) = Ø, or bit 5 of (ØØDØ) = 1, the routine exits via D8CB. (A = Ø, return.)

Otherwise D7C2 is called to read a character from the screen. If it returns with A = Ø, the routine returns. Otherwise A is pushed, and C664 is called to perform cursor right.

D916 A is pulled, the routine returns.

A stray part of the VDU routine is next, called from C4D5:

D918 Bits 2 and 6 of (ØØDØ) are zeroed, C951 is called to set the normal cursor, A = &ØD, and the routine returns. This is the response to &ØD as a termination of an edit line.

OSBYTE 132: Read bottom of display RAM address: D923

OSBYTE 133: Read lowest address for given mode: D926

D923 X = (Ø355), mode.

D926 Y = X AND 7. X = (C44Ø + Y), the RAM size key. A = (C45E + X), the corresponding high byte of the start address. X = Ø. If bit 7 of (Ø28E) = 1, the routine jumps to D93E. (32K RAM) Otherwise, A = A AND &3F. If Y is less than 4, A = X.

D93E Y = A, the routine returns.

Review

That completes the VDU control system. It is something of a jungle, with many subroutines scattered here and there without too much relation to their functions, but that is almost inevitable in a complex system. It proved impossible to separate out any particular functional groups, but the treatment of the whole block in sequence should make location of a given routine easier.

Chapter 10
SAVE AND LOAD

The operating system save and load functions are accessed via the Command Line Interpreter. Save enters at E23E, Load at E23C. However, some subsidiary modules come first in address order:

E2ØE A is pushed, and (Ø2EE/F1 + X) = Ø. A is pulled. The routine returns. This clears a 32-bit shift register used to hold file data. It is called with X = &Ø2, &Ø6, &ØA, and &ØE.

E21F (ØØE6) = Y. A = A * 16. Y = 4.

E227 A = 2*A. (Ø2EE/F1 + X) are rotated left, taking the previous bit 7 of A into the shift register. If carry is then set, it indicates that the register has overflowed, and "Bad Address" is reported by a jump to E267.

Otherwise, Y is decremented, and if Y ≠ Ø the routine loops to E227 to perform another shift. If Y = Ø, Y = (ØØE6) and the routine returns.

This routine shifts the lower nibble of A into the shift register, setting up an address or other data.

The main routine now begins:

E23C A = &FF, signalling that Load is to be performed.

E23E (ØØF2/3) = X/Y, the start of the command line after the command word. (Ø2EE/F) = X/Y sets the same data in the two locations just below the shift register. A is pushed. For Save, it will hold Ø, the value of the last byte in the CLI table line.

Then EØ2E is called with X = 2 to clear the shift register. Y = &FF, and (Ø2F4) = Y. Y is incremented.

EA1D (GSINIT) is called to prepare for reading the text line.

E257 EA2F is called to read a code from the text line. If it returns with carry clear, the routine loops to E257. When the end of the text string is reached, carry is set and A is pulled and pushed again. If A = Ø, the routine jumps to E2C2, to implement Save.

Otherwise E2AD is called to set up the file block. If it returns with carry set the routine jumps to E2AØ, while a return with EQ set gives a jump to E2A5. Otherwise;

E267 Text "Bad Address".

The next block is not relevant to Save/Load. Then:

E2AØ If NE is set the routine jumps to E31Ø to report "Bad Command". Otherwise (Ø2F4), previously set to &FF, is incremented to zero. This is the first byte of the execution address.

E2A5 X = &EE, Y = 2, A is pulled, and the routine jumps to OSFILE at FFDD. (See Files.)

X/Y give the file block address, Ø2EE, and A instructs that a Save should be executed if it holds Ø, or that a load should be executed if it holds &FF. All further action is handled by the filing system, which can save to tape, and load from tape or ROM.

The file block is set up by the following routine:

E2AD EØ3A is called to look for newline, skipping spaces. EØ8F is called, returning with carry set if it finds a hex digit. If it returns with carry clear E2ØE is called to flush the shift register and return.

E2B8 E21F is called to shift the lower nibble of A into the shift register, and EØ8F is again called to check for a hex digit. If it returns with carry set, the routine loops to E2B8. Otherwise the routine returns with carry set.

For Load, much information comes from the tape, but for Save the information has to be defined, and more work is needed.

E2C2 X = &ØA, and E2AD is called to set up (Ø2F8/B) from hex data. If it returns with carry clear, a jump to E31Ø reports "Bad Command".

Otherwise V is cleared, and A = ((ØØF2) + Y) to read the next byte from the text line. If the code is not &2B (+), the routine jumps to E2D4. Otherwise, the next hex group defines length, not an end address. V (and MI) is set, and Y is incremented to point to the hex group.

E2D4 E2AD is called with X = &ØE to set up (Ø2FC/F). If it returns with carry clear, a jump to E31Ø reports "Bad Command". Otherwise, P is pushed, and if V is clear the routine jumps to E2ED. There is an explicit end address.

Otherwise, X = &FC, and;

E2E1 (Ø2ØØ + X) = (Ø2ØØ + X) + (Ø1FC + X). X is incremented, and if it is non-zero the routine loops to E2E1. This adds the length data to the start address, putting the result as the end address.

E2ED X = 3.

E2EF (Ø2F4 + X) = (Ø2F8 + X), (Ø2FØ + X) = (Ø2F8 + X). X is decremented. If it is positive, the routine loops to E2EF. This copies the start address to the load address and execution address.

P is pulled, and if EQ is set the end of the command line has been reached. The routine jumps to E2A5 to call OSFILE to execute Save.

Otherwise, X = 6, and E2AD is called to set up (Ø2F4/7), the execution address, from hex data. A return with carry clear gives a jump to E31Ø for a "Bad Command" report.

An EQ return leads to E2A5, and the actual Save process. Otherwise, E2AD is called with X = 2 to set up a load address in (Ø2FØ/3). As usual, return with carry clear gives "Bad Command", while EQ gives a jump to E2A5 to execute a Save. Failing that, "Bad Command" is reported.

The file block may be summarised:

(Ø2EE/F): Address of filename start
(Ø2FØ/3): Load Address
(Ø2F4/7): Execution address
(Ø2F8/B): Start address of data in Save, File Length in Load.
(Ø2FC/F): End address of data.

Chapter 11
THE SOUND SYSTEM

The sound system falls into three main parts: the OSWORD 7 routine, which sets up sound data; the OSWORD 8 routine, which sets up envelope data, and the executive routine called from the 1Ø mS interrupt handler. The routines are complex, and the use of different formats, especially for volume data, can be confusing.

The OSWORD 7 call assumes that a block of eight bytes has been set up, starting at an address defined by the X,Y parameters of the call, this address being copied to (ØØFØ/1).

E82D A is set from the second of the eight bytes, which holds the 'H/S' data from the original BASIC command. H may be 1 or Ø, S may be 1 to 3, so the normal range of H/S is Ø to &13. Provision is made, however, for a value of &FF, which jumps to E88D in the speech system, while other values greater than &1F lead to E7CA with X = 8. This is an entry in the OSBYTE control system.

For normal values of H/S, subroutine E8C9 (see below) is called, with Y = Ø. This returns with A holding C, the channel number, and with carry set if F = 1. X = A OR 4 converts the channel number to the corresponding buffer number, and if carry is set E1AE is called to flush buffer X, as requested by F = 1.

Then E8C9 is called again, this time with Y = 1. It returns with A = S and with carry set if H = 1. S is copied from A into (ØØFA), and P is pushed.

Next, the seventh byte in the table (duration) is read and pushed, and the same process is applied to the fifth byte (pitch). The third byte (volume) is read into A, and this is combined with H and S as follows:

A is rotated left, bringing in H from carry, and two is subtracted. Now, the volume parameter may hold a number in the Ø to − 15 range, indicating an explicit volume, or a number in the 1 to 16 range identifying an envelope. For a volume specification, the above process willl produce a result in the range &EØ to &FE, while an envelope number will give a result in the range Ø to &1E.

In either case the result is multiplied by 4, and (ØØFA) is added. This produces the following structure;
Bit 7 is Ø for an envelope, 1 for an explicit volume.
Bits 3-6 give the envelope number less 1, or the volume plus 15.
Bit 2 holds the H parameter.
Bits Ø - 1 hold the S parameter.

The composite byte is transferred to buffer X by calling E1F8. If this returns with carry set, a successful transfer has been made, and the routine jumps on to E887. Otherwise three bytes are pulled off the stack to clear it, and — for no obvious reason — X is set from (ØØDØ), the VDU status word, before the routine returns.

The next block is used to set up sound data for BELL (VDU 7):

E86F P is pushed and interrupts are barred.

X = (Ø263) AND 7 or 4. This sets up the buffer number for a sound channel, usually channel 3.

A = (Ø264), and E4BØ is called to put that value, usually &9Ø, into the chosen buffer. &9Ø specifies a volume level of −14.

A = (Ø266) and is pushed. This is duration data, usually 6.

A = (Ø265) and is pushed. This is pitch data, usually &64.

E887 C is set and (Ø8ØØ + X) is rotated right to pass carry to bit 7. This is the channel set flag, and warns the executive routine that the channel is active. The routine jumps to E8A4.

The next block is mainly used for speech control, but also for sound:

E88D P is pushed. A is set from the third byte and pushed, then from the fourth byte and pushed, then from the first byte. X = 8 to select the speech buffer, and E1F8 is called to pass A to that buffer. If E1F8 returns with carry set, the process is aborted, and the stack is cleared, as for the sound routine. Otherwise, bit 7 of (Ø2D7) is zeroed to show that the related buffer is set.

E8A4 A is pulled and E4BØ is called to enter the contents of A in the buffer specified by X. This process is repeated, then P is pulled and the routine returns.

Next we have OSWORD 8: Envelope. Once again, it is assumed that a data block has been set up, in this case containing fourteen bytes:

E8AE X = (A–1)*16 OR &ØF. As this is an OSWORD function, A has already been set from the first byte of the data block, and holds the envelope number. A displacement pointer to the top of the appropriate storage area is set up in X. Then A = Ø, Y = &1Ø.

E8BB If Y exceeds &ØD, the routine jumps to E8C1, and a zero is set. Otherwise, A = ((ØØFØ) + Y).

E8C1 (Ø8CØ + X) = A. X and Y are decremented, and if Y is not zero the routine loops to E8BB, otherwise retiring.

The thirteen upper bytes of the fourteen-byte block, but not the envelope number, are copied into the chosen sixteen-byte area. The top three bytes of the area are zeroed. The data pattern set up is:

(Ø8CØ + &1Ø*E)	Bits Ø - 6 give step length in 10 mS periods. Bit 7 is false if repeat is required.
(Ø8C1/3+&1Ø*E)	Change of pitch per step.
(Ø8C4/6+&1Ø*E)	Steps per section.
(Ø8C7/A+&1Ø*E)	Amplitude change in phases.
(Ø8CB/E+&1Ø*E)	Target levels at ends of phases.

E is the envelope number less 1.

To complete the sound setting routines we need:

E8C9 A = ((ØØFØ) + Y). If Y exceeds &ØF, carry is set. A = A AND 3. Y is incremented, and the routine returns.

Now we must face the executive sound routines. The entry point, which can be found by reference to the 1Ø mS interrupt handler, is here EB47, but the routines are dealt with in order of address sequence for convenience of reference. The first block handles outputs to the sound chip, which have the following format:

Ø	X	F9	F8	F7	F6	F5	F4	Upper frequency, current channel
1	Ø	Ø	Ø	F3	F2	F1	FØ	Lower frequency, tone 3
1	Ø	Ø	1	A3	A2	A1	AØ	Volume, tone 3
1	Ø	1	Ø	F3	F2	F1	FØ	Lower frequency, tone 2
1	Ø	1	1	A3	A2	A1	AØ	Volume, tone 2
1	1	Ø	Ø	F3	F2	F1	FØ	Lower frequency, tone 1
1	1	Ø	1	A3	A2	A1	AØ	Volume, tone 1
1	1	1	Ø	X	FB	NF1	NFØ	Set noise type
1	1	1	1	A3	A2	A1	AØ	Volume, noise channel

The volume data runs from 15 (silence) to Ø (maximum), and is thus equal to the number in the BASIC command plus 15.

The frequency data is equal to 125ØØØ divided by the required frequency, expressed as a ten-bit word. The four lowest bits are passed to a specific channel, the upper eight bits pass to the last channel addressed.

The chip control routine has four entry points. EBØ3 is used to silence a sound channel, EBØA to set a volume. EB21/2 are used to set pitch.

EBØ3 (Ø8Ø8 + X) = 4. This is the 'phase counter', and 4 is the end of the 'release' phase. A = &CØ, which at this stage in the proceedings is the code for zero volume, &4Ø being added to the coding studied earlier.

EBØA (Ø8Ø4 + X) = A. This sets the basic sound level for the buffer X channel. However, if (Ø262) ≠ Ø, sound suppression is being applied, and A = &CØ.

Next, A = A – &4∅, and the result is divided by eight. This brings the volume data into bits ∅-3, where it is needed, and in the form in which it is needed, once these bits have been inverted to balance an inversion in the calling routine. Then the upper four bits of the data must be set to identify the required channel. This is done by reference to a four-byte look-up table, which effectively performs the calculation A = A + (32*(11 – X)), and &1∅ is added to indicate that volume is being set.

EB21 P is pushed to balance the stack in cases where this has not already been done.

EB22 Interrupt is barred, then (FE43) = &FF, setting Port A of the internal VIA to output on all bits. This Port drives the sound chip as well as the keyboard and other functions. A is then output on Port A, but the sound chip will take no notice until it is enabled by (FE4∅) = ∅, an output on Port B. After a short delay loop, (FE4∅) = 8 disables the chip again, and there is a further delay before P is pulled and the routine returns.

The main executive routine follows, with the overall entry point at EB47. The 'staging jump' at EB44 allows conditional jumps in the early part of the routine to reach EC59.

EB47 (∅83B) = ∅, but if (∅838) is also zero (∅83B) is incremented to 1, and (∅838) is decremented to &FF. (∅838) is set from the S parameter when synchronous operation is required, and when it reaches zero the required number of channels have been set up. The change to (∅83B) then allows action to proceed.

X = 8, preparing for entry to a loop in which X takes successive values from 7 to 4.

EB59 This is the loop point. X is decremented, and if (∅8∅∅ + X) = ∅ a jump to EC59 via EB44 skips the rest of the loop. No sound is set up for this channel.

If (∅2CF + X) is negative, the relevant buffer is empty, and the routine jumps on to EB69. Otherwise, if (∅818 + X), the main duration count, is not zero, a jump to EB6C is taken.

EB69 Subroutine EC6B (below) is called. This checks the situation, and if necessary picks up a new sound. An empty buffer may well mean that a buffer has been flushed in response to the F parameter of a new call.

EB6C The main duration count in (Ø818 + X) is again checked. If it is zero, a jump to EB84 is taken. If it holds &FF, the jump is to EB87, this meaning that the sound is of indefinite duration.

If the duration count is at neither extreme, (Ø81C + X) is decremented. This is the 1Ø mS count, and if it has reached zero it is reset to 5 and (Ø818 + X) is decremented. This action occurs every 5Ø mS, the period of the main duration count. If the main count is still not zero, a jump to EB87 is taken.

EB84 Subroutine EC6B is called to see whether further data needs to be set up. This only arises if the main duration count reaches zero before or after the decrement above.

EB87 If (Ø824 + X) = Ø the routine jumps to EB91. This is the step progress counter, set to zero if no envelope is involved. If it has not reached zero, it is decremented, and a non-zero result gives a jump to EC59 via EB44, skipping the rest of the loop. No action is needed until the end of a step is reached.

EB91 Y = (Ø82Ø + X). This is the displacement of the envelope data relative to Ø8CØ, but is set to &FF if no envelope is involved. In this case, a jump to EC59 via EB44 skips the rest of the loop.

Otherwise, step length is set up by (Ø824 + X) = (Ø8CØ + Y) AND &7F. The AND zeroes the 'Repeat' bit.

A new step has begun, but if (Ø8Ø8 + X) = 4 the release phase has been completed, and the routine jumps to ECØ7.

Otherwise, A = (Ø8CB + (Ø8Ø8 + X) + (Ø82Ø + X)) – &3F. Ø8CB is the base for the 'target values' in the envelope, (Ø8Ø8 + X) is the phase count, and (Ø82Ø + X) is the displacement of the envelope in use.

The target value is set in (Ø83A), and (Ø839) = (Ø8C7

+ (Ø8Ø8 + X) + (Ø82Ø + X)), giving the amplitude change per step in the current phase.

The base volume level in (Ø8Ø4 + X) is read and pushed for future reference, and A = (Ø8Ø4 + X) + (Ø839). This may well produce an overflow. If it does not, the routine jumps to EBCF.

An overflow is handled by putting bit 7 of A into carry. If the bit is Ø, A = &CØ. If the bit is true, A = &3F.

A pause is necessary at this point to look at the volume level coding again. The original BASIC command levels Ø to −15 are represented here by values &CØ to &38 at intervals of 8. The lowest three bits are ignored. Therefore &3F represents maximum volume, &CØ represents silence.

EBCF (Ø8Ø4 + X), setting the new volume level. Then A is rotated left, putting the msb into carry. A = A EOR (Ø8Ø4 + X), and if the result is positive bits 6 and 7 of (Ø8Ø4 + X) are the same, and a jump is taken to EBE1. Otherwise A = &3F if carry is clear, and &CØ if carry is set. (Ø8Ø4 + X) = A.

EBE1 (Ø839), holding the amplitude change per step, is decremented. Then A = (Ø8Ø4 + X) − (Ø83A), subtracting the target value. Next, A = A EOR (Ø 839), a negative result leading to a jump to EBF9. This result means that the current trend set by (Ø839) is correct. Otherwise, (Ø8Ø4 + X) = (Ø83A), the target value, and (Ø8Ø8 + X) is incremented to indicate that a new phase has been entered.

EBF9 A is pulled, obtaining the old volume level, and the new level is compared with the old. If they are the same, the routine jumps to ECØ7, otherwise EBØA is called to set the new level.

ECØ7 If (Ø81Ø + X) = 3, the routine jumps to EC59, skipping the rest of the loop. All sections have been executed. Otherwise, if (Ø814 + X) ≠ Ø, the current section is not complete, and the routine jumps to EC3D.

If (Ø814 + X) = Ø, a section change must be implemented. (Ø81Ø + X) is incremented to show entry to the next section. If the result is not 3 the routine jumps on to EC2D.

If (Ø81Ø + X) = 3, the question of repeat arises. A is set from (Ø8CØ + (Ø82Ø + X)), the first envelope byte, and if the result is negative the routine jumps on to EC59. There is no repeat.

Otherwise, (Ø83Ø + X) = Ø, this being the differential pitch, and (Ø81Ø + X) = Ø, restarting the section sequence.

EC2D A = (Ø8C4 + (Ø81Ø + X) + (Ø82Ø + X)), picking up the number of steps in the new section. The result is set in (Ø814 + X), and if it is zero the routine jumps to EC59.

EC3D (Ø814 + X) is decremented, and A = (Ø8C1 + (Ø82Ø + X) + (Ø81Ø + X)), picking up the rate of pitch change. This is added to the differential pitch in (Ø83Ø + X), and the result is added to (Ø8ØC + X), the base pitch. EDØ1 is called to set the new pitch.

EC59 If X = 4, the routine jumps to EC6A. Otherwise the routine loops back to EB59.

Next we have a routine that clears all sound channels. It is called by initialise:

EC6Ø X = 8.

EC62 X is decremented and ECA2 is called to clear channel X. If X ≠ 4, the routine loops to EC62, otherwise returning.

Next comes the block called to check whether there is further sound data to be set up:

EC6B If (Ø8Ø8 + X) = 4, the routine jumps to EC77. Otherwise, (Ø8Ø8 + X) = 3. A value of 4 means that release is complete, a value of 3 means that release is in progress.

EC77 If (Ø2CF + X) = Ø, a jump to EC9Ø is taken. The buffer is not empty. Otherwise, (Ø2CF + X) = Ø, the sync flags in (Ø82C/F) are cleared to zero, the duration count in (Ø818 + X) is zeroed, and the sync count in (Ø838) is set to &FF.

EC9Ø If (Ø828 + X), the synchronising flag, is zero the routine jumps to ECDB, the synchronising routine. If

(Ø83B) is Ø, a jump to ECDØ is taken. Otherwise, (Ø282 + X) = Ø, and the routine goes to ED98 to pick up and interpret data.

The next block clears channel X:

ECA2 Subroutine EBØ3 is called to silence the channel, returning with Y = Ø. (Ø818 + X) = Ø, zeroing the main count, (Ø2CF + X) = Ø, marking the buffer as not empty. (Ø8ØØ + X) = Ø to state that the channel is dormant. The sync flags in (Ø82C/F) are zeroed, and (Ø838) = &FF. EDØ6 follows to command zero pitch.

The subroutine which follows is called from ECDE to check for a sound termination:

ECBC P is pushed and interrupt is barred. If (Ø8Ø8 + X) ≠ 4, the end of release phase has not been reached, and the routine jumps to ECCF. Otherwise the buffer is examined by subroutine E45B, and if the buffer is not empty a jump to ECCF is taken. Otherwise, (Ø8ØØ + X) = Ø, marking the channel as dormant.

ECCF P is pulled.

ECDØ If (Ø82Ø + X) = &FF, EBØ3 is called to terminate sound. (No envelope.)

ECDA The routine returns.

Next comes the synchronising routine:

ECDB Subroutine E45B is used to examine the buffer. If the buffer is empty, the routine jumps to ECBC. The next word in the buffer is in A, and if A AND 3 = Ø the routine jumps to ED98 via EC9F. S = Ø, and the remaining buffer data can be picked up.

If (Ø838) = Ø a jump to ECFE is taken. The synchronising count is complete. Otherwise (Ø828 + X) is incremented, setting the sync flag. If (Ø838) is positive, a value of S has already been set, and the routine jumps to ECFB.

Otherwise, E45B is again called to obtain the first byte, and bits Ø-1 of this are set in (Ø838). ECFE follows. (This jump is unconditional, since it is known that S is 1 – 3.)

ECFB (Ø838) is decremented.

ECFE ECDØ follows to silence the channel if envelope is not in use.

The next block deals with pitch setting. The coding method adopted makes this rather complex. The commanded pitch defines a number of eighth tones above an arbitrary base note. Now, an eighth tone interval implies a frequency ratio of 1.Ø145453/1, and a direct calculation on that basis would be difficult. The method adopted is to determine the octave in which the note lies and then use a look-up table giving semitone values and eighth tone differences, finally dividing by two for each octave involved:

EDØ1 If A = (Ø82C + X), the pitch is unchanged, and the routine returns via ECDA.

EDØ6 (Ø82C + X) = A, to register the pitch being set. If X ≠ 4, a jump to ED16 enters the tone-setting routine. Noise is set thus:

A = A AND &ØF OR (32*(11 − X)). This is a familiar format from the chip control routine, which is entered at EB22 (via ED95) after P has been pushed.

ED16 A is pushed, and (Ø83C) = A AND 3. This is the eighth tone surplus. (Ø83D) = Ø.

A is then pulled and divided by four, to give the semitone number.

A is then divided by twelve, with the result in (Ø83D) and the remainder in A. (Ø83D) then defines the octave, A the position within the octave. Y = A.

(Ø38D) is pushed, and then set from a look-up table with Y as a displacement pointer. The look-up table may conveniently be given here:

EDFB	&FØ	EEØ7	&E7	&3FØ =	1ØØ8	Diff = 14
EDFC	&B7	EEØ8	&D7	&3B7 =	951	Diff = 13
EDFD	&82	EEØ9	&CB	&382 =	898	Diff = 12
EDFE	&4F	EEØA	&C3	&34F =	847	Diff = 12
EDFF	&2Ø	EEØB	&B7	&32Ø =	8ØØ	Diff = 11
EEØØ	&F3	EEØC	&AA	&2F3 =	755	Diff = 1Ø
EEØ1	&C8	EEØD	&A2	&2C8 =	712	Diff = 1Ø
EEØ2	&AØ	EEØE	&9A	&2AØ =	672	Diff = 9
EEØ3	&7B	EEØF	&92	&27B =	635	Diff = 9
EEØ4	&57	EE1Ø	&8A	&257 =	599	Diff = 8
EEØ5	&35	EE11	&82	&235 =	565	Diff = 8
EEØ6	&16	EE12	&7A	&216 =	534	Diff = 8

The base frequency value is made up from the two least significant bits of the second table followed by the byte from the first table. It will be found that successive values show a ratio of 1.Ø59/1, the pitch of a semitone. The differences come from the upper nibble of the bytes in the second table, and are roughly proportional to the main figures.

For purists, A = 44Ø would require a frequency setting of 568. The nearest table value is 565, which gives 442 Hz.

(Ø38D) having been set from the first table, A is set from the second and pushed. Then (Ø83E) = A AND 3, completing the ten-bit basic number. A is pulled and Ø83F) = A ÷ 16, copying the upper nibble. Next, (Ø83D/E) = (Ø83D/E) – (Ø 83F) * (Ø83C) adjusting for the surplus eighth tones.

The octave number pushed earlier is now pulled, and (Ø83D/E) is divided by two to the power of the octave number, raising the pitch the appropriate number of octaves.

The chip is now set up, two accesses being required. The first is based on (Ø83D) AND &ØF OR (32*(11 – X)). P is pushed and interrupt is barred, and EB21 is called. Then (Ø83D/E) = (Ø83D/E) + 4, and A = (Ø83D) + 4, forming the command for setting the upper bits of the frequency definition. EB22 is called, since P has been pushed already. The routine returns.

The last sound routine picks up and interprets buffer data:

ED98 P is pushed and interrupt barred. Then E46Ø is called to read a byte from the buffer. The result is pushed, then A = A AND 4 to isolate the 'H' bit. If this is Ø, the routine jumps to EDB7.

Otherwise, A is pulled to balance the stack, and if (Ø82Ø + X) = &FF, indicating that envelope is not in use, EBØ3 is called to silence the channel. E46Ø is called twice to clear the buffer of redundant data, P is pulled, and the routine jumps to EDF7 to set the main duration count, using the last byte from the buffer.

If H is true, the current sound is prolonged. If H is false, the next routine deals with the data:

EDB7 A is pulled, and bits Ø - 2 are zeroed, leaving only the volume data. A left shift puts bit 7 into carry, and if the bit is Ø (envelope) a jump to EDC8 is taken. Otherwise A is inverted, shifted right logically, and &4Ø is subtracted. EBØA is called to set volume. A = &FF.

EDC8 (Ø82Ø + X) = A. This will be &FF if no envelope is used, otherwise the envelope number less one multiplied by 16, which provides a displacement pointer to the envelope storage space.
(Ø81C + X) = 5. This sets the duration sub-counter.
(Ø824 + X) = 1. This sets the phase counter.
(Ø814 + X) = Ø. This sets the step counter.
(Ø8Ø8 + X) = Ø. This is envelope phase.
(Ø83Ø + X) = Ø. This is pitch differential.
(Ø81Ø + X) = Ø. This is step count.

E46Ø is now called to read pitch, which is set in (Ø8ØC + X).

Duration is similarly read from the buffer, but not immediately. P is pulled, and A is pushed, saving duration. Then EDØ1 is called with A = (Ø8ØC + X) to set pitch.

EDF7 The duration counter (Ø818 + X) is set from a value pulled off the stack, and the routine returns.

Review

That completes the sound routines. They are confusing, but yield to tracing through with pencil and paper, noting the various codings involved.

A striking point is that a nominal table of eight data bytes is boiled down to a mere three bytes on the buffer. This suggests that there could be simpler ways of setting up a sound, though it would be necessary to make use of the buffer handler, rather than attempting direct entry.

In other respects, the routines leave little scope for ingenuity and enterprise, being so closely integrated that it would be difficult to provide alternatives.

Chapter 12
FILES

In the cassette version of OS 1.2Ø, the filing system is closely related to Save and Load, and is complicated by the use of the serial system for both cassette and RS423 functions. Files are also related to the speech facility, and ROMs may be used as file sources.

The relevant routines include some which are widely scattered from E275 onwards, and then in a continuous block from F1C4. The routines are examined here in address sequence, for ease of reference, though this means that some of the earlier routines, concerned with speech processing, are of limited interest.

The main entry points can be identified as follows:

*SPOOL	E281	(Via CLI)
OSARGS	F18E	(Via FFDA, (Ø214))
OSFILE	F27D	(Via FFDD, (Ø212))
*RUN	F3Ø5	(Via CLI)
*CAT	F32B	(Via CLI)
OSFIND	F3CA	(Via FFCE, (Ø21C))
OSBGET	F4C9	(Via FFD7, (Ø216))
OSBPUT	F529	(Via FFD4, (Ø218))
*OPT	F54D	(Via CLI)
*EXEC	F68D	(Via CLI)

There are also OSBYTE calls involved:

OSBYTE 119:	Close SPOOL/EXEC Files: E275
OSBYTE 139:	Select File Options: F54D
OSBYTE 140:	Select Tape Filing System: F135
OSBYTE 141:	Select ROM Filing System: F135
OSBYTE 143:	Paged ROM Service Request: F168
OSBYTE 158:	Read from Speech Processor: EE6D
OSBYTE 159:	Write to Speech Processor: EE7F

OSBYTE 119: Close SPOOL/EXEC Files: E275 *SPOOL: E281

E275 F168 is called with X=&1Ø to offer ROM service. If this sets EQ the routine returns, else F68B closes the current file, and A = Ø. Then:

E281 If A = Ø, the file is closed. P is pushed, and (ØØE6) – Y, the file handle. Y=(Ø257), the current file number, and (Ø257) = A. If Y ≠ Ø, OSFIND is called at FFCE to close file (Ø257), else Y = (ØØE6) and P is pulled. If EQ is set, the routine returns, otherwise OSFIND is called with A = &8Ø to open file Y for output. Y = A, and if A = Ø "Bad Command" is reported. Otherwise (Ø257) = A, and the routine returns.

OSBYTE 137: Switch Cassette Motor: E67F

E67F A = (Ø282), RAM copy of the last output to the serial ULA. Y = A. If X is greater than zero, bit 7 of A is set true. The routine then jumps to E6A7, where the serial ULA and RAM copy are set from A. A = Y, X = A, and the routine returns. (X = Ø gives motor off, X ≥ 1 gives motor on.)

The next routine checks for 'Cassette Critical':

E7DC A = (ØØEB), the flag indicating SPOOL or EXEC in use. If bit 7 = 1, the routine jumps to E812, giving A = Ø, return. If bit 3 of (ØØE2) = 1 (CAT in use), the routine returns. Otherwise A = (ØØBB) AND &88, which picks out the 'ignore error' bits of the cassette options byte, and the routine returns.

The routines which follow relate to Speech. In the absence of a speech facility comment will necessarily be limited:

EE13 (ØØF5) = &EF. This is the ROM file number. The routine returns.

EE18 X = &ØD. (ØØF5) is incremented and copied to Y. If Y is positive, a paged ROM is selected, and the routine jumps to EE59. Otherwise, a Phrase ROM is selected, and (ØØF6/7) = ØØØ1, this being a pointer to the selected ROM. EEBB is called, and X = 3.

EE2C EE62 is called. If A ≠ (DFØC + X), the routine jumps to EE18. Otherwise X is decremented, and if it is positive the routine loops to EE2C. (This looks for '(C)' in the ROM, no ROM being valid without the copyright symbol . . .)

EE3B EEBB is called, then X = &FF.

EE4Ø EE62 is called, then Y = 8.

EE45 A is shifted left, and (ØØF7 + X) is shifted right. This is repeated eight times, using Y as a counter. The result is that the contents of A are set in (ØØF6) in reverse order. Then X is incremented, and if X = Ø the routine loops to EE4Ø to set up another byte and transfer it to (ØØF7). If X ≠ Ø EEBB follows with carry clear.

The next group deal with ROM service:

EE51 X = &ØE, Y = (ØØF5), and if Y is negative (pointing to a PHROM) the routine jumps to EE62, otherwise Y = &FF, and;

EE59 P is pushed, and F168 is called to offer paged ROM service. P is pulled. If A is greater than zero, carry is set. The routine returns with A = Y.

EE62 P is pushed and interrupt barred. EE7F (OSBYTE 159) is called with Y = &1Ø. The routine jumps to EE84 with Y = Ø.

OSBYTE 158: Read from Speech Processor: EE6D

EE6D The routine jumps to EE82 with Y = Ø.

EE71 A is pushed while EE7A is called. Then A is rotated right four times, bringing the upper nibble to the lower nibble position.

EE7A Y = A AND &ØF OR &4Ø, forming a command for the Speech Processor.

Then:

OSBYTE 159: Write to Speech Processor: EE7F

EE7F A = Y, Y = 1. P is pushed and interrupt barred.

EE84 If bit 7 of (Ø27B) = Ø, the Speech Processor is not fitted, and the routine jumps to EEAA. Otherwise (FE43) = (FØ75 + Y). This sets DDRA of VIA 1 to &ØØ for Y = 1, giving eight-bit input, or to &FF for Y = 2, giving eight-bit output. (See table below.) Then (FE4F) = A, which will send A to the Speech Processor if output is selected. (FE4Ø) = (FØ77 + Y) is an output to Port B of VIA 1, selecting the read or write condition in the Speech Processor, according to the value of Y.
The routine now loops until the Speech Processor reports ready by pulling bit 7 of Port B low. Then A = (FE4F), reading Speech Processor data if input is selected. (FE4Ø) = FØ79 + Y) then resets the Speech Processor.

EEAA P is pulled, Y = A, the routine returns.

The table used above is fitted in between two character code blocks used in the keyboard routine. It is:

FØ75 ØØ FF Ø1 Ø2 Ø9 ØA

EEAD (ØØF6/7) = (Ø3CB/C), setting the ROM displacement pointer from the 'spare' area of the heading block. If (ØØF5) is positive, a paged ROM is selected, and the routine returns. For a PHROM:

EEBB P is pushed and interrupt barred. A = (ØØF6), and EE71 is called to pass the two nibbles of A to the Speech Processor. (ØØFA) = (ØØF5). A series of shifts then replaces the two most significant bits of A by the two least significant bits of (ØØFA). EE71 is called to pass A to the Speech Processor in two nibbles, and then A = (ØØFA), which has been divided by four by the shifts. EE7A is called to pass the lower nibble to the Speech Processor.

We can now move on to more general routines:

OSBYTE 140: Select Tape Filing System: F135

OSBYTE 141: Select ROM Filing System: F135

F135 A = A EOR &8C, which gives Ø for OSBYTE 14Ø (&8C), and 1 for OSBYTE 141 (&8D). A is doubled, and stored in (Ø247), the cassette/ROM selection flag, which thus holds Ø for cassette, 2 for ROM.

If X is greater than 2, carry is set, while if X = 3, EQ is set. F14B follows. (X selects baud rate.)

F14Ø This point is entered from DB35 in initialise. P is pushed and (ØØE3) = &A1, setting the cassette options byte, the implication of which may be summarised thus:

Lower nibble relates to Sequential access; upper nibble relates to Save and Load.

ØØØØ Ignore errors, no messages
ØØØ1 Abort if error, no messages
ØØ1Ø Retry after error, no messages
1ØØØ Ignore error, short messages
1ØØ1 Abort if error, short messages
1Ø1Ø Retry after error, short messages
11ØØ Ignore error, long messages
11Ø1 Abort if error, long messages
111Ø Retry after error, long messages.

The condition set is thus:

Sequential access: Abort if error, no messages.
Save and Load: Retry after error, short messages.

Long messages provide additional data, as will be seen.

(Ø3D1) = &19 sets the standard inter-block gap, and P is pulled.

F14B P is pushed, and F1B1 is called via EØ31 with A = 6. This closes all files. (See below.) X = 6, and P is pulled. If the EQ condition was set earlier, X is decremented to 5. (ØØC6) = X. If (ØØC6) = 5, 3ØØ baud is selected, while (ØØC6) = 6 selects 12ØØ baud. Then X = &ØE.

F15B (Ø211 + X) = (D951 + X), X is decremented, and if it is not zero the routine loops to F15B. (This resets vector links (Ø212) to (Ø21E), which can be annoying for anyone who has modified them, but as they all relate to file functions it seems a reasonable precaution.)

(ØØC2) = X = Ø, X = &ØF, then;

OSBYTE 143: Paged ROM Service Request: F168

F168 A = (ØØF4), the number of the paged ROM currently selected. A is pushed, and A = X, X = &ØF.

F16E If (Ø2A1 + X) is positive, ROM X has no service entry, and the routine jumps on to F183. Otherwise, (ØØF4) = X, (FE3Ø) = X to enable ROM X, and 8ØØ3 is called, this being the 'service entry'.

X = A, and if A = Ø the routine exits via F186, else X = (ØØF4).

F183 X is decremented, and if the result is positive the routine loops back to F16E to check the next ROM, otherwise;

F186 A is pulled and copied to (ØØF4) and (FE3Ø), selecting the original ROM again. A = X, which may hold Ø or &FF. (Note that A is not preserved by this call, as stated elsewhere.) The routine returns.

OSARGS: F18E

F18E If A ≠ Ø, or Y ≠ Ø, the routine returns. A = (ØØC6) AND &FB. Then A = A OR (Ø247), A is doubled and again A = A OR (Ø247). A is halved, and the routine returns. The result in A is not as described in the User Guide. If (ØØC6) holds 5, AND &FB gives 1, while if it holds 6 the result is 2. If cassette is selected, (Ø247) = Ø, and the result stands. If ROM is selected, (Ø247) = 2, so the result is 6 or 7. Note that only A = Ø, Y = Ø are accepted as input parameters.

The routine returns.

An important link table follows. It gives addresses less 1, for a reason which will appear in the subsequent routine.

F1A3	4C	F5	*OPT:	F54D
F1AD	1D	F6	EOF?	F61E
F1A7	Ø4	F3	*RUN	F3Ø5
F1A9	ØF	E3	Bad Command	E31Ø
F1AB	Ø4	F3	*RUN	F3Ø5
F1AD	2A	F3	*CAT	F32B
F1AF	74	E2	OSBYTE 119:	E275

F1B1 This is entered via EØ31 = (Ø21E) in most cases. If A is greater than 6, the routine returns. Otherwise (ØØBC) = X, X = 2*A, A = (F1A4 + X), and A is pushed, A = (F1A3 + X) and A is pushed. X = (ØØBC), and the routine returns to the artificial return link, which is incremented by the RTS instruction.

Note that A, on entry at F1B1, holds the qualifying byte from the Command Line Interpreter table, or its equivalent.

The next block is used in load operations. It is entered from OSFILE with A = &FF, and from *RUN with A = Ø and (Ø3C2) = &FF.

F1C4 P and A are pushed, and FB27 is called to copy the load/save cassette options into (ØØBB), set (ØØC7) = 6, and claim the serial system for cassette use, if necessary waiting until the system is free. The ACIA is reset.

A = (Ø3C2), and is pushed. F631 is called to search for the required file and to read the header. A is pulled. If it holds Ø, the routine jumps to F1ED, else;

F1D7 A loop copies (Ø3BE/C1) to (ØØB3), this being the file load address. If all the bytes copied hold &FF, FAE8 is called to tidy up, and a jump to E267 reports 'Bad address'. Otherwise:

F1ED A = (Ø3CA), the Block Flag, and carry is set from bit Ø. A is pulled, restoring the value on entry to F1C4. If A = Ø, the routine jumps to F2Ø2. Otherwise, if carry is clear the routine jumps to F2Ø9. If A ≠ Ø and carry is set, FAF2 is called to tidy up, and the report 'Locked' follows.

The 'Locked' report is avoided if bit Ø of (Ø3CA = Ø, making carry clear, or A = Ø, indicating entry from *RUN. This does not accord with descriptions given elsewhere.

F202 If carry is clear, the routine jumps to F2Ø9, otherwise (Ø258) = 3. This is the Escape/Break flag, and a value of 3 disables Escape, and clears store if Break is pressed.

F2Ø9 If (ØØBB) AND &3Ø = Ø, the 'ignore error' condition is set for save and load, and the routine jumps to F213. Otherwise, if (ØØC1) ≠ Ø the routine jumps to F21D.

F213 Y is pushed, and FBBB is called to check for the presence of a second processor, accessing the appropriate routine if one is found to be present. Y is pulled, and F7D5 is called to check block length, setting (ØØC2) = Ø or 4.

F21D F9B4 is called to perform the load action. If it returns with NE set, the routine jumps to F255, returning to search by calling F637 and jumping back to F2Ø9. Otherwise FB69 is called to pick and increment the block number, setting the result in (ØØBE/F).

If bit 7 of (Ø3CA), the block flag byte, is 1, the current block is the last, and the routine jumps to F232. Otherwise F96A is called to increment (ØØB1/3), the block (page) count, and F77B is called to set up another block read. The routine loops to F2Ø9.

F232 Data is stored in the parameter block used to control OSFILE actions. The start address of the block is given by (ØØC8/9). The settings are:

((ØØC8) + &ØA) = (ØØCC)
((ØØC8) + &ØB) = (ØØCD)
((ØØC8) + &ØC) = Ø
((ØØC8) + &ØD) = Ø.

In save, these bytes hold the start address of data, but in load they hold length of file. (Provision is made for four bytes for the sake of the second processor system.)

P is pulled.

F246 FAE8 is called to release the serial system.

F249 If bit 7 of (ØØBA) = Ø, the routine jumps to F254 = return.

F24D P is pushed, and FA46 is called. This displays the data which follows the call, in this case &ØD, calling newline. P is pulled, and the routine returns.

The next routine caters for retry after a failure:

F255 F637 is called to search, and a jump to F2Ø9 follows.

Now filenames are read, using Command Line Interpreter routines:

F25A (ØØF2/3) = X/Y, setting up the start address for the filename. Y = Ø and EA1D is called to look for a ' " ' symbol. X = Ø.

F265 EA2F is called to get a character code, a return with carry set indicating the end of a character string, in response to which the routine jumps to F277. A return with EQ set causes a jump to F274. Otherwise (Ø3D2 + X) = A, storing the character found. X is incremented, and if it has not reached &ØB the routine loops to F265, else;

F274 This point is reached if an invalid character is found or the filename is too long. A jump to EA8F reports 'Bad String'.

F277 (Ø3D2 + X) = Ø, terminating the filename copy. The routine returns.

OSFILE: F27D

F27D OSFILE is accessed through FFDD, (Ø212). It requires a parameter block starting at address X/Y. A is pushed, and (ØØC8/9) = X/Y. The first two bytes of the parameter block are picked up in X/Y, giving the address of the start of the filename. F25A is called to pick up and copy the filename.

F29Ø A loop copies the parameter bytes 2 to 9 (Load address and execution address) to (Ø3BE/C5) and (ØØBØ/7). (As elsewhere, four bytes are allowed for these addresses, though only two are used internally.)

A is pulled. If it holds Ø, the routine jumps to the save process at F2A7. If it holds &FF, the routine jumps to the load process at F1C4. For any other value, the routine returns. (The other six options listed are not available with the cassette system.)

The save process follows:

F2A7 (Ø3C6/7) = Ø, this being the block number. Then parameter bytes 1Ø to 17 are copied to (ØØBØ/7), being the data start address, four bytes, and the data end address, four bytes.

If X = Ø, no filename was found, and a jump to F274 reports 'Bad String'. Otherwise, FB27 is called to set up the load/save options, set (ØØC7) = 6 and claim the serial system for cassette use. F934 is called to report 'Bad Command' if an attempt is being made to write to a ROM.

Then FBBD is called with A = Ø to check for a second processor. FBE2 switches on the motor, and resets the ACIA, checking for Escape in passing.

F2C8 Carry is set, and X = &FD.

F2CB (Ø2CB + X) = (FFB7 + X) − (FFB3 + X). X is incremented, and if it is non-zero the routine loops to F2CB. This sets (Ø3C8/A) to (ØØB4/6) − (ØØBØ/2), the number of pages (blocks) to be saved. If the last byte transferred, the most significant, is non-zero, the routine jumps to F2E8. Otherwise, A = 1 − (Ø3C9), less 1 if (Ø3C8) ≠ Ø. If this does not generate a carry, the routine jumps to F2E8, otherwise X = &8Ø and F2FØ follows.

F2E8 (Ø3C9) = 1, (Ø3C8) = X.

F2FØ (Ø3CA) = X. F7EC is called to save one block. If the return shows negative, the routine returns via F341, the last block having been saved. Otherwise, F96A is called to increment (ØØB1/3), the page of the start address for the next block, and (Ø3C6/7), the block number, is incremented. The routine loops to F2C8.

The calculations above need some thought. (Ø3C8/9) are intended to hold the block length, not expected to exceed FFFF, in which case (Ø3CA) will be set to zero, and there is then a question of how small the block is. If it is Ø1ØØ, (Ø3C8) = Ø, (Ø3C9) = 1. There will be a carry from A = 1 − 1, so (Ø3CA) = &8Ø, indicating 'last block', whereas a length of Ø1Ø1 would mean no carry, and (Ø3C9) = 1, (Ø3C8) = Ø, and (Ø3CA) = Ø. That, at least, appears to be the mechanism.

*RUN: F3Ø5

F3Ø5 F25A is called to pick up a filename, and F1C4 is called with (Ø3C2), the execution address, set to &FF. A file is loaded. If bit 7 of (Ø27A) = Ø there is no second processor, and the routine jumps to F31F.

Otherwise, if (Ø3C4/5), the upper half of the

execution address, is not FFFF, the routine jumps to F322, otherwise;

F31F The routine jumps to (Ø3C2), the lower half of the execution address.

F322 X/Y = Ø3C2, A = 4, and the second processor is entered via FBC7.

*CAT: F32B

F32B A = 8, and F344 is called to set bit 3 of (ØØE2), the status flag. FB27 is called to set up the load/save options, set (ØØC7) = 6, and claim the serial system.

F348 is called with A = Ø to check whether ROM or tape is involved, then FAFC is called to perform a read. A = &F7, ready to clear bit 3 of (ØØE2).

F33D A = A AND (ØØE2).

F33F (ØØE2) = A. The routine returns.

The meaning of (ØØE2) can conveniently be given here:

Bit Ø: 1 if input file open
Bit 1: 1 if output file open
Bit 2: Not used
Bit 3: 1 if CAT in use
Bit 4: Not used
Bit 5: Not used
Bit 6: 1 if End of File
Bit 7: 1 if End of File Warning.

F342 A = &4Ø, to set bit 6 of (ØØE2).

F344 A = A OR (ØØE2). The routine jumps to F33F.

The next block deals with search:

F348 A is pushed, and if (Ø247) = Ø F359 follows. Tape is selected. Otherwise EE13 is called to set (ØØF5) = &EF, then EE18 checks ROM type. A return with carry clear gives a jump to F359, otherwise F39A is entered with V clear.

F359 F77B is called to read data. When it returns, the block number is copied from (Ø3C6/7) to (ØØB4/5). (Ø3DF) = &FF, clearing the flags of the last block read, and (ØØBA) = Ø. F376 follows.

F370 This is a loop point. FB69 sets (ØØBE/F) to the block number plus 1, then F77B reads the next block.

F376 If (0247) ≠ ∅ (ROM, not tape), and V is clear, the routine jumps to F39A. Otherwise;

F37D A is pulled and pushed. It would appear that the result should be &FF, but if it is ∅ the routine jumps to F3AE. Otherwise FA72 is called to check the filename, a return with NE set indicating a match. This results in a jump to F39C. Otherwise, if (∅∅BB) AND &3∅ = ∅, which means 'ignore errors', the routine jumps to F39A, else if (∅∅B6) ≠ (∅3C6), the lower byte of the block number, the routine jumps to F39C.

F39A P is pulled, the routine returns.

F39C If (∅247) = ∅ (tape, not ROM), the routine jumps to F3AE, else;

F3A1 EEAD is called to set a ROM displacement address.

F3A4 The block number in (∅3C6/7) is set to FFFF, and the routine loops to F37∅ to attempt another read, beginning with block ∅.

F3AE If V is set, F7D7 is called with A = &FF to set (∅∅BC/D) = ∅∅FF and to set (∅∅C2) = X.

Then F9D9 is called with X = ∅ to report 'Data?'. If (∅247) = ∅, the routine jumps to F3C3 to service tape needs, else if bit 6 of (∅∅BB) = ∅ the routine jumps to F3A1. (Long messages not required.)

F3C3 If bit 7 of the block flags in (∅3CA) = 1, indicating that the last block has been read, the routine jumps to F3A4, else loops to F37∅.

OSFIND: F3CA

F3CA X and Y are pushed via A, A being held in (∅∅BC) meanwhile. If A is non-zero (open a file), the routine jumps to F3F2. Otherwise A = Y, which holds the file handle for file closure, or zero if all files are to be closed. If Y ≠ ∅, the routine jumps to F3E3, else E275 is called to close all files, and then F478 is called to tidy up.

F3DD (∅∅E2) is shifted right and left logically to zero bit ∅. If the bit was ∅, no input file was open, and the routine exits via F3EF to F471, else;

F3E3 If bit Ø of A = 1, the routine loops back to F3DD to close the input file. If bit 1 of A = 1, the routine jumps to F3EC to close the output file. Otherwise, the error 'Channel' is reported, since the cassette system only supports one input file and one output file.

F3EC F478 is called to close the output file, then the routine exits via F471 to tidy up.

The next block deals with file opening, input file first:

F3F2 F25A is called to get a filename, which starts at address X/Y. If bit 6 of (ØØBC), holding A at entry, is Ø, the request is not for an input file, and the routine jumps to F436. Otherwise, it is assumed that an input file is wanted.

(Ø39E) = Ø, this being the BGET offset pointer. (Ø3DD/E), the next block number for BGET, is set to ØØØØ. F33D is called with A = &3E to clear bits Ø, 6 and 7 of (ØØE2), indicating status as input file closed, not end of file, not EOF warning. FB1A is called to set sequential access options in (ØØBB), and to claim the serial system.

P is pushed while F631 is called to search for the file named, it being assumed that the cassette recorder is switched to Read or Play. F6B4 is called to check the protection bit of block status and respond appropriately. P is pulled, and X = &FF.

F416 X is incremented, and (Ø3A7 + X) = (Ø3B2 + X), the routine looping to F416 until (Ø3B2 + X) = Ø. This copies the filename. F344 is called with A = 1 to set bit Ø of (ØØE2), showing input file open. If (Ø2EA/B) = ØØØØ, the block length of the input file is zero, and F342 is called to set bit 6 of (ØØE2), end of file. A = (Ø247) OR 1, and the routine exits via F46F.

The opening of an output file is handled next:

F436 A = X, and if X = Ø the report 'Bad String' is given. The filename is of zero length. Otherwise;

F43C X = &FF.

F43E X is incremented, and (Ø38Ø + X) = (Ø3D2 + X), the routine looping to F43E until (Ø3D2 + X) = Ø, copying the filename. X = 8, A = &FF.

F44B (Ø38B + X) = A. X is decremented, and the routine loops to F44B until X = Ø, setting (Ø38C/93) to &FF. X = &14, A = Ø.

F454 (Ø38Ø + X) = A. X is incremented, and the routine loops to F454 until X = &1E. This zeroes (Ø394/D).

(Ø397) is rotated left. As the preceding loop left carry set, this makes (Ø386/7), block number, equal to ØØØ1.

FB27 is called to set up the load/save options in (ØØBB) and claim the serial system. F934 is called to check for (Ø247) ≠ Ø, which gives 'Bad Command', since it is pointless to output to ROM . . .

FAF2 is called to set up the serial system, and F344 is called with A = 2 to set bit 1 of (ØØE2), meaning output file open. A = 2.

F46F (ØØBC) = A.

F471 Y and X are pulled via A, A = (ØØBC), and the routine returns.

Subsidiary functions for the above now follow:

F478 If bit 1 of (ØØE2) = Ø, output file closed, the routine returns. Otherwise (Ø397) = Ø, (Ø396) = (Ø39D). This sets block length to the current value of the BPUT offset, and then (Ø398) = &8Ø, marking the current block as the last.

F496 is called to save the current block of the file. F33D is entered with A = &FD to zero bit 1 of (ØØE2), indicating output file closed.

F496 FB1A is called to set sequential options in (ØØBB) and claim the serial system. X = &11.

F49B (Ø3BE + X) = (Ø38C + X). X is decremented, and while it is positive the routine loops to F49B. This copies the header block, less filename, from (Ø38C/9D) to (Ø3BE/CF).

(ØØB2/3) = FFFF, (ØØBØ/1) = Ø9ØØ, the start of the cassette output buffer. FB81 is called with X = &7F to copy the filename from (Ø38Ø/B) to (Ø3D2/C). (Ø3DF) = A = Ø, this being a block flag copy. FB8E switches the motor on. FBE2 sets up the ACIA, F7EC performs the save, and when it returns the block number in (Ø394/5) is incremented. The routine returns.

The above routines carry a warning. They assume that the tape in the cassette recorder is correctly positioned, and that Record and Play are selected as appropriate. They are closely analogous to disc routines, but whereas the read and write modes of the disc system are controllable, the cassette is not, so you have to do the job yourself.

The transfer of data to and from the files is controlled by OSBGET and OSBPUT:

OSBGET: F4C9

F4C9 X and Y are pushed via A, and then FB9C is called with A = 1 to check that the conditions necessary to OSBGET are established.

If bit 7 of (ØØE2) = 1, end of file warning, the report 'EOF' is given by a jump to F523. If bit 6 of (ØØE2) = Ø, not EOF, the routine jumps to F4E3. Otherwise F344 is called with A = &8Ø to set bit 7 of (ØØE2), and the routine exits to F51B with A = &FE.

F4E3 X = (Ø39E), the offset of the next byte to be read, and if X + 1 ≠ (Ø2EA), block size, the routine jumps to F516 to read a byte.

Otherwise, if bit 7 of (Ø2EC) = 1 (last block), the routine jumps to F513 to signal EOF before reading the byte.

Otherwise, A = (Ø2ED), which holds the last character in the current block, and A is pushed. FB1A is called to set sequential options in (ØØBB), and to claim the serial system. P is pushed, and F6AC reads in a new block. P and A are pulled (from data set from X and Y), and (ØØBC) = A. Carry is cleared.

If bit 7 of (Ø2EC) = Ø, not last block, the routine jumps to F51D. If (Ø2EA/B), the block size, is non-zero, the routine jumps to F51D. Otherwise F342 is called to set bit 6 of (ØØE2), showing EOF, and the routine jumps to F51D.

F513 F342 is called to set bit 6 of (ØØE2), EOF. Then;

F516 X is equal to (Ø39E) when this point is reached. X is decremented, giving the offset to the last byte read, carry is cleared, and A = (ØAØØ + X), reading the byte from the cassette input buffer.

F51B (ØØBC) = A, which may be the byte just read, or may be &FE if the data has run out.

F51D (Ø39E), the offset pointer, is incremented. The routine exits via F471.

F523 Text 'EOF'.

The displayed report 'EOF' can be disconcerting, but it can be avoided by taking note of EOF warning before calling OSBGET.

OSBPUT: F529

F529 The byte to be entered is held in A, and is copied to (ØØC4). X and Y are pushed, and FB9C is called with A = 2 to check that the conditions necessary to OSBPUT are established.

X = (Ø39D), the BPUT offset pointer, and A is restored from (ØØC4). (Ø9ØØ + X) = A sets the byte in the cassette output buffer. Then X is incremented, and if X = Ø F496 is called to prepare for a write to tape, the file being full. FAF2 is called to set up the serial system. Whatever the contents of X, action continues.

F545 (Ø39D), the offset, is incremented. A is set from (ØØC4), and the routine exits via F46F.

OSBYTE 139: Select File Options: F54D *OPT:F54D

F45D If X = Ø, default values are to be set, and the routine jumps to F57E. If X = 3, the routine jumps to F573 to set interblock gap. If, otherwise, Y is greater than 2, the message 'Bad Command' is given, by a jump to E31Ø via F55E.

If X = 1 message control is involved, and the routine jumps to F561.

If X = 2, error responses are to be changed, and F568 follows.

Barring any of these jumps:

F55E The routine jumps to E31Ø to report 'Bad Command'.

F561 For message control, the two lower bits of each nibble of (ØØE3) have to be set. A = &33 to provide an appropriate mask. Y = Y + 3, and F56A follows.

F568 For error response control, the mask is A = &CC, and;

F56A Y is incremented, and (ØØE3) = (ØØE3) AND A OR (F581 + Y). The routine returns.

F57E Default values are set by Y = A = Ø and a jump to F56D.

F581 Table: A1 ØØ 22 11 ØØ 88 CC.

We now begin to encounter lower level subroutines of wider usage. The first is called from FAE2, and also from DCBØ in Interrupt.

F588 (ØØCØ) is decremented. If (Ø247) = Ø, tape, not ROM, the routine jumps to F596. Otherwise, EE51 is called to service a ROM, Y = A, and the routine exits via F5BØ with carry clear.

F596 A = (FEØ8), reading ACIA status. A is pushed. If bit 1 of A = 1, the transmit register is occupied, and the routine jumps to F5A9. Otherwise, if (ØØCA) = Ø, F5A9 again follows. A is pulled to clear the stack, then (FEØ9) = &BD, setting the ACIA to divide by 16, deal with eight bits with odd parity and stop bit, ready to send low, both transmit and receive interrupts enabled. The routine returns.

F5A9 Y = (FEØ9), picking up ACIA data. A is pulled, and bit 2 is shifted into carry, this being the data carrier detect bit from (FEØ8). (Active low.)

F5BO If (ØØC2) = Ø, the routine returns via F61D. If (ØØC2) ≠ 1, the routine jumps to F5BD. If (ØØC2) = 1 and carry is clear the routine returns via F61D, but if carry is set an exit via F61B with Y = 2 sets (ØØC2) = 2. ((ØØC2) is a progress index marking the stage reached in a serial transfer process.)

F5BD If (ØØC2) ≠ 2, the routine jumps to F5D3.

If (ØØC2) = 2; If carry is set the routine returns via F61D. If carry is clear the data byte is transferred from Y to A, and FB78 is called to set (ØØBE/CØ) = Ø. Y = 3.

If A = &2A, the synchronising byte, the routine exits via F61B, setting (ØØC2) = 3. Failing that, FB5Ø is called to control the cassette system, and the routine exits via F61B with Y = 1, setting (ØØC2) = 1.

F5D3 If (ØØC2) ≠ 3, the routine jumps to F5E3.

If (ØØC2) = 3; if carry is set the routine jumps to F5DC, otherwise (ØØBD) = Y, the character read, and the routine returns via F61D.

F5DC (ØØCØ) = &8Ø. The routine returns via F61D.

F5E2 If (ØØC2) ≠ 4 the routine jumps to F6ØE.

If (ØØC2) = 4; if carry is set the routine jumps to F616 to set (ØØC2) = Ø, otherwise A = Y and F7BØ is called to continue the reading process.

Then Y = (ØØBC) and (ØØBC) is incremented. If bit 7 of (ØØBD) = 1, the routine jumps to F6ØØ. ((ØØBD) holds the last byte read.)

FBD3 is called to check second processor involvement (setting X = A), and a return with A = Ø gives a jump to F5FD. Otherwise, (FEE5) = X, and the routine jumps to F6ØØ.

F5FD A = X, restoring the value before the call to FBD3, ((ØØBØ) + Y) = A, setting the last byte read in store. (Y = (ØØBC))

F6ØØ Y is incremented, and if Y ≠ (Ø3C8), the low byte of block length, the routine returns via F61D. Otherwise (ØØBC) = 1, and the routine jumps to F61B with Y = 5, setting (ØØC2) = 5.

F6ØE A = Y. F7BØ is called to continue the process. (ØØBC) is decremented, and the routine returns via F61D.

F616 FB46 is called to reset the ACIA. Y = Ø.

F61B (ØØC2) = Y.

F61D The routine returns.

The next routine is accessed by way of F1B1, and implements OSBYTE 127: Check for End of File:

F16E A and Y are pushed. Y = A = X, and FB9C is called with A = 3 to check options, reporting 'Channel' if appropriate.

A = (ØØE2) AND &4Ø, reading EOF status. X = A, and Y and A are pulled. The routine returns.

The search routine comes next, with entry at F631 from F1CD and F4ØD, or at F637 from F255 and F7Ø2:

F631 (ØØB4/5) = ØØØØ

F637 A = (ØØB4) and A is pushed. (ØØB6) =A. A = (ØØB5), and A is pushed. (ØØB7) = A. (This makes two copies of (ØØB4/5), one on the stack, the other in (ØØB6/7)) FA46 is called to output the following text and then continue with subsequent code:

F644 'Searching'

F64F F348 is called with A = &FF. When it returns, (ØØB4/5) is recovered from the stack. If (ØØB6/7) ≠ Ø, the routine jumps to F66D. Otherwise (ØØB4/5) = ØØØØ. If (ØØC1) ≠ Ø the routine jumps to F66D, else FB81 is called with X = &B1 to copy the filename from (Ø3B2) on to (Ø3D2) on.

F66D If (Ø247) = Ø (tape), or if V is set, the routine jumps to F685. Otherwise 'File not found' is reported, as an error.

F685 (Ø3AF) = Y = &FF. The routine returns.

*EXEC: F68D

Also called at F68B from E27C and FA31. This is equivalent to *EXEC Ø.

F68B A = Ø.

F68D P is pushed, and (ØØE6) = Y. The EXEC file handle in (Ø256) is copied to Y, and reset from A. If Y ≠ Ø, OSFIND is called to close the current file.

F69B Y is reset from (ØØE6), and P is pulled. If EQ is set, the routine returns via F6AB. Otherwise OSFIND is called with A = &4Ø to open an input file. Y = A. If

Y = Ø, a jump to F674 reports 'File not found'. Otherwise, (Ø256) = A, setting the file handle.

The next routine is entered from F4F9 to read a block:

F6AC FB81 is called with X = &A6 to copy a filename from (Ø3A7) on to (Ø3D2) on. F77B is called to read data.

F6B4 A = (Ø3CA), the block flag byte. Bit Ø is shifted into carry. If it is Ø F6BD follows, else F1F6 to report 'Locked'.

F6BD (ØØB4/5) = (Ø3DD/E), the number of the next block expected. (ØØBØ/1) = ØAØØ, the start of the cassette input buffer. (ØØB2/3) = FFFF. F7D5 is called to set conditions, and F9B4 is called to report 'Loading' or a query, as appropriate. If the return is NE, F7Ø2 follows, else;

(Ø2ED) = (ØAFF), saving the last character in the cassette input buffer. FB69 is called to set (ØØB4/5) = (Ø3C6/7) + 1, as block number, and this returns with X/Y = (ØØB4/5), from which (Ø3DD/E) is set. (Next block expected.)

F6EE (Ø3C8/A) = (Ø2EA/C), being block size and block flags. If bit 7 of (Ø2EC) = Ø, this is not the last block, and the routine jumps to F6FF, otherwise F249 is called to execute a new line if bit 7 of (ØØBA) = 1.

F6FF The routine exits to FAF2.

F7Ø2 F637 is called to perform a search. If it returns NE, the routine jumps to F6BA to check for the 'Locked' condition, else;

F7Ø7 If A = &2A, the synchronising byte, the routine jumps to F742. If A ≠ &33, the substitute for a header in ROM files, the routine jumps to F71E to report 'Bad ROM'. Otherwise, the block number in (Ø3C6/7) is incremented, X = &FF and the routine jumps to F773 with V (and MI) set.

F71E F33D is called with A = &7F to clear bit 3 of (ØØE2), and the error report 'Bad Rom' follows.

The next routine picks up a header. Its entry point is F77B, but for tape there is an immediate jump to F72D:

F72D FB9Ø is called with Y = &FF to set (ØØC3) = Y and call OSBYTE 137,1,Y to switch the motor on. Then (ØØC2) = 1 and FB5Ø is called to set up the serial system.

F739 F995 is called to check for Escape, the routine looping to F739 until (ØØC2) = 3. (Note that this is possible because F588 is called by interrupt.)

F742 FB7C is called with Y = Ø to set (ØØBE/F) = ØØØØ.

F747 F797 is called to check the situation. If V is clear, the routine jumps to F766. Otherwise (Ø3B2 + Y) = A. If F797 set EQ, the routine jumps to F757. Otherwise Y is incremented, and if Y ≠ &ØB, the permitted filename length, the routine jumps to F747. The filename is cleared by this, since A and Y are initially zero. Y is decremented.

F757 X = &ØC.

F759 F797 is called again to check the situation, and if V is clear a jump to F766 follows. Otherwise (Ø3B2 + X) = A, X is incremented, and if X ≠ &1F the routine loops to F759, clearing the remainder of the header block.

F766 A = Y, X = A, and A = Ø. (Ø3B2 + Y) = A. (ØØC1) = (ØØBE) OR (ØØBF).

F773 FB78 is called to set (ØØCØ) = Ø, (ØØBE/F) = ØØØØ. Then (ØØC2) = Y and if A ≠ Ø the routine returns via F7D4.

F77B If (Ø247) = Ø (tape), the routine jumps to F72D.

F78Ø EE51 is called to offer paged ROM service. If A = &2B, the ROM file terminator, the routine jumps to
F7Ø7. If bit 3 of (ØØE2) = 1, F24D is called to give a new line.

F79Ø EE18 is called, and if carry is clear the routine loops to F78Ø, otherwise V is cleared and the routine returns.

F797 If (Ø247) = Ø (tape), the routine jumps to F7AD. Otherwise X and Y are pushed, and EE51 is called. (ØØBD) = A, (ØØCØ) = 1. X and Y are pulled.

F7AD F884 is called to check for Escape and loop until bit 7 of (ØØCØ) = 1.

F7BØ P and A are pushed. Carry is set and transferred to bit 7 of (ØØCB) by a rotate right. (ØØBF) = (ØØBF) EOR A.

F7B9 A = (ØØBF), and is rotated left. If carry is then clear, the routine jumps to F7CA. Otherwise a rotate right restores A, and (ØØBF) = (ØØBF) EOR 8, (ØØBE) = A EOR &1Ø. Carry is set.

F7CA (ØØBE/F) is rotated left, and (ØØCB) is shifted right logically. If this results in zero, the routine loops back to F7B9. Otherwise A and P are pulled and the routine returns.

The next block sets (ØØC2):

F7D5 A = Ø.

F7D7 (ØØBD) = A, (ØØBC) = X = Ø. If V is clear, the routine jumps on to F7E9. Otherwise if (Ø3C8/9) = ØØØØ, the routine jumps to F7E9. If neither jump is taken, X = 4.

F7E9 (ØØC2) = X. The routine returns.

The next routine, called from F4BD, saves a block:

F7EC P is pushed, X = 3, A = Ø.

F7F1 (Ø3CB + X) = A. X is decremented, and if it is positive the routine loops to F7F1, clearing (Ø3CB/E). If (Ø3C6/7), the block number, = Ø, the routine jumps to F8Ø4, otherwise F892 is called to create a five-second delay, and F8Ø7 follows.

F8Ø4 F896 is called to create the inter-block gap delay.

F8Ø7 A = &2A, the sync byte, and (ØØBD) = A. FB78 is called to set (ØØCØ) = Ø and (ØØBE/F) = ØØØØ. FB4A is called to set the ACIA, and F884 is called to check Escape. Y is decremented.

F815 Y is incremented, and (Ø3B2 + Y) = (Ø3D2 + Y). F875 is called to output A to tape, this being a filename character. If the return is NE, the filename is not complete, and the routine loops to F815. Otherwise X = &ØC.

F823 A = (Ø3B2 + X), and F875 is called to output A to tape. X is incremented, and if X ≠ &1D the routine loops to F823. This deals with the remainder of the header. F87B is then called to prepare for data output. If (Ø3C8/9), block length, is zero, the routine jumps to F855, there being no data to be saved. Otherwise Y = Ø and FB7C is called to set (ØØBE/F) = ØØØØ.

F83E A = ((ØØBØ) + Y), picking up a data byte, and FBD3 is called to check for a second processor. If the return is NE, X = (FEE5).

F848 A = X, and F875 is called to save the byte. Y is incremented, and if Y ≠ (Ø3C8) the routine loops to F83E, else F878 is called to reset pointers.

F855 F884 is called twice, then FB46 is called to reset the ACIA. F898 is called with A = 1 to give a short delay. P is pulled, and F8B9 is called to set up a report. If bit 7 of (Ø3CA) = Ø, this is not the last block, and the routine returns via F874. Otherwise, P is pushed, F892 is called for a five second delay, and F246 is called to release the serial system and present a report. P is pulled, and;

F874 The routine returns.

This routine saves a byte:

F875 F882 is called, and the routine returns via F7BØ to set up (ØØBE/F) and other variables.

F87B A = (ØØBF), and F882 is called. Then A = (ØØBE).

F882 (ØØBD) = A.

F884 F995 is called to look for Escape and 'Cassette Critical'. The routine loops to F884 until bit 7 of (ØØCØ) = 1. (ØØCØ) = Ø and A = (ØØBD). The routine returns.

Next comes a multi-purpose delay routine.

F892 A = &32, giving a five second delay. F898 follows.

F896 A = (ØØC7), the inter-block gap.

F898 X = 5.

F89A (Ø24Ø) = A. This is the location which is decremented by each Frame Sync interrupt, at 20 mS intervals.

E89D F995 is called to check Escape and 'Cassette Critical', the routine looping back to F89D until bit 7 of (Ø24Ø) = 1, i.e. until the count goes negative. When the loop drops out, X is decremented, and if X ≠ Ø the routine loops back to F89A, resetting the inner count. When X = Ø, the routine returns. The total delay is 5 * A * 20 mS.

We now reach the generation of screen reports:

F8A9 If (Ø3C6/7) = ØØØØ (block number), the routine jumps to F8B6, else if bit 7 of (Ø3DF) = Ø (block flags), the routine jumps to F8B9. Otherwise;

F8B6 If block number is non-zero, or the block last read completed the task, F249 is called to report progress.

F8B9 Y = Ø, (ØØBA) = Y. (Ø3DF) = (Ø3CA) (block flags). E7DC is called to check system status. If it returns with A = Ø, the routine returns via F933. The cassette system is busy. Otherwise, a newline is output by calling OSWRCH with A = &ØD.

F8CD A = (Ø3B2 + Y), a character in the filename. If A = Ø F8E2 is entered. If A is otherwise less than &2Ø, the routine jumps to F8DA. If A is otherwise less than &7F, the routine jumps to F8DC.

F8DA A = &3F (?)

F8DC OSWRCH is called to display the character. Y is incremented, and if Y ≠ Ø the routine loops to F8CD.

F8E2 If (Ø247) = Ø (tape), the routine jumps to F8EB, else if bit 6 of (ØØBB) = Ø the routine returns via F933. (Not long messages.)

F8EB F991 is called to output a space. Y is incremented, and if Y is less than &ØB the routine loops to F8EB, filling out the maximum filename length. Then X = A = (Ø3C6), the low byte of the block number. F97A is called to output the number in hexadecimal, and if bit 7 of (Ø3CA) = Ø the routine returns via F933.

Otherwise, this is the last block, and X = A, A = A + (Ø3C9), the upper byte of block length (normally zero). (ØØCD) = A, and F975 is called to output A in hexadecimal with a preceding space. Then A = (Ø3C8), the lower byte of block length, (ØØCC) = A, and F97A is called to output A in hexadecimal (without a preceding space).

If bit 6 of (ØØBB) = Ø, long messages are not required, and the routine returns via F933. Otherwise, X = 4 and;

F917 F991 is called to display a space. X is decremented, and the routine loops to F917 until X = Ø. Then X = &ØF, and F9027 is called to display the load address held in (Ø3BE/C1). X = &13.

F927 Y = 4.

F929 A = (ØØ3B2 + X), and F97A is called to output A in hexadecimal. X and Y are decremented, and if Y ≠ Ø the routine loops to F929. Otherwise;

F933 The routine returns.

With X = &13, the routine outputs (Ø3C2-5), the execution address.

Next, a routine entered from F2BD and F462, a control for Save:

F934 If (Ø247) = Ø, F93C follows, otherwise E31Ø, giving 'Bad Command', since you can't save to a ROM.

F93C FB8E is called to zero (ØØC3) and start the motor. Then FBE2 sets up the ACIA, and E7DC checks for 'Cassette Critical'. If it returns with A = Ø, the routine returns via F933. Otherwise the message 'RECORD then Return' is output, using FA46.

F94A The message text.

F95D F995 is called to check for Escape, and OSRDCH is called to look for the Return key pressed. The routine loops to F95D until the key is pressed, otherwise returning via FFE7, giving newline.

The next routine is simple:

F96A Increment (ØØB1/3). This advances the load address by one block. The routine returns.

The hex output routine is also reasonably simple:

F975 A is pushed and F991 is called to output a space. A is pulled.

F97A A is pushed and divided by 16, bringing the upper nibble to the lower nibble position. F983 outputs the nibble in hex. Then A is pulled ready for the original lower nibble to be output;

F983 Carry is cleared, and A = A AND &ØF + &3Ø, producing the ASCII code if the nibble is Ø - 9. If the result is less than &3A, the routine jumps to F98E, else A = A + 7 to correct the code for A - F.

F98E The routine returns via OSWRCH, displaying the character code in A.

F991 A = &20, and the routine jumps to F98E, displaying a space.

The next block is called from several places to check for Escape:

F995 P is pushed. If bit 7 of (ØØEB) = 1, 'Cassette Critical', the routine jumps to F99E. If bit 7 of (ØØFF) = 1, the routine jumps to F9AØ (escape condition). Otherwise;

F99E P is pulled. The routine returns.

F9AØ F33B is called to close the input file. FAF2 is called to free the serial system, and OSBYTE 126 acknowledges Escape. The message 'Escape' is output.

F9AB The text 'Escape'.

Now the loading module is reached:

F9B4 A = Y. If A = Ø, the routine jumps to F9C4. Otherwise FA46 outputs the text.

F9BA 'Loading'.

F9C4 (ØØBA) = A, X = &FF, A = (ØØC1). If A ≠ Ø the routine jumps to F9D9, else FA72 is called to compare filenames. P is pushed. X = &FF, Y = &99, A = &FA. This sets Y/A to point to the message 'File?'. If FA72 returned with NE set, the routine jumps to F9F5 to report a query (unexpected file name). Otherwise;

F9D9 Y = &8E, making Y/A point to 'Data?'. (CRC check error). If (ØØC1) = Ø there is no such error, and the routine jumps to F9E3, otherwise to F9F5 to report.

F9E3 If the block number in (Ø3C6/7) is equal to (ØØB4/5), the routine jumps to FAØ4, else;

F9F1 Y/A = FAA4, pointing to 'Block?'' (Unexpected block number.)

F9F5 If this point is reached, an error has been found. A, Y and X are pushed, and F8B6 is called to display a report in the usual form. X, Y and A are pulled, and the routine jumps to FA18.

FAØ4 X is pushed, and F8A9 is called to report. FAD6 is then called to check for Escape and other conditions. X is pulled. If (ØØBE/F) = Ø, the routine returns via FA8D, otherwise Y/A = FA8E, pointing to 'Data?', and;

FA18 (ØØBA) is decremented, and A is pushed. If bit 7 of (ØØEB) = 1 (Cassette Critical) the routine jumps to FA2C. Otherwise, if X AND (Ø247) = Ø, the same point is reached. If X AND &11 AND (ØØBB) = Ø (Ignore errors), FAC3 follows, else;

FA2C A is pulled and (ØØB8/9) = Y/A. F6BB is called to tidy up, (ØØEB) is halved, clearing bit 7, FAE8 is called to sound 'Bell' and reset the serial system. A jump to (ØØØB/9) displays the required error report. It will respond to the selected error system.

FA3C A is pulled, and Y/A is incremented.

FA43 A and Y are pushed.

FA46 E7DC is called to check Cassette Critical. (ØØB8/9) is set from the value of Y/A on the stack. A = Y, and P is pushed.

FA52 (ØØB8/9) is incremented, and if the location it points to holds zero the routine jumps to FA68. Otherwise P is pulled and pushed again. If EQ is set, the routine loops to FA52. Otherwise OSASCI is called to display the character pointed to by (ØØØB8/9), and the routine loops to FA52. (Note that no display occurs if EQ is set by Y = Ø.)

FA68 P is pulled, (ØØB8/9) is incremented, and the routine jumps to (ØØB8/9), which will now point to the location following the text.

As the double increment of the pointer skips the initial zero and the error number, the texts do not cause an error condition, and action can continue.

Now come the filename comparisons:

FA72 X = &FF.

FA74 X is incremented, and A = (Ø3D2 + X), a character of the filename. If A ≠ Ø, the routine jumps to FA81, otherwise the routine returns with A = Ø, X = Ø, or if X is already zero with A = (Ø3B2 + X).

FA81 E4E3 is called to set carry if the code in A is not upper case alphabetic, A = A EOR (Ø3B2 + X), and if carry is clear bit 6 of A is zeroed, converting lower case to upper. If A = Ø the filename characters match, and the routine loops to FA74. Otherwise the routine returns with A ≠ Ø.

FA8E Text : "Data?" . FAAE follows.

FA99 Text : "File?" . FAAE follows.

FAA5 Text : "Block?" . FAAE follows.

FAAE If (ØØBA) = Ø the routine jumps to FAD3, otherwise if X = Ø the routine jumps to FAD3, otherwise if (ØØBB) AND &22 = Ø (no retry) the routine jumps to FAD3. Y = A, and FA4A is called to output.

FAC2 "Rewind tape".

FAD2 The routine returns.

FAD3 F24D is called to output newline.

FAD6 If (ØØC2) = Ø, the routine returns via FAD2. Otherwise F995 is called to check Escape, etc. If (Ø247) ≠ Ø F588 is called. In any case, the routine loops to FAD6.

Next comes the routine which releases the serial system:

FAE8 E7DC is called to check 'Cassette Critical', and if it leaves A = Ø OSWRCH is called with A = 7 to sound 'Bell'.

FAF2 FBBD is called with A = &8Ø to look for a second processor. X = Ø.

FAFC FB95 is called to switch off the cassete motor. P is pushed and interrupt barred. (FE1Ø) = (Ø282), restoring the previous setting of the serial ULA. (ØØEA) = Ø, setting serial system timeout. FBØB follows.

FBØA P is pushed.

FBØB FB46 is called to release the ACIA by (FEØ8) = 3. A = (Ø25Ø), the last setting of the ACIA, and then the routine exits via E189, which sets (Ø25Ø) and (FEØ8) from A, pulling P before returning.

Now, the routines that claim the serial system. There are separate entries for cassette (FB27) and sequential access (FB1A):

FB14 This is a loop point. P is pulled, and if bit 7 of (ØØFF) = Ø (Not Escape), the routine jumps to FB31, otherwise returning.

FB1A (ØØBB) = (ØØE3) * 16, putting the sequential access options in the upper nibble of (ØØBB). A = (Ø3D1), the sequential block gap, and the routine jumps to FB2F.

FB27 (ØØBB) = (ØØE3) AND &FØ, picking out the cassette options. A = 6.

FB2F (ØØC7) = A.

FB31 Interrupt is allowed, P is pushed, and interrupt is barred. If bit 7 of (Ø24F) = Ø (serial system busy), or bit 7 of (ØØEA) = 1 (RS423 timeout count in progress), the routine loops through FB14. Otherwise, (ØØEA) = 1, claiming the serial system for cassette use. FB46 is called to reset the ACIA with (FEØ8) = 3. P is pulled, and the routine returns.

Further setting of the serial system follows:

FB46 A = 3, and an exit via FB65 sets (FEØ8) = A, which resets the ACIA.

FB4A (ØØCA) = A = &3Ø, and FB63 follows.

FB5Ø (FE1Ø) = 5, selecting a transmit baud rate of 300, modified by the ACIA to 12ØØ baud. A short delay follows, with X counting from &FF down to Ø. Then (ØØCA) = X, (FE1Ø) = &85, resetting the serial ULA to motor on, 300 baud transmit, 192ØØ baud receive, cassette mode. A = &DØ. (Note that the cassette motor is switched off during the delay count, which explains the odd clicks that are heard from time to time when the cassette recorder is in use.)

FB63 A = A OR (ØØC6).

FB65 (FEØ8) = A. The routine returns.

This may set the ACIA to 3 (Reset), or &35 (8 bits + stop bit, divide by 16, transmit interrupt enabled) or &36 (the same, except that division is by 64, giving 300 baud working), &D5 (8 bits + stop bit, receive interrupt enabled, divide by 16) or &D6 (the same, except that division is by &64).

Miscellaneous routines follow:

FB78 Y = Ø, (ØØCØ) = Y.

FB7C (ØØBE) = Y, (ØØBF) = Y. The routine returns.

Now, a copy routine:

FB81 Y = &FF.

FB83 X and Y are incremented. (Ø3D2 + Y) = (Ø3ØØ + X). The routine loops to FB83 until (Ø3ØØ + X) = Ø, when the routine returns.

FB8E Y = Ø.

FB9Ø Interrupt is permitted. X = 1, (ØØC3) = Y.

FB95 OSBYTE 137 is called. X = Ø switches the cassette motor off, X = 1 switches the motor on. Y = Ø for write, Y = 1 for read.

The next block is called from F4CF in OSBGET with A = 1, from F531 in OSBPUT with A = 2, and from F625 with A = 3. Y holds the file handle, 1 for input, 2 for output.

FB9C (ØØBC) = A. Y = Y EOR (Ø247), reversing bit 1 if ROM files are selected. A = (ØØE2) AND (ØØBC), and bit Ø of A is shifted into carry. Y is decremented, and if it is then zero the routine jumps to FBAF. Otherwise, the original bit 1 of A is shifted into carry, and Y is again decremented. If Y ≠ Ø, the routine jumps to FBB1 to report 'Channel', otherwise;

FBAF If carry is set, the routine returns via FBFE, else;

FBB1 Text 'Channel'. (An error report).

Next, the check for a second processor:

FBBB A = 1.

FBBD FBD3 is called to perform checks. If it returns with A = Ø, the routine returns via FBFE. Otherwise A = X, X = &BØ, Y = Ø.

FBC7 A is pushed, and A = &CØ.

FBCA Ø4Ø6 is called, this being a routine set up when a second processor is in use. If it returns with carry clear, the routine loops to FBCA, else A is pulled and the routine exits to Ø4Ø6.

FBD3 X = A. If (ØØB2/3) = FFFF, the routine returns via FBE1, a 16-bit address being implied. Otherwise, A = (Ø27A) AND &8Ø, which will be zero if no second processor is fitted.

FBE1 The routine returns.

Finally, a block to control the motor and ACIA:

FBE2 (FE1Ø) = &85. The serial ULA is set for motor on, cassette mode, transmit baud rate 3ØØ. FB46 is called to reset the ACIA, and then FB63 is called with A = &1Ø to set up the ACIA. This will set either &15 (8 bits + stop bit, divide by 16, interrupts disabled) or &16 (the same, but divide by 64).

FBEF F995 is called to check Escape, and A = (FEØ8)AND 2. If A = Ø the transmit data register is set and the routine returns. Otherwise (FEØ9) = &AA passes data to the ACIA. The routine returns.

This completes the routines related to Files.

Chapter 13
THE BASIC INTERPRETER

Unlike the Operating System, the BASIC Interpreter does not have a number of well-defined entries which can be used as starting points for explorations. There is the main entry at 8ØØØ, and there may or may not be a 'service entry' at 8ØØ3. We must therefore begin our trek at 8ØØØ, where we find a jump to 8Ø1F, the start of a short initialising routine.

Before going further, however, there is an interesting experiment to try. Enter the statement ?&E3 = &EE to switch on 'long messages', and load a short program. The final report will give, in addition to the usual data, two eight-digit hexadecimal numbers. The first is the load address, the second the execution address, which gives a start point for execution of the program. This is normally the start of the short initialising routine, which may differ from one version of the ROMs to another, which would appear to make a tape record compatible only with a machine having a given version of the ROMs.

Fortunately, the execution address is not used by CHAIN, while LOAD ignores both load address and execution address for a BASIC program, loading from OSHWM upwards, even if that location has been moved by PAGE.

The load and execution addresses are only relevant for the Operating System commands, and hence *RUN may not work with a BASIC program saved on a different machine.

This is an example of the way the BASIC system takes control once it is entered, and a warning that the conditions which it imposes must always be taken into account in interpreting its actions.

Initialisation

8Ø1F OSBYTE 132 is called to read HIMEM, and the result is set in (ØØØ6/7). OSBYTE 131 is called to read OSHWM, and the high byte of this is copied to (ØØ18). (ØØ1F) = Ø, (Ø4Ø2/3) = ØØØØ, and (Ø4ØØ/1) = ØAØA. This sets ØØØØØAØA in (Ø4ØØ/3), which is the @% variable. (This does not quite agree with the statement in the User Manual that the default setting is @% = 1Ø.)

If ((ØØ11) AND 1) OR (ØØØ0) OR (ØØØE) OR (ØØØF) OR (ØØ1Ø) = Ø, then (ØØØD) = &41, (ØØØE) = &52, (ØØØF) = &57.

Then (Ø2Ø2/3) = B433, a most important setting, as it determines the BRK vector, which is used to enter the error-handling routine. (See the section on Interrupt.)

(ØØ23) = &FF, and the routine jumps on to 8A8Ø.

This enters the second instruction in the NEW routine, which leads into the Ready function, and then into the interpreter heart.

NEW and Ready

We expect NEW to destroy any existing BASIC program, though not so completely that OLD cannot restore it. We then expect to be given a signal that the system is ready to accept commands. These may be new lines for entry into a program, or may be for immediate execution, and the interpreter must take appropriate action. This gives us some idea of what to expect.

8A7D This is the NEW entry. 981Ø is called to set up pointers, check that the NEW statement is properly terminated, and check for Escape, which causes an error report.

8A8Ø A = &ØD, ready to enter a line termination, but the pointer for this has to be set up first, (ØØ12/3) being set to OSHWM by reference to (ØØ18). (ØØ2Ø) = Ø. (This is one of a number of minor settings that need not be examined for the moment, though we might make a note of it in passing.)

Then ((ØØ12) + Y) = A, setting the termination. Y is incremented from Ø to 1, and ((ØØ12) + Y) = &FF sets the second part of the termination. Y is again incremented, and (ØØ12) = Y, adjusting the pointer to OSHWM + 2.

8A96 This is a major loop point, reached after a new line has been added to a program; after OLD, DELETE, RENUMBER; and from AUTO. BD38 is called to reset pointers and clear (Ø48Ø/FF).

8A99 This is another loop point, reached after END, STOP, and a number of other places where the Ready state is expected to follow.

(ØØØB/C) = Ø7ØØ, the point where the command line entry will start. (ØØ16/7) = B443, which is the start of a BASIC line in ROM that is used to implement error reports. BC1D is then called with A = &3E to display '>' to indicate that the system is ready for a command, and to read in the command line at Ø7ØØ on, using OSWORD Ø. The permittted code range is &2Ø to &FF, and the maximum line length is 238 bytes.

8AAE This is the entry from the RUN routine, which first resets (ØØØB/C) to scan the stored program, not the input line. The setting (ØØ16/7) = B443 is repeated.

8AB6 This is the return point after error. (ØØ28) = &FF, (ØØ3C) = &FF, S, the stack pointer, is set to &FF, and BD52 is called to reset pointers. OSBYTE 126 is called to clear Escape, and (ØØ37/8) = (ØØØB/C). (ØØØA) = Ø, this being the displacement pointer associated with (ØØØB/C), and (ØØØ3B) = Ø.

At this point, 88D9 is called to check syntax and tokenise keywords. If it finds a line number, it prefaces the edited line with the token &8D, as a warning that entry, not immediate execution, is required. 97AE is then called to analyse the line, returning with carry clear if the first byte was not &8D, otherwise with carry set.

If carry is clear, the routine jumps to 8AE1 to execute the command line, otherwise BCAA is called to insert the line in the program, and the routine loops to 8A96 above.

Execution

8AE1 8A1E is called to read the next code in the line, skipping space codes. If the code is less than &C6, the routine jumps to 8B30, otherwise to 8B22.

And what is the significance of &C6? To discover that, we must jump on to 8B22, where we find that (ØØ37/8) is set by reference to two tables, and the routine then jumps to (ØØ37/8). We now have essential evidence, which we must put to work at once.

First dump 8ØØØ - 9ØFF in alphanumerics, using the program given in the Appendix. You will see the start of the keyword table. Note the address of the 'A' in 'AND', calling it START. Then note the base addresses used to reference the ROM tables at 8B22 on, calling the one used to set (ØØ37) TABLOW and the one used to set (ØØ38) TABHI. Insert the three values you have noted in the following program:

```
1ØØ CLS
11Ø @% = Ø
12Ø A% = START
13Ø B% = ?A%
14Ø A% = A% + 1
15Ø IF B% > &7F THEN 18Ø
16Ø PRINT CHR$(B%);
17Ø GOTO 13Ø
18Ø C% = ?A%
19Ø D% = Ø
2ØØ IF B% < &8F THEN 22Ø
21Ø D% = ?(TABLOW + B%) + 256*?(TABHI + B%)
22Ø PRINT TAB(1Ø);~B%;"  ";
23Ø IF C% < 16 PRINT "  ";
24Ø PRINT ~C%;"  ";
25Ø IF D% <>Ø PRINT ~D% ELSE PRINT
26Ø A% = A% + 1
27Ø IF A% > = TABLOW + &8F STOP
28Ø GOTO 13Ø.
```

The program will display or print a tabulation in four columns. The first column gives the keyword, the second its token, the third its qualifier, used in syntax checking, and the fourth its link address, if any. This is indeed a 'map of the camp', since it tells us where we can find the routine which executes a given keyword, and that identifies a very large part of the interpreter system.

However, the map is not quite complete, since a number of tokens have no addresses, and there are other operators which even have no tokens, such as +, −, * and /.

Evaluate

To find operator links, we must look at Evaluate. First check the link address for EVAL. At that address there is a subroutine call to the true evaluation routine:

AE1B Y = (ØØ1B), (ØØ1B) is incremented, and A = ((ØØ19) + Y). This picks up the next code of the statement under examination.
If A = &2Ø (space), the routine loops to AE1B to get the next code.
If A = &2D (-), the routine jumps to ADAE to negate (ØØ2A/D).
If A = &22 ("), the routine jumps to ADF8 to handle text.
If A = &2B (+), AE34 is called, and the routine continues.
If A is otherwise less than &8F, the routine jumps to AE3F.
If A exceeds &C5, the routine jumps to AE3F to report 'No such variable', though the code is, in fact, a token for a command, appearing in an invalid position.

Otherwise, the routine jumps to 8B22, where — as we have seen — a link address is set up to match the token, and the link point is entered.

AE3F Codes less than &8F are examined further. If A exceeds &3E, the routine jumps to AE4F, while if A is otherwise greater than &2D the jump is to AE59. If A = &26 (&), a jump to AE9C enters the hex-to-binary converter. If A = &28 (open bracket), AE85 follows, else;

AE4F (ØØ1B) is decremented, and 95A9 is called to look for a variable name. If it returns with EQ set, no valid name has been found, and AE5F follows. Otherwise B35B enters the variable value in (ØØ2A/D), then returns.

AE59 AØ6C is called to accept a numeric input, and if it returns with carry clear 'No such variable' is reported. Otherwise the routine returns.

AE5F If (ØØ28) AND 2 ≠ Ø, the routine reports 'No such variable'. The same result is produced by carry set. Otherwise (ØØ1B) = X, A/Y = (Ø44Ø/1), and AF19 follows to set up (ØØ2A/D).

AE72 Error text 'No such variable'.

AE85 9BØ3 is called, (ØØ1B) is incremented, and if X ≠ &29 (close bracket) a jump to AE9Ø reports 'Missing)'.

AE9Ø Error text 'Missing)'.

The Operator Ladder

The call to 9BØ3 at AE85 enters the 'operator ladder', a series of linked subroutines:

9BØ3 9B4C is called, and the routine jumps on &84 (OR) and &82 (EOR), otherwise decrementing (ØØ1B), setting (ØØ27) and Y from A, and returning.

9B4C 9B76 is called, and the routine jumps on &8Ø (AND), otherwise returning.

9B76 9C1D is called, and the routine jumps on &3C to &3E (<, =,>), otherwise returning.

9C1D 9DAE is called, and the routine branches on &2B (+) and &2D (−), otherwise returning.

9DAE 9DFD is called, and the routine jumps on &2A (*), &2F (/), &83 (MOD), and &81 (DIV), otherwise returning.

9DFD AE1B, the evaluation routine from which we started, is called, and after spaces have been skipped the next byte is read. The routine jumps on &5E (∧), otherwise returning.

This links a number of operators to processing routines, and others will be found in routines with which they are associated. For example, TAB(will be looked for in the PRINT routine, while TO and STEP will appear in the FOR routine.

Even so, the list is still not quite complete, and we need to do a little more digging. We broke off our search at the jumps to 8B3Ø and 8B22, and the best course will be to continue in address sequence:

8AEA A jump to 8A99, entering the Ready state.

8AED This is the entry for DATA, DEF, and REM, all of which are commands which mark the rest of the statement as non-executable. A = &ØD, Y = (ØØØA) − 1.

8AF2 Y is incremented, and A is compared with ((ØØØB + Y). If equality is not found, the routine loops to 8AF2, scanning on until the terminating &ØD code is reached.

8AF7 If this point is entered with A = &8B (ELSE), the routine jumps to 8AED. The IF has led to execution of THEN, and ELSE is skipped.

Otherwise, if (ØØØC) = 7 the (ØØØB/C) pointer is still within the Ø7ØØ - Ø7FF range, and the routine jumps to 8A99 via 8AEA. The pointer value indicates that an input line is being scanned.

Otherwise, a stored program is being scanned, and 9861 is called to reset pointers for a continuation of the scan. 8A14 follows.

We now come to three major loop points, reached when it appears that a statement is complete. The choice of 8BØ7, 8BØ9 or 8BØC depends on the type of action which precedes the entry:

8BØ7 (ØØØA) is decremented.

8BØ9 981Ø is called to check for colon, newline or ELSE, reporting Syntax error if none of these are found, and to reset (ØØØB/C) and (ØØØA) to point to the next statement.

8BØC Y = Ø, A = ((ØØØB) + Y). If A ≠ &3A (colon), the routine jumps to 8AF7 to check the type of statement being scanned.

8B14 Y = (ØØØA) and (ØØØA) is incremented. A = ((ØØØB + Y), and if A = &20 the routine loops to 8B14, skipping spaces. Otherwise, if A is less than &CF, and therefore not a command word, the routine jumps to 8B3Ø, else;

8B22 As we have already seen, the routine jumps to a link which depends on the value of the token found.

If the first code in the statement is less than &CF, it must be assumed that a LET command is understood, but some preliminary checking is needed:

8B3Ø (ØØ19/A) = (ØØØB/C), forming a new scan pointer. (ØØ1B) = Y to set up an associated displacement pointer. 95A9 is called to look for a variable name. If it returns NE, a variable has been found or established, and the routine jumps to 8B5C in LET.

Otherwise, if carry is set the routine jumps to 8B8E, which branches on & 3D (=), &2A (*), and &5B ([), revealing three more entry points, including those giving access to the Command Line Interpreter and the Assembler.

We can find more: The routine at 95A9 jumps to 955D if A holds a code less than &4Ø, and 955D branches on &21 (!), &3F (?) and &24 ($).

You should now have a list of almost all the important entry points other than some of those relating to mathematical functions. This is essential for further analysis, but is of little use to anyone wishing to call the routines from an external machine code program, since each routine jumps back to the central control system and cannot be called as a subroutine, which is possible in other versions of BASIC.

A more profitable line of exploration relates to the mathematical routines, which will be dealt with next.

Floating Point

Some general comments on floating point working may be useful by way of introduction. The BBC BASIC floating point numbers are held in five bytes, one byte for the exponent and four for the mantissa. The exponent has a 'bias' of &8Ø, so its effective value is given by $2^{E - \&8\emptyset)}$, where E is the actual exponent byte.

The value of the mantissa is found by making the most significant bit 1, calculating the resulting binary value and dividing by 2^{32}. The original state of the most significant bit indicates the sign of the number, Ø for positive and 1 for negative, but the true value of the bit is always 1.

The overall value of the number is founded by multiplying the exponent and mantissa values together. There is a special case for zero value, the exponent holding zero.

There are forty-three floating point constants stored in ROM, and they can be located thus:

Each number occupies five bytes, the first byte (the exponent) being in the range &75 to &86. In some instances there are single bytes between the floating point numbers, these identifying a group of numbers for use as constants in a power series.

There are ten numbers after the LN routine
There are ten numbers before the COS routine
There are fourteen numbers before the EXP routine
There are nine numbers before the ADVAL routine:

One the numbers have been located, they can be displayed in decimal form by the following routine:

```
100 INPUT ADD$
110 ADD = EVAL("&" + ADD$)
120 A% = ?ADD - &80
130 E = 2 ^ A%
140 M = 0
150 FOR N = 1 TO 4
160     F = ?(ADD + N)
170     M = M * 256 + F
180     NEXT
190 IF M > 2 ^ 31 THEN G = 1 ELSE G = 0
200 M = M/(2 ^ 32)
210 IF G = 0 THEN M = M + 0.5
220 IF G = 1 THEN PRINT "-";
230 PRINT M*E
150 GOTO 100
```

The address of the exponent is input, and the value of the exponent is calculated as E. The binary value of the mantissa is then assembled in M, and G is set according to sign. The value of M is then calculated, 0.5 being added for a positive number to correct for the zeroed sign bit. For a negative number, a minus sign is displayed. The overall value is then displayed.

Among the resulting numbers you may recognise $\log_{10} e$, $\log_e 2$, e, ? PI/2, PI/18Ø, 18Ø/PI, the remaining numbers being mostly power series constants.

These numbers are in 'normalised' form, with the most significant bit of the mantissa set to 1. Halving the mantissa and adding one to the exponent would give the same value, but the number would then be 'denormalised'.

When two floating point numbers are added together, their exponents are added together and their mantissas are multiplied together on a 'fractional binary' basis, which stipulates that 8ØØØØØØØ multiplied by itself is 4ØØØØØØØ (the square of ½ is ¼). The result must be normalised.

A similar method is used for division.

Addition and subtraction are a different matter. The two floating point numbers involved must be adjusted so that their exponents are equal, after which addition or subtraction may be performed on the mantissas.

All other numeric manipulations are based ultimately on the four basic functions — multiply, divide, add and subtract.

Floating Point Storage

There are two 'expanded' hold buffers for floating point numbers, one at (ØØ2E/35) and the other at (ØØ3B/42):

(ØØ2E) and (ØØ3B) hold the sign of the number.
(ØØ2F/3Ø) and (ØØ3C/D) hold the exponent.
(ØØ31/4) and (ØØ3E/41) hold the normal mantissa.
(ØØ35) and (ØØ42) hold a mantissa extension.

These buffers can hold denormalised numbers, and are used where the ranges of exponent and mantissa exceed the usual bounds. After normalisation, only (ØØ3Ø/4) and (ØØ3D/41) are relevant.

A four-byte location at (ØØ43/46) is used to hold a mantissa during multiply and divide.

There are also four floating point hold buffers at (Ø46C/7Ø), (Ø471/75), (Ø476/A), and (Ø47B/F). These are usually accessed by setting an appropriate pointer in (ØØ4B/C). Only normalised numbers can be held in these locations.

Other pointers used to pick up floating point numbers include (ØØØ4/5), while (ØØ4B/C) is also used to pick up constants.

It should be noted that the floating point routines are complemented by a full set of integer processes, and the system reserves the right to convert an integral floating point number to integer form, if it is within the necessary magnitude range. Similarly, an integer may be converted to floating point if it is outside that range.

The integer processes can be traced via the Operator Ladder, but a different approach is needed for the floating point functions.

Floating Point Functions

Look back at the Evaluate routine, and consider what happens if a number is found. A hexadecimal number, prefaced by &, will be converted to a binary integer in (ØØ2A/D). A numeric in the &30 - &39 range will cause a jump to AE3F because it is less than &8F, and then the routine will jump to AE59 on codes &2E to &3E. This will cover a number starting with a decimal point (&2E). At AE59, AØ6C is called to accept a numeric input in ASCII decimal form and convert it into a floating point number in (ØØ3Ø/4):

AØ63 This is a loop point. Carry is cleared, (ØØ35) = X, A1CB is called to check for a zero number, and the routine returns with A = &FF.

AØ6C (ØØ31/5) and (ØØ48/9) are zeroed. If A = &2E (.), the routine jumps to AØ91. If the code in A is not numeric, the routine exits via AØ63, otherwise the code is converted to a binary number in A, and (ØØ35) = A.

AØ8A Y is incremented, and A = ((ØØ19) + Y) picks up the next code. If it is not &2E (.), the routine jumps on to AØ99, Otherwise, if (ØØ48) ≠ Ø, indicating that a decimal point has already been found, the routine jumps to AØD9, else (ØØ48) is incremented, and the routine loops to AØ8A.

(ØØ48) is non-zero after a decimal point has been recognised, and (ØØ49) counts input digits while (ØØ48) ≠ Ø.

A099 If A = &45 (E), the routine jumps to A0D2 to process the decimal exponent. If the code in A is not numeric, the routine jumps to A0D9, otherwise the binary value of the number is held in A. If (0031) holds less than &18, the routine jumps to A0B3.

Otherwise, there is a risk of overspill. If (0048) ≠ 0 a decimal point has been found, and the routine loops to A08A. Further digits will be accepted, but ignored. If (0048) = 0, (0049) is incremented, and A08A follows. (Note that carry was set by CPX#18.)

A0B3 If (0048) ≠ 0, (0049) is decremented, marking a digit after the decimal point. Then A188 is called to multiply (0031/5) by ten, and A (preserved by the subroutine) is then added to (0031/5) by ten, and A (preserved by the subroutine) is then added to (0031/5). The routine loops to A08A to look for another digit.

A0D2 A131 is called to process the decimal exponent, the result being added to (0049), which keeps count of decimal places.

A0D9 (001B) = Y, and if (0048/9) = 0000 the routine jumps on to A110. The number is an integer, requiring no decimal corrections. Otherwise A1CB is called to zero (002E/30) if the number itself is zero, in which case A10C follows.

A0E6 The number must now be converted to floating point form. (0030) is set to &A8, corresponding to an exponent value of 2^{40} (002E/F) = 0000. A2F4 is called to normalise the number.

If (0049) is negative, the routine jumps to A102. If (0049) = 0, the jump is to A109.

A0F9 A1E5 is called to multiply the floating point number by ten, (0049) is decremented, and if (0049) ≠ 0 the routine loops to A0F9. Otherwise, the routine jumps to A109.

A102 A23E is called to divide the floating point number by ten. (0049) is incremented, and if it is not zero the routine loops to A102.

A109 A667 is called to perform a rounding adjustment.

A1ØC Carry is set, A = &FF, the routine returns.

That is only the main routine, and a number of subsidiaries follow. The first deals with an integer input:

A11Ø If (ØØ48/9) = Ø, consideration must be given to storing the number as an integer. (ØØ2D) = (ØØ32). A = (ØØ32) AND &8Ø OR (ØØ31), and if the result is not zero the routine jumps to AØE6. The number is too large to be stored as an integer. Otherwise, (ØØ2A) = (ØØ35), (ØØ2B) = (ØØ34), (ØØ2C) = (ØØ33). Note that the byte order is reversed, to meet the integer number convention. A = &4Ø, carry is set and the routine returns. (Note that &FF signals floating point, &40 signals integer. In both cases carry is set unless the input data is not numeric after all, giving a return via AØ31.)

Next comes the routine for picking up a decimal exponent. The entry point is A131, A12A being a loop point.

A12A A13C is called to execute the normal process, but the result is complemented, and the routine returns with carry set.

A131 Y is incremented, and A = (ØØ19) + Y). If A = &2D (−), the routine jumps to A12A. If A ≠ 2B (+), a jump to A13F is taken, the positive sign otherwise being understood.

A13C Y is incremented, and A = ((ØØ19) + Y).

A13F If A does not hold a numeric code, the routine exits via A135. Otherwise, the binary value of the digit is set in (ØØ4A). Y is again incremented, and A = ((ØØ19) + Y). If A does not hold a numeric code the routine exits via A161, otherwise the binary value of the digit is set in (ØØ43). (ØØ4A) is multiplied by ten, and (ØØ43) is added, the result being held in A. The routine returns.

A161 There is only one digit. A = (ØØ4A), and the routine returns with carry clear.

A165 There is no exponent. A = Ø, and the routine returns with carry clear.

Next, an adding routine.

A169 (ØØ31/5) = (ØØ31/5) + (ØØ3E/42). The routine returns.

The next block multiplies (ØØ31/5) by ten. It starts at A188, and that is all there is to be said about it.

The zero-check routine follows.

A1CB If (ØØ31/5) = Ø, the routine jumps to A1DE, else if (ØØ2E) ≠ Ø the routine returns with A = (ØØ2E), else with A = 1.

A1DE (ØØ2E/3Ø) = Ø. The routine returns.

Now a floating point number is multiplied by ten:

A1E5 The tentative exponent in (ØØ2F/3Ø) is increased by three, which implies multiplication by eight.

A1FØ A2ØF copies (ØØ31/5) to (ØØ3B/42). Then A233 is called twice, dividing (ØØ3E/42 by four.

A1F9 A169 adds (ØØØ3E/42) to (ØØ31/5), which now holds 5/4 times its original value. The change to the exponent multiplies the overall value by eight, giving a multiplication by ten.

A1FC If no carry was generated by the last addition, the routine returns via A2ØE. Otherwise (ØØ31/5) is halved, shifting in the carry, and (ØØ2F/3Ø) is incremented. The overall value is unaltered.

A2ØE The routine returns.

A2ØF (ØØ3B/42) = (ØØ2E/35). The routine returns.

A23Ø A2ØF is called.

A233 (ØØ3E/42) is halved. The routine returns.

Now, a floating point number is divided by ten. This is done by multiplying by $(1 + 2^{-1})^* (1 + 2^{-4})^* (1 + 2^{-8})^* (1 + 2^{-16})^* (1 + 2^{-32})/16$. Work that out, and you will find it equals Ø.1!

A23E (ØØ2F/3Ø) is reduced by four, implying division by 16.

A249 A23Ø copies (ØØ2E/35) to (ØØ3B/42) and halves the result. A1F9 then adds (ØØ3E/42) to (ØØ31/5), which has been multiplied by 1½. A23Ø is called again, and A233 is called three times, followed by A1F9. This multiplies (ØØ31/5 by (1 + 2^{-4}). Next (ØØ3E/42) is set to (ØØ31/5) divided by 256, and A1F9 completes the multiplication by (1 + 2^{-8}). Then (ØØ3E/42) = (ØØ32/5) divided by 65536, and A1F9 completes multiplication by (1 + 2^{-16}). Finally, A = (ØØ31), and carry is set if bit 7 of (ØØ32) = 1, and;

A295 A and carry are added to (ØØ31/5), performing the last of the multiplications. If the final addition gives a carry, A1FC is entered to halve the mantissa and increment the exponent, otherwise the routine returns.

We now reach the normalising routine, which adjusts exponent and mantissa until the most significant bit of the mantissa is most the significant true bit.

There are three entry points. A2AF is used where the number is in integer form in (ØØ2A/D), and is to be converted to floating point form. A2DE is used where numeric data in A is to be converted to floating point form, and A2F4 is used where the number is already in denormalised form with the exponent data in (ØØ2E/3Ø) and the mantissa in (ØØ31/5).

A2AF (ØØ35) = (ØØ2F) = X = Ø. If (ØØ2D), the most significant byte of the integer number, is positive, the routine jumps to A2BE, else ADB5 is called to negate (ØØ2A/D) and then X is set to &FF.

A2BE (ØØ2E) = X. (ØØ31/4) = (ØØ2A/D) with byte order reversed. (ØØ3Ø) = &AØ, representing an exponent value of 2^{32}. A2F4 follows.

A2D7 (ØØ2E) = (ØØ2F) = (ØØ3Ø) = A. (A = Ø) The routine returns.

A2DE A is pushed, and A691 is called to zero (ØØ2E/35). A is pulled. If A = Ø, the routine returns, its task done. If A is positive, the routine jumps to A2EE. Otherwise (ØØ2E) = A, and A = –(ØØ2E). This puts the absolute value of the input number in A, and the signed value in (ØØ2E), which provides for future setting of the sign bit.

A2EE (ØØ31) = A, and (ØØ3Ø) = &88, giving an exponent value of 2^8.

A2F4 If (ØØ31) is negative, the normalisation is complete, and the routine returns. Otherwise, if (ØØ31/5) = Ø the routine jumps to A2D7 to set up the zero case. Otherwise A = (ØØ3Ø), the exponent.

A3Ø4 Y = (ØØ31). If Y is negative, the routine returns. If it is non-zero, the routine jumps to A32B. Otherwise (ØØ31/5) is multiplied by 256 (with (ØØ35) = Ø), and A = A − 8. (ØØ3Ø) = A, and if the subtraction generated a borrow (ØØ2F) is decremented. A3Ø4 follows.

A327 Y = (ØØ31). If Y is negative, the routine returns via A2DD.

A32B (ØØ31/5) is doubled, A is decremented, and (ØØ3Ø) = A. If the decrement created a borrow, (ØØ2F) is decremented. A327 follows.

The scheme is simple enough. If the most significant byte of the mantissa is zero, the mantissa is multiplied by 256 and then the exponent is reduced by eight. If the most significant byte is positive, the mantissa is doubled and the exponent is decremented. To allow room for manoeuvre, a five-byte mantissa is used as an input to normalise, with a two-byte exponent, but the surplus bytes are later shed.

Mathematical Functions

It would be neither convenient nor necessary to trace out all the mathematical functions in detail, since there would be a great deal of repetition, so the LOG function will be taken as an example illustrative of all the rest.

LOG is entered at ABCD:

ABCD A8Ø4 (LN) is called to calculate the Naperian logarithm. We will examine that in a moment. Next, Y/A = A856, pointing to a constant, which is in fact $\log_{10}e$. A661 is called to multiply the result of LN by the constant, which is first copied to ((ØØ4B)). The routine returns with A = &FF to indicate a floating point result.

To multiply (ØØ3Ø/4) by any constant or variable, it is only necessary to call A661 with (ØØ4B/C) pointing to the number in question. The two blocks immediately following the LOG routine provide for setting up AA7C (PI/18Ø), and AA81 (18Ø/PI), these being the constants for RAD and DEG. A short routine immediately before the LN entry allows the setting of Ø46C, Ø471, Ø476 or Ø47B, these being holds for floating point numbers. The variables, also held in page 4, can be picked up in a similar manner.

Now that LOG has demonstrated the general concept, LN will show how it can be extended.

The entry for LN is at A8Ø4, with an auxiliary entry at A8Ø7.

A8Ø4 92AC is called to evaluate the independent variable or expression, check type, and call normalise if a floating point number is involved.

A8Ø7 A1CB is called to check for a zero number. If zero is found, the routine jumps to A8ØE to report 'Log range'. Otherwise, if the number is positive A81A follows, else the report 'Log range' is again reached.

A8ØE Error text 'Log range'.

A81A A = (ØØ3Ø), the exponent of the independent variable, and A is pushed. A463 is called to set (ØØ3B/42) to zero. (ØØ3E) = &CØ, and (ØØ3Ø) = (ØØ3B) = (ØØ3D) = &81. This sets up a floating point number in (ØØ3D/41) as 81 CØ ØØ ØØ ØØ. The value of the number is 1.5.

A513 is now called, to subtract (ØØ30/5) from (ØØ3B/42), with the result in (ØØ3Ø/5). (ØØ3Ø) is incremented, to double the result, and then A889 is called with A/Y = A86Ø, pointing to a group of floating point constants preceded by a single byte. This is the power series routine, which is used for other calculations with other sets of constants.

A is pulled, and A = A − &81, giving the original exponent of the independent variable less &81, or the effective value less one. The single-byte normalise routine is called at A2DE, and then (ØØ4B/C) is set to A85B, pointing to the constant Log_e 2. A661 is called to multiply the contents of (ØØ3Ø/5 by this constant, then (ØØ4B/C) = Ø46C and

A5ØE is called to perform a subtraction. The routine returns with A = &FF to indicate a floating point result.

The power series routine is too important to pass without comment, especially as it takes a rather unusual form:

A889 (ØØ4D/E) = A/Y, the pointer to the group of constants. Then A376 is called to set (ØØ3Ø/4) in (Ø46C/7Ø). The byte pointed to by (ØØ4D/E) is picked up and stored in (ØØ48) as a counter, and (ØØ4D/E) is incremented to point to the first constant. (ØØ4B/C) = (ØØ4D/E). A3A6 then copies the constant to (ØØ3Ø/4).

A8A7 A7FB is called to set (ØØ4B/C) = Ø46C, and A6B8 is called to copy (ØØ2E/35) to (ØØ3B/42), copy (Ø46C/7Ø) to (ØØ3Ø/4), and then divide (ØØ3Ø/4) by (ØØ3D/41), result in (ØØ3Ø/4).

(ØØ4D/E) is increased by five, to point to the next constant, then (ØØ4B/C) = (ØØ4D/E). A5ØE is called to subtract (ØØ3Ø/4) from the constant, then (ØØ48) is decremented, and if it is non-zero the routine loops to A8A7, otherwise returning.

The power series is unusual in that it uses divide and subtract, rather than multiply and add.

Other mathematical functions follow the same principles, and tracing them out is a matter of recognising what the subroutines do. The subroutines are complex, the calling routines relatively simple, but in many cases it is possible to express the action of a subroutine in a few words covering many bytes.

Using The Routines

It appears impossible to make use of the command routines, as they are not subroutines, but jump back firmly to the interpreter core. Using the mathematical subroutines also presents problems, because they make type checks and monitor the action in other ways, which can lead to a return to BASIC control when it is not wanted. Moreover, the mathematical subroutines sometimes expect to pick up data from a statement, and if there is no statement there are problems.

This will be a disappointment to many, since the practice of using BASIC interpreter routines in machine code programs is popular. The situation is not as bad as it might appear, for two main reasons. First, there are many functions which can be accessed via the Operating System, and these will suffice in most cases.

Secondly, there is an unexpected way out, which we can discover by examining the error reporting system. There are two key addresses for this: B433, set in (Ø2Ø2/3) as the entry point to be used when a BRK code is found, and B443, set in (ØØ16/7) in the 'Ready' routine.

B433 B3FC is called to set the variable ERL, indicating the line which was being executed when the error occurred, zero being set if an immediate instruction was involved. Then (ØØØB/C) = (ØØ16/7) = B433. The routine jumps to 8AB6, and the system then executes the BASIC statement at B433:

&F6 &3A &E7 &9E &3C &3E &3Ø &F1 &22 &2Ø &61 &74 &2Ø
REPORT: IF ERL < > Ø PRINT " space a t space

&6C &69 &6E &65 &20 &22 &3B &9E &3B &ØD &ØØ &ØØ
1 i n e space " ; ERL ; RET End of program

Now here is a twist! The system is designed to allow machine code to be used as an insert in a BASIC program, but here is a way a BASIC statement can be used as an insert in a machine code program. All that is needed is to set (ØØØB/C) to point to the start of the statement, and to terminate the line by a USR call returning action to the machine code. A little ingenuity, using indirection, may be needed to transfer variables, but that should not be too difficult.

A supreme advantage of the method is that there is no need to know too much about the routines that are invoked, since they will act exactly as in normal BASIC, making appropriate checks and picking up data as it is needed.

Excuse me . . . I must go and experiment . . .

Appendix
DISASSEMBLER AND SORT PROGRAMS

The exploration of machine code needs to be tackled systematically. Simply disassembling the whole program can lead to errors and confusion, though experienced explorers may be able to get away with this approach. Even they need, sooner or later, a tidy version which shows data as data, text as text, and code as code, with clear separation between the various blocks.

Listing 1 offers the necessary facilities. It will display or print disassembled code, hex values, or alphanumerics. A printer is extremely useful, but not absolutely essential. In general, it is possible to abort an operation and return to the menu by pressing 'E', but it should be noted that this will not work if the output is held up in Paged Mode, though the sequence space/E will then secure a return.

Start and end addresses should be input in hexadecimal form, without the preparatory '&', which the program supplies.

Listing 2 performs another useful function. In tracing out a program, an ordered list of link addresses is invaluable, but preparing such a list is tedious. The sort program will accept up to 1ØØØ inputs of the form XXXX YYYY, where XXXX is a link destination and YYYY is the address of a jump or call to the link. Inputs of more or less than nine characters are rejected, as a precaution against error, the computer bleating at you as a warning. Errors can be deleted by selecting menu item 3 and keying in the erroneous entry. If the entry is not found, the computer says not found. Option 4, Sort, will then put the entries into sequential order, and they can be displayed or printed out. The display is in three columns, the printout in seven columns. If your printer will not take seven columns, change the value of E at line 35Ø to the number of columns you require.

Note that there are some 225Ø links in the BASIC ROM alone, so it is advisable to process them in sections, or enlarge the three arrays. This, however, could make the sorting process a little slower, but it will still be faster than a 'bubble sort' by a considerable margin.

LISTING 1:DISASSEMBLER

```
100 DIM MNEM$(56),PRE$(13),POST$(13)
110 DIM OPM(256),OPS(256),N(13)
120 FOR I=1 TO 13
130 READ N(I)
140 NEXT
150 REPEAT
160 READ A,B,C
170 OPS(A)=B:OPM(A)=C
180 UNTIL A = 255
190 FOR I=1 TO 13
200 READ PRE$(I),POST$(I)
210 NEXT
220 FOR I = 0 TO 56
230 READ MNEM$(I)
240 NEXT
250 PFLAG%=0
260 CLS
265 VDU3
270 *FX15,1
280 PRINT TAB(12,6);"Select Option"'
290 PRINT TAB(7);"1: Decompile"
300 PRINT TAB(7);"2: Dump codes"
310 PRINT TAB(7);"3: Dump Alpha"
320 PRINT TAB(7);"4: Printer On"
330 PRINT TAB(7);"5: Printer Off"
340 PRINT TAB(7);"To return to Menu, press E"
350 PRINT TAB(7);"To continue, press Space"
360 PRINT ' TAB(7);
370 INPUT "Your choice ",C%
380 IF C%<1 OR C%>5 GOTO 360
390 CLS
400 ON C% GOTO 800,450,620,410,430
410 PFLAG%=1
420 GOTO 260
430 PFLAG%=0
440 GOTO 260
450 GOSUB 1100
460 REPEAT
470 CLS
480 REPEAT
490 R%=(ADD MOD 128)/8
500 PRINT TAB(0);~ADD;
510 REPEAT
520 N%=ADD MOD 8
530 B%=?ADD
```

```
540 PRINT TAB(5+3*N%-(B%<16));~B%;
550 ADD=ADD+1
560 UNTIL N%=7 OR ADD>ENDA
570 UNTIL R%=15 OR ADD>ENDA
580 F=GET-69
590 *FX15,1
600 UNTIL F=0
610 GOTO 260
620 GOSUB 1100
630 REPEAT
640 CLS
650 REPEAT
660 R%=(ADD MOD 256)/16
670 PRINT TAB(0);~ADD;
680 REPEAT
690 N%= ADD MOD 16
700 B%=?ADD
710 IF B%<32 OR B%> 126 THEN B%=32
720 PRINT TAB(5+2*N%);CHR$ B%;
730 ADD=ADD+1
740 UNTIL N%=15 OR ADD>ENDA
750 UNTIL R%=15 OR ADD>ENDA
760 F=GET-69
770 *FX15,1
780 UNTIL F=0
790 GOTO 260
800 GOSUB 1100
810 N(0)=1
820 @%=&A00
830 CLS
840 PRINT "ADDRESS    CODE    MNEMONIC"
850 REPEAT
860 OPERAND=?ADD
870 MO = OPM(OPERAND)
880 PRINT~ADD;"    ";
890 FOR J=1 TO N(MO)
900 IF ADD?(J-1)<16 PRINT "0";
910 PRINT ~ADD?(J-1);" ";
920 NEXT
930 PRINT TAB(20);MNEM$(OPS(OPERAND));PRE$(MO);
940 IF MO <>11 THEN 970
950 IF ADD?1<128 PRINT ~(ADD+2 + ADD?1) ELSE PRINT
~(ADD-256 +2 + ADD?1)
960 GOTO 1040
970 IF N(MO)=1 THEN 1030
980 IF N(MO)<2 THEN 1030
990 FOR J=ADD +N(MO)-1 TO ADD+1 STEP - 1
1000 IF ?J<16 PRINT "0";
1010 PRINT~?J;
1020 NEXT
1030 PRINT POST$(MO)
1040 ADD=ADD+ N(MO)
1050 Q=OPS(OPERAND)
1060 IF Q=28 OR Q=42 OR Q=43 THEN PRINT:I=I+1
1070 UNTIL (INKEY(-35) OR (ADD>ENDA))
1075 *FX 15,1
1080  IF ADD>ENDA F%=GET
1090 GOTO 260
```

```
1100 PRINT '' TAB(7);
1110 INPUT "Start Address",ADD$
1120 ADD = EVAL("&"+ADD$)
1130 PRINT TAB(7);
1140 INPUT "End Address",AEND$
1150 ENDA=EVAL("&"+AEND$)
1160 IF PFLAG%=1 THEN VDU 2
1170 RETURN
1180 DATA 1,1,3,2,2,3,3,2,2,2,2,3,2
1190 DATA &6D,1,3,&65,1,4,&69,1,5,&7D,1,6,&79,1,7,
&61,1,8,&71,1,9,&75,1,10
1200 DATA &2D,2,3,&25,2,4,&29,2,5,&3D,2,6,&39,2,7,
&21,2,8,&31,2,9,&35,2,10
1210 DATA 10,3,2,14,3,3,6,3,4,&1E,3,6,22,3,10,&90,4,
11,&B0,5,11,&F0,6,11,&2C,7,3,&24,7,4
1220 DATA 48,8,11,&D0,9,11,16,10,11,0,11,1,&50,12,
11,&70,13,11,&18,14,1,&D8,15, 1
1230 DATA &58,16,1,&B8,17,1,&CD,18,3,&C5,18,4,&C9,
18,5,&DD,18,6,&D9,18,7,&C1,18,8,&D1,18,9,&D5,18,10
1240 DATA &EC,19,3,&E4,19,4,&E0,19,5,&CC,20,3,&C4,
20,4,&C0,20,5,&CE,21,3,&C6,21,4,&DE,21,6,&D6,21,10,
&CA,22,1,&88,23,1
1250 DATA &4D,24,3,&45,24,4,&49,24,5,&5D,24,6,&59,
24,7,65,24,8,&51,24,9,&55,24,10
1260 DATA &EE,25,3,&E6,25,4,&FE,25,6,&F6,25,10
1270 DATA &E8,26,1,&C8,27,1,&4C,28,3,&6C,28,12,32,
29,3,&AD,30,3,&A5,30,4,&A9,30,5,&BD,30,6,&B9,30,7,
&A1,30,8,&B1,30,9,&B5,30,10
1280 DATA &AE,31,3,&A6,31,4,&A2,31,5,&BE,31,7,&B6,
31,13,&AC,32,3,&A4,32,4,160,3  2,5,&BC,32,6,&B4,
32,10
1290 DATA &4A,33,2,&4E,33,3,&46,33,4,&5E,33,6,&56,
33,10
1300 DATA &EA,34,1,13,35,3,5,35,4,9,35,5,&1D,35,6,
&19,35,7,1,35,8,17,35,9,21,35,10
1310 DATA &48,36,1,8,37,1,&68,38,1,&28,39,1,&2A,40,
2,&2E,40,3,&26,40,4,&3E,40,6,&36,40,10
1320 DATA &6A,41,2,&6E,41,3,&66,41,4,&7E,41,6,&76,
41,10
1330 DATA 64,42,1,96,43,1,&ED,44,3,&E5,44,4,&E9,44,
5,&FD,44,6,&F9,44,7,&E1,44,8,&F1,44,9,&F5,44,10
1340 DATA &38,45,1,&F8,46,1,&78,47,1,&8D,48,3,&85,
48, 4,&9D,48,6,&99,48,7,129,48,8,&91,48,9,&95,48,10
1350 DATA &8E,49,3,&86,49,4,&96,49,13,&8C,50,3,&84,
50,4,&94,50,10
1360 DATA &AA,51,1,&A8,52,1,&BA,53,1,&8A,54,1,&9A,
55,1,&98,56,1,255,0,0
1370 DATA "","",A,"",&,"",&,"",£,"",&,",X",&,",Y",
(&,",X)",(&,"),Y",&,",X",&,"",(&,),&,""
1380 DATA Invalid,ADC,AND,ASL,BCC,BCS,BEQ,BIT,BMI,
BNE,BPL,BRK,BVC,BVS,CLC,CLD,CLI,CLV,CMP
1390  DATA CPX,CPY,DEC,DEX,DEY,EOR,INC,INX,INY,JMP,
JSR,LDA,LDX,LDY,LSR,NOP,ORA
1400 DATA PHA,PHP,PLA,PLP,ROL,ROR,RTI,RTS,SBC,SEC,
SED,SEI,STA,STX,STY,TAX,TAY,TSX,TXA,TXS,TYA
>
```

LISTING 2: FAST SORT

```
100 N=-1
110 CLS
120 DIM A(1000)
130 DIM B(1000),C(1000)
140 CLS:PRINT "Select Mode"
150 PRINT TAB(5);"1; Enter New List"
160 PRINT TAB(5);"2; Continue Old List"
170 PRINT TAB(5);"3; Delete Entry"
180 PRINT TAB(5);"4; Sort"
190 PRINT TAB(5);"5; Output"
200 PRINT TAB(5);"6; Print"
210 INPUT "INPUT 1 - 6",F
220 IF F<1 OR F>6 THEN 140
230 ON F GOSUB 260,280,890,640,400,340
240 GOTO 140
250 REM Data entry routine.
260 N=-1
270 FOR X=0 TO 1000:A(X)=0
280 GOSUB 560
290 IF LEFT$(D$,1)="G" RETURN
300 N=N+1
310 A(N)=H
320 GOTO 280
330 REM Print routine.
340 VDU 2
350 E = 7
360 GOSUB 420
370 VDU3
380 RETURN
390 REM Display routine.
400 CLS
410 E = 3
420 K=INT(N/E)+1
430 FOR P=0 TO (K-1)
440 FOR Q=0 TO E-1
450 R=A(P+Q*K)
460 IF (P+Q*K)>N THEN 500
470 H=INT(R/65536)
480 J=R-65536*H
490 PRINT TAB(10*Q);~H;" ";~J;
500 NEXT Q
510 PRINT
520 NEXT P
530 PRINT
540 INPUT X:RETURN
550 REM Input routine.
560 INPUT D$
570 IF LEFT$(D$,1)="G" RETURN
580 IF LEN(D$)<>9 THEN VDU7:GOTO 560
590 J=EVAL("&"+LEFT$(D$,4))
600 H=EVAL("&"+RIGHT$(D$,4))
610 H=H+65536*J
620 RETURN
630 REM Sort routine
```

```
640 FB=0:PRINT"Sorting"
650 NA=0:NB=0:NC=0:FA=0
660 FOR X=0 TO 1000:B(X)=0:C(X)=0:NEXTX
670 HA=A(NA)
680 IF FA=0 THEN 710
690 C(NC)=HA:NC=NC+1
700 GOTO 720
710 B(NB)=HA:NB=NB+1
720 NA=NA+1:IF NA>N THEN 760
730 IF HA<=A(NA) THEN 670
740 FA=(FA+1)AND 1
750 GOTO 670
760 NA=0:NB=0:NC=0:HA=0
770 IF B(NB)=0 THEN 840
780 IF C(NC)=0 THEN 830
790 IF B(NB)>=HA AND C(NC)>=HA THEN 820
800 IF B(NB)>=HA THEN 830
810 IF C(NC)>=HA THEN 840
820 IF B(NB)>C(NC) THEN 840
830 HA=B(NB):NB=NB+1:GOTO850
840 HA=C(NC):NC=NC+1
850 A(NA) = HA:NA=NA+1
860 IF NA <= N THEN 770
870 FB=FB+1:PRINT FB:IF C(0)=0 THEN RETURN
880 GOTO 650
890 GOSUB560
900 C=-1
910 FOR X=0 TO N
920 IF H=A(X) THEN C=X
930 NEXT X
940 IF C<0 THEN PRINT "Not found":P$=INKEY$(150)
:RETURN
950 FOR X=C TO (N-1)
960 A(X)=A(X+1)
970 NEXT
980 N=N-1
990 RETURN
>
```

Index

85

A

A/D Channel, Select, OSBYTE 16 39
ACIA Setting and Ram Copy, Update, OSBYTE 156 54
Acknowledge Escape, OSBYTE 126 40
ADVAL, OSBYTE 128 41
Alter CRT Controller Bias, OSBYTE 144 42
Animation, Wait for, OSBYTE 19 40
*BASIC 85

B

BASIC Interpreter 2, 199
  Evaluation of Operators 203
  Execution of Programs 202
  Initialisation 200
Baud Rate, Receive, Select, OSBYTE 7 38
Baud Rate, Transmit, Select, OSBYTE 8 38
BPUT for TUBE, OSBYTE 157 43
BRK Instruction 19
Buffer, Flush Specific, OSBYTE 21 57, 60
Buffer, Get Byte from, OSBYTE 145 58
Buffer, Put Byte in, OSBYTE 138 57
Buffer Class, Flush Selected, OSBYTE 15 57, 60
Buffer Status, Examine, OSBYTE 152 58
Buffers 57
Byte to Input Buffer, Checking Escape, OSBYTE 153 58

C

Cancel Paged Mode, VDU 15 99
Cassette Motor, Switch, OSBYTE 137 168
*CAT 85, 177
Character Analysis 96
Character at Text Cursor Position, Read, OSBYTE 135 146
Character Definition, Read, OSWORD 10 119
Character to Printer, Next, VDU 1 98
Characters, Define, VDU 23 111
Characters, Explode, OSBYTE 20 120
Clear Escape Condition, OSBYTE 124 40
Clear Graphics Screen, VDU 16 106
Clear Screen, VDU 12 104
Clock, Internal VIA Interrupt 6 27
Clock, Read, OSWORD 1 45
Clock, Write, OSWORD 2 46
Close SPOOL/EXEC Files, OSBYTE 119 168
*CODE 87
Colour, Duration of First, OSBYTE 9 38
Colour, Duration of Second, OSBYTE 10 38
Colour, Graphics, Define, VDU 18 106
Colour, Text, Define, VDU 17 106
Colours, Default, VDU 20 109
Colours, Logic, Define, VDU 19 110
Command Line Interpreter 81
Conventions 3
Conversion, End of, Internal VIA Interrupt 4 29
Conversion, Start, OSBYTE 17 39
CRT Controller Bias, Alter, OSBYTE 144 42
Cursor, Graphics, Select, VDU 5 100
Cursor, Home, VDU 30 104
Cursor, Text, Position, VDU 31 105
Cursor, Text, Select, VDU 4 99
Cursor Down, VDU 101 103
Cursor Left, VDU 8 100
Cursor Position, Read, OSBYTE 134 143

Cursor Position (Text), Read Character at, OSBYTE 135 146
Cursor Positions, Graphic, Read Last Two, OSWORD 13 142
Cursor Right, VDU 9 102
Cursor Up, VDU 11 102

D
Default 85
Default Colours, VDU 20 109
Define Characters, VDU 23 111
Define Graphics Colour, VDU 18 106
Define Graphics Window, VDU 24 115
Define Logic Colours, VDU 19 110
Define Text Colour, VDU 17 106
Define Text Window, VDU 28 103
Delete, VDU 32 116
Disable Display, VDU 21 99
Disable Event, OSBYTE 13 39
Disassembler 219
Display, Disable, VDU 21 99
Display OS version number, OSBYTE 0 35
Display Ram Address, Read Bottom of, OSBYTE 132 149
Duration of First Colour, OSBYTE 9 38
Duration of Second Colour, OSBYTE 10 38

E
Enable Event, OSBYTE 14 39
End of Conversion, Internal VIA Interrupt 4 29
End of File Check, OSBYTE 127 41
Enter Language ROM, OSBYTE 142 15
Escape, Acknowledge, OSBYTE 126 40
Escape Condition, Clear, OSBYTE 124 40
Escape Flag, Set, OSBYTE 125 40
Evaluation of BASIC Operators 203
Event, Disable, OSBYTE 13 39
Event, Enable, OSBYTE 14 39
Examine Buffer Status, OSBYTE 152 58
*EXEC 185
Execute Code via User Vector, OSBYTE 136 42
Execution of BASIC Programs 202
Exit Routine 30
Explode Characters, OSBYTE 20 120
External VIA Interrupt 1: Printer 25

F
File Check, End of, OSBYTE 127 41
File Options, OSBYTE 139 41, 182
Files 167
Files, Close SPOOL/EXEC, OSBYTE 119 168
Floating Point Numbers 206-214
Flush Selected Buffer Class, OSBYTE 15 57, 60
Flush Specific Buffer, OSBYTE 21 57, 60
Frame Sync, Internal VIA Interrupt 1 24
Function Keys, Reset, OSBYTE 18 90
*FX 87

G
Get Byte from Buffer, OSBYTE 145 58
Graphic Cursor Positions, Read Last Two, OSWORD 13 142
Graphics Colour, Define, VDU 18 106
Graphics Cursor, Select, VDU 5 100
Graphics Origin, Set, VDU 29 116
Graphics Screen, Clear, VDU 16 106
Graphics Window, Define, VDU 24 115
GSINIT 90
GSREAD 90

H
Home Cursor, VDU 30 104

I
I/O Processor Memory, Read, OSWORD 5 46
I/O Processor Memory, Write to, OSWORD 6 46
Initialisation
  Switch-on, 6
  BASIC Interpreter 200
Input and Output 51
Input Buffer, Byte to, Checking Escape, OSBYTE 153 58
Input Devices, Select, OSBYTE 2 37
Internal VIA Interrupt 0: Keyboard 29
Internal VIA Interrupt 1: Frame Sync 24
Internal VIA Interrupt 4: End of Conversion 29
Internal VIA Interrupt 5: Speech 26
Internal VIA Interrupt 6: Clock 27
Interrupts 19
Interrupts, Serial System 22
*KEY 87

K
Key, Read With Time Limit, OSBYTE 129 75
Key Pressed Data, Write, OSBYTE 120 71
Keyboard 65
Keyboard, Internal VIA Interrupt 0 29
Keyboard Matrix 79

Keyboard Repeat Delay,
OSBYTE 11 36
Keyboard Repeat Period,
OSBYTE 12 36
Keyboard Scan, OSBYTE 121 72
Keyboard Scan from &10,
OSBYTE 122 72

L
Language ROM, Enter, OSBYTE 142 15
LEDs, Set to Keyboard Status,
OSBYTE 118 66
Load and Save 151
Logic Colours, Define VDU 19 110

M
Mathematical Functions 214
Memory, Read a Line to, OSWORD 0 44
Mode, Read Lowest Address for,
OSBYTE 133 149
Mode, Select, VDU 22 111
*MOTOR 87

N
NEW 200
Newline, VDU 13 105
Next Character to Printer, VDU 1 98
Numbers, Floating Point 206-214

O
Operators, BASIC 203-204
Operating Systems 2
*OPT 87
OS version number, Display,
OSBYTE 0 35
OSARGS 172
OSBGET 181
OSBPUT 182
OSBYTE calls 33, 47
OSBYTE 0: Display OS version
number 35
OSBYTE 2: Select Input Devices 37
OSBYTE 6: Suppressed Printer
Character 36
OSBYTE 7: Select Receive Baud
Rate 38
OSBYTE 8: Select Transmit Baud
Rate 38
OSBYTE 9: Duration of First Colour 38
OSBYTE 10: Duration of Second
Colour 38
OSBYTE 11: Keyboard Repeat Delay 36
OSBYTE 12: Keyboard Repeat
Period 36
OSBYTE 13: Disable Event 39
OSBYTE 14: Enable Event 39
OSBYTE 15: Flush Selected Buffer
Class 57, 60
OSBYTE 16: Select A/D Channel 39
OSBYTE 17: Start Conversion 39
OSBYTE 18: Reset Function Keys 90
OSBYTE 19: Wait for Animation 40
OSBYTE 20: Explode Characters 120
OSBYTE 21: Flush Specific Buffer 57, 60
OSBYTE 117: Read VDU Status 40
OSBYTE 118: Set LEDs to Keyboard
Status 66
OSBYTE 119: Close SPOOL/EXEC
Files 168
OSBYTE 120: Write Key Pressed
Data 71
OSBYTE 121: Keyboard Scan 72
OSBYTE 122: Keyboard Scan
from &10 72
OSBYTE 123: Warn Printer Going
Dormant 54
OSBYTE 124: Clear Escape
Condition 40
OSBYTE 125: Set Escape Flag 40
OSBYTE 126: Acknowledge Escape 40
OSBYTE 127: End of File Check 41
OSBYTE 128: ADVAL 41
OSBYTE 129: Read Key With Time
Limit 75
OSBYTE 130: Read Higher Order
Address 75
OSBYTE 131: Read OSHWM 71
OSBYTE 132: Read Bottom of Display
Ram Address 149
OSBYTE 133: Read Lowest Address for
Given Mode 149
OSBYTE 134: Read Cursor Position 143
OSBYTE 135: Read Character at Text
Cursor Position 146
OSBYTE 136: Execute Code via User
Vector 42
OSBYTE 137: Switch Cassette
Motor 168
OSBYTE 138: Put Byte in Buffer 57
OSBYTE 139: File Options 41, 182
OSBYTE 140: Select Tape Filing
System 170
OSBYTE 141: Select ROM Filing
System 170
OSBYTE 142: Enter Language ROM 15
OSBYTE 143: Paged ROM Service
Request 172
OSBYTE 144: Alter CRT Controller
Bias 42
OSBYTE 145: Get Byte from Buffer 58
OSBYTE 146: Read from FC00-FCFF 42

OSBYTE 147: Write to FC00-FCFF 42
OSBYTE 148: Read from FD00-FDFF 42
OSBYTE 149: Write to FD00-FDFF 42
OSBYTE 150: Read from FE00-FEFF 43
OSBYTE 151: Write to FE00-FEFF 43
OSBYTE 152: Examine Buffer Status 58
OSBYTE 153: Byte to Input Buffer, Checking Escape 58
OSBYTE 154: Set Video ULA 43
OSBYTE 155: Write to Palette Register 43
OSBYTE 156: Update ACIA Setting and Ram Copy 54
OSBYTE 157: BPUT for TUBE 43
OSBYTE 158: Read from Speech Processor 169
OSBYTE 159: Write to Speech Processor 169
OSBYTE 160: Read VDU Parameters 40
OSBYTE 166-255: Reset variables 36
OSFILE 175
OSFIND 178
OSWORD calls 43, 47
OSWORD 0: Read a Line to Memory 44
OSWORD 1: Read Clock 45
OSWORD 2: Write Clock 46
OSWORD 3: Read Timer 45
OSWORD 4: Write Timer 46
OSWORD 5: Read I/O Processor Memory 46
OSWORD 6: Write to I/O Processor Memory 46
OSWORD 9: Read a Pixel 104
OSWORD 10: Read Character Definition 119
OSWORD 11: Read Palette 104
OSWORD 12: Write Palette 110
OSWORD 13: Read Last Two Graphic Cursor Positions 142
Output and Input 51

P

Paged Mode, Cancel, VDU 15 99
Paged Mode, Set, VDU 14 99
Paged ROM Service Request, OSBYTE 143 172
Palette, Read, OSWORD 11 104
Palette, Write, OSWORD 12 110
Palette Register, Write to, OSBYTE 155 43
Pixel, Read a, OSWORD 9 104
Plot, VDU 25 113
Position Text Cursor, VDU 31 105
Printer, External VIA Interupt 1 25
Printer, Next Character to, VDU 1 98
Printer, Warn Going Dormant, OSBYTE 123 54
Printer Character, Suppressed, OSBYTE 6, 36
Printer Off, VDU 3 99
Printer On, VDU 2 99
Put Byte in Buffer, OSBYTE 138 57

R

Read a Line to Memory, OSWORD 0 44
Read a Pixel, OSWORD 9 104
Read Bottom of Display Ram Address, OSBYTE 132, 149
Read Character at Text Cursor Position, OSBYTE 135 146
Read Character Definition, OSWORD 10 119
Read Clock, OSWORD 1 45
Read Cursor Position, OSBYTE 134 143
Read from FC00-FCAA, OSBYTE 146 42
Read from FD00-FFAE, OSBYTE 148 42
Read from FE00-FEFF, OSBYTE 150 43
Read from Speech Processor, OSBYTE 158 169
Read Higher Order Address, OSBYTE 130 75
Read I/O Processor Memory, OSWORD 5 46
Read Key With Time Limit, OSBYTE 129 75
Read Last Two Graphic Cursor Positions, OSWORD 13 142
Read Lowest Address for Given Mode, OSBYTE 133 149
Read OSHWM, OSBYTE 131 71
Read Palette, OSWORD 11 104
Read Timer, OSWORD 3 45
Read VDU Parameters, OSBYTE 160 40
Read VDU Status, OSBYTE 117 40
Reset Function Keys, OSBYTE 18 90
Reset variables, OSBYTE 166-255 36
*ROM 88
ROM, Paged, Service Request, OSBYTE 143 172
ROM Filing System, Select, OSBYTE 141 170
Routines, Finding 2
*RUN 85, 176

S

Save and Load 151
Screen, Clear, VDU 12, 104
Screen, Graphics, Clear, VDU 16, 106
Select A/D Channel, OSBYTE 16, 39
Select Graphics Cursor, VDU 5 100
Select Input Devices, OSBYTE 2 37

Select Mode, VDU 22 111
Select Receive Baud Rate,
OSBYTE 7 38
Select ROM Filing System,
OSBYTE 141 170
Select Tape Filing System,
OSBYTE 140 170
Select Text Cursor, VDU 4 99
Select Transmit Baud Rate,
OSBYTE 8 38
Serial System Interrupts 22
Set Default Windows, VDU 26 114
Set Escape Flag, OSBYTE 125 40
Set Graphics Origin, VDU 29 116
Set LEDs to Keyboard Status,
OSBYTE 118 66
Set Paged Mode, VDU 14 99
Set Video ULA, OSBYTE 154 43
Sort Programs 219
Sound System 155
Speech, Internal VIA Interrupt 5 26
Speech Processor, Read from,
OSBYTE 158 169
Speech Processor, Write to,
OSBYTE 159 169
Start Conversion, OSBYTE 17 39
Suppressed Printer Character,
OSBYTE 6 36
Switch Cassette Motor,
OSBYTE 137 168
*TAPE 88

T

Tape Filing System, Select,
OSBYTE 140 170
Text Colour, Define, VDU 17 106
Text Cursor, Position, VDU 31 105
Text Cursor, Select, VDU 4 99
Text Cursor Position, Read Character at,
OSBYTE 135 146
Text Window, Define, VDU 28 103
Timer, Read, OSWORD 3 45
Timer, Write, OSWORD 4 46
TUBE, BPUT for, OSBYTE 157 43
*TV 88

U

Update ACIA Setting and Ram Copy,
OSBYTE 156 54

V

Variables 3
Variables, Reset, OSBYTE 166-255 36
VDU 1: Next Character to Printer 98
VDU 2: Printer On 99
VDU 3: Printer Off 99
VDU 4: Select Text Cursor 99
VDU 5: Select Graphics Cursor 100
VDU 8: Cursor Left 100
VDU 9: Cursor Right 102
VDU 11: Cursor Up 102
VDU 12: Clear Screen 104
VDU 13: Newline 105
VDU 14: Set Paged Mode 99
VDU 15: Cancel Paged Mode 99
VDU 16: Clear Graphics Screen 106
VDU 17: Define Text Colour 106
VDU 18: Define Graphics Colour 106
VDU 19: Define Logic Colours 110
VDU 20: Default Colours 109
VDU 21: Disable Display 99
VDU 22: Select Mode 111
VDU 23: Define Characters 111
VDU 24: Define Graphics Window 115
VDU 25: Plot 113
VDU 26: Set Default Windows 114
VDU 28: Define Text Window 103
VDU 29: Set Graphics Origin 116
VDU 30: Home Cursor 104
VDU 31: Position Text Cursor 105
VDU 32: Delete 116
VDU 101: Cursor Down 103
VDU Control 93
VDU Control, Variables for Page 3 95
VDU Function Link Table 94
VDU Parameters, Read, OSBYTE 160 40
VDU Status, Read, OSBYTE 117 40
VIA Interrupt, *see* External VIA Interrupt;
Internal VIA Interrupt
Video ULA, Set, OSBYTE 154 43

W

Wait for Animation, OSBYTE 19 40
Warn Printer Going Dormant,
OSBYTE 123 54
Windows, Set Default, VDU 26 114
Write Clock, OSWORD 2 46
Write Key Pressed Data,
OSBYTE 120 71
Write Palette, OSWORD 12 110
Write Timer, OSWORD 4 46
Write to FC00-FCFF, OSBYTE 147 42
Write to FD00-FDFF, OSBYTE 149 42
Write to FE00-FEFF, OSBYTE 151 43
Write to I/O Processor Memory,
OSWORD 6 46
Write to Palette Register,
OSBYTE 155 43
Write to Speech Processor,
OSBYTE 159 169

Write to Us

Melbourne House is always interested in receiving letters from its readers.

Publishing Ideas

If you have written a book or program that you think would be of interest to other computer users, we want to hear from you.

We are always interested in discussing new ideas for books with authors. If you think you have a good book idea, please send a detailed outline first. We prefer to work with authors as early as possible in the writing process.

BASIC programs are wanted for inclusion in our books, and machine language programs are wanted for our list of adventure and game software. Always send a tape or disk and, if possible, a code printout with your submission letter.

Fees and royalties are negotiated according to the quality and ingenuity of the submission, and are more than competitive with those of other publishing houses.

Send your book or program to the Melbourne House office closest to you — see the back of the title page for the address. Mark your letter to the attention of the Editorial Department to ensure an early review of your idea and a prompt reply.

Bugs and Problems

Every effort is made to ensure that our books are error-free. Occasionally, however, you may have difficulties — in such instances, do not hesitate to write to Melbourne House. Send your letter to the Melbourne House office closest to you — see the back of the title page for the address.

So that we can process your query as quickly as possible, mark your letter to the attention of Customer Support. Quote the title of this book in your letter, together with the printing and edition numbers, and the year of publication. This information is on the back of the title page at the foot.

Describe your problem precisely, quoting the program title and the offending line numbers.

Guide to the BBC ROMS

Customer Registration Card

Please fill out this page (or a photocopy of it) and return it so that we may keep you informed of new books, software and special offers. Post to the appropriate address on the back.

Date . . . . .19 . . . .

Name . . . .

Street & No. . . . .

City . . . . .Postcode/Zipcode . . . .

Model of computer owned . . . .

Where did you learn of this book:

☐ FRIEND ☐ RETAIL SHOP

☐ MAGAZINE (give name) . . . .

☐ OTHER (specify) . . . .

Age? ☐ 10-15 ☐ 16-19 ☐ 20-24 ☐ 25 and over

How would you rate this book?

QUALITY: ☐ Excellent ☐ Good ☐ Poor

VALUE: ☐ Overpriced ☐ Good ☐ Underpriced

What other books and software would you like to see produced for your computer?

. . . .

. . . .

. . . .

EDITION 7 6 5 4 3 2 1

Melbourne House addresses

Put this Registration Card (or photocopy) in an envelope and post it to the appropriate address:

United Kingdom

Melbourne House (Publishers) Ltd
Castle Yard House
Castle Yard
Richmond, TW10 6TF

United States of America

Melbourne House Software Inc.
347 Reedwood Drive
Nashville TN 37217

Australia and New Zealand

Melbourne House (Australia) Pty Ltd
2nd Floor, 70 Park Street
South Melbourne, Victoria 3205

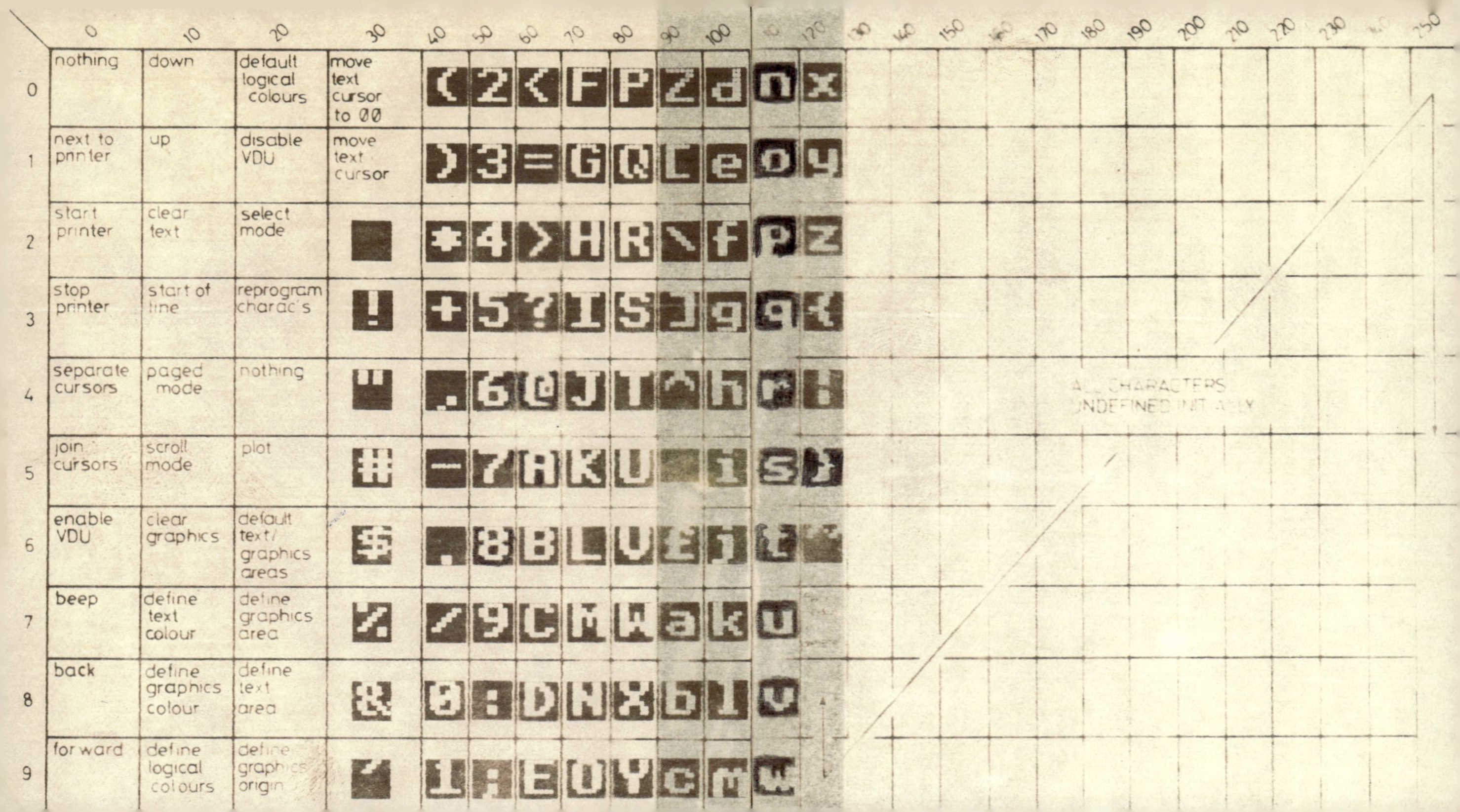

	0	10	20	30	40	50	60	70	80	90	100	110	120
0	nothing	down	default logical colours	move text cursor to 00	(	2	<	F	P	Z	d	n	x
1	next to printer	up	disable VDU	move text cursor	)	3	=	G	Q	[	e	o	y
2	start printer	clear text	select mode		*	4	>	H	R	\	f	p	z
3	stop printer	start of line	reprogram charac's	!	+	5	?	I	S	]	g	q	{
4	separate cursors	paged mode	nothing	"	,	6	@	J	T	^	h	r	|
5	join cursors	scroll mode	plot	#	-	7	A	K	U	_	i	s	}
6	enable VDU	clear graphics	default text/ graphics areas	$	.	8	B	L	V	`	j	t	~
7	beep	define text colour	define graphics area	%	/	9	C	M	W	a	k	u	
8	back	define graphics colour	define text area	&	0	:	D	N	X	b	l	v	
9	forward	define logical colours	define graphics origin	'	1	;	E	O	Y	c	m	w	

130–250: ALL CHARACTERS UNDEFINED INITIALLY